TRANSITIVE CULTURES

TRANSITIVE CULTURES

Anglophone Literature
of the Transpacific

CHRISTOPHER B. PATTERSON

RUTGERS UNIVERSITY PRESS
New Brunswick, Camden, and Newark, New Jersey, and London

Library of Congress Cataloging-in-Publication Data

Names: Patterson, Christopher B., author.
Title: Transitive cultures : Anglophone literature of the transpacific / Christopher B.
    Patterson.
Description: New Brunswick, New Jersey : Rutgers University Press, [2017] |
    Includes bibliographical references and index.
Identifiers: LCCN 2017033672| ISBN 9780813591902 (cloth : alk. paper) |
    ISBN 9780813591865 (pbk. : alk. paper)
Subjects: LCSH: Southeast Asian literature (English)—History and criticism. |
    Literature and transnationalism—Malaysia. | Literature and transnationalism—
    Philippines. | Transnationalism in literature. | Pacific Area—In literature.
Classification: LCC PR9645.5 .P38 2017 | DDC 820.9/95—dc23 LC record available at
    https://lccn.loc.gov/2017033672

A British Cataloging-in-Publication record for this book is available from the British
Library.

♾ The paper used in this publication meets the requirements of the American National
Standard for Information Sciences—Permanence of Paper for Printed Library
Materials, ANSI Z39.48–1992.

www.rutgersuniversitypress.org

Manufactured in the United States of America

For Y-Dang and Kai

Imperialism consolidated the mixture of cultures and identities on a global scale. But its worst and most paradoxical gift was to allow people to believe that they were only, mainly, exclusively, white, or Black, or Western, or Oriental.

—Edward W. Said, *Culture and Imperialism*

And I saw that what divided me from the world was not anything intrinsic to us but the actual injury done by people intent on naming us, intent on believing that what they have named us matters more than anything we could ever actually do.

—Ta-Nehisi Coates, *Between the World and Me*

Now, the talk-show hosts … get it if I'm making fun of myself and if I'm a punch line for them, but not as a human being. They would have a transsexual on because a transsexual is saying, "This is who I really am. I'm real." I'm saying, "No, I'm not real. I'm actually everything and nothing at all."

—RuPaul, "Real Talk with RuPaul," *Vulture.com*

CONTENTS

TRANSITIVE CULTURES

INTRODUCTION

Pluralism, Transition, and the Anglophone

In his 1993 novel *In a Far Country*, K. S. Maniam explores the spiritual effects of cultural pluralism in Malaysia, where the four official races—Chinese, Malays, Indians, and Others—make up a single national identity. Maniam's protagonist, Rajan, is an assimilated second-generation Indian, whose desire for social mobility has outweighed his own sense of self. Despite his success in real estate, Rajan is filled with "a terrifying emptiness" (25) that leads him to seek three mentors who each symbolize one of the races of postcolonial Malaya: 1) his father, the spiritual link to Rajan's homeland of India; 2) his Chinese colleague, Lee Shin, who cultivates a Chinese identity displayed as orientalist chinoiserie;[1] and 3) the Malay mystique Zulkifli, who speaks of the tiger as a symbol for the Malay community's "traditional, mystical attitude to the landscape" (12). Rajan rejects each of these possible mentors, finding little in Indian, Chinese, or Malay identity that speaks to his own experiences. His journey is not one of ethnic self-discovery, but a political odyssey that leads him to understand how people "build up walls" that "prevent us from knowing each other, knowing ourselves" (39).

Maniam's metaphor of cultural identity as a wall that blocks us from knowing ourselves distinguishes many Anglophone novels that come from the former "tropical dependencies" of Southeast Asia, particularly colonial Malaya (peninsular Malaysia and Singapore), the Philippines, and the various English-speaking diasporas in North America. From a North American point of view, seeing cultural identity as a "wall" seems at odds with the histories of racial organizing that claim cultural identity as a gateway to greater understanding and social commitments. But from a Southeast Asian context, Maniam's narrative probes the premises of cultural pluralism as a mode of governance instituted by colonial rule, which separated populations according to their racial identities as a means of enforcing order and providing social legibility. The novel's dreamy, reflective style undermines realist representations of cultural identity that have been reinforced through narratives of racial harmony. *In a Far Country* forgoes the notion that one's ascribed identity should provide spiritual fulfillment, and instead echoes the sentiments of Anglophone writers who see ascribed cultural identities as a remnant of colonial governance. What does it mean to understand oneself and others not through cultural identity, but through what Maniam calls "the crossovers" that are the material reality of diversity?[2]

Transitive Cultures asks how English-language writing from Southeast Asia and its diasporas in North America can be read together to reveal forms of pluralist governance in sites across the transpacific, in Asia as well as in North America.[3] It builds upon a wide range of scholarship in Asian American studies and Southeast Asian studies and theories of diaspora, postcolonialism, and cultural studies to ask how Anglophone narratives deracinate the primary optics of multiculturalism by forgoing the presumption that given nationalist and ethnic identities should be the primary means for providing one's spiritual, social, or even political fulfillment. Anglophone literature from Malaya (Malaysia/Singapore), the Philippines, and their diasporic populations in Hawai'i, the mainland United States, and Canada traces how terms like "diversity," "racial harmony," and "tolerance" are embedded in a transnational history of imperial networks and colonial governance. Narratives in English from Southeast Asia and its migrants often depict the Southeast Asian as an individual who is expected to perform an "authentic" and "tolerable" identity that is diasporic, empowered, and hypervisible, as well as imperial, confining, and monolithic. Since Southeast Asian migrants often have a long history of migrancy, where the "original homeland" is already several homelands away, these writers see even their own given racial and diasporic identities as contributing a structural role through the hypervisibility of cultural practices and traditions, so that, for instance, the traditional needlework of the Malays becomes a mark of talent for working in microprocessor factories, and the matronly affection of Filipinas becomes a mark of talent for domestic servitude and nursing. How do these narratives allow us to shift from seeing identity as an ascribed characteristic to be praised or empowered, to seeing categories of identity as imperial strategies of appropriation, social stratification, and incorporation, which are needed to represent the nation (and global corporations) as multiculturalist, and thus exceptional?

To navigate these landscapes, Anglophone texts consider seriously the potentialities of crossover. In K. S. Maniam's 1997 essay, "The New Diaspora," he fleshes out his metaphor of the tiger as a symbol of an ethnic nationalism that requires "the continual and ritualistic immersion into the spirit of the land so as to be reaffirmed." The tiger represents a clinging to an inherited sense of culture, and rejects a more complex inward journey that lies beyond ready-made identities and histories. Maniam contrasts this figure of the tiger with that of the chameleon, "the blending into whatever economic, intellectual, and social landscapes that are available." The tiger's promise of stability and mutual respect leaves one in a "cultural entrapment" that neglects the perspectives offered by other cultures, while the chameleon "seeks to inhabit, simultaneously, different intellectual, cultural, and imaginative spaces." While the tiger is strong in purity, and defends its young against outside forces, the chameleon remains aware of and knowledgeable about the cultures around it. The chameleon thus is not necessarily a migrant or minority subject, but an "insider and outsider at the same time," an individual "exiled within [his or her] own homelands." Whereas the tiger represents an affiliation with "pragmatic tolerance," the chameleon imagines a form of dealing with one's cultural and historical context without relying on the identity-based optics of capital and the state to find one's essence. The chameleon rejects the "culture of fear" brought about through multicultural contexts—the fear that violent racialized factions will emerge. Maniam's metaphor speaks to multiplicity as a "true nature" by emphasizing the act of adapting to varied perceptions and expectations.[4]

Maniam's metaphor of the chameleon echoes other literary artists and thinkers within Southeast Asia. In the 1970s, the writer Lloyd Fernando also wrote of Malaysian and Singaporean pluralism as a colonial legacy that ultimately needed to be reevaluated in the wake of the race riots of the 1960s. Fernando envisioned an alternative type of cultural form that saw migrant cultures as partaking in "an unceasing process" that is "capable of continuing as if in infinite series" (*Cultures in Conflict* 14). Written in the wake of the 1960s crises that saw multiple race riots across Malaya, Fernando's essays theorized a cultural form based on the conscious ability to transition among multiple racial "types." These transitions were not occurring merely to access positions of privilege, as one might envision cosmopolitan subjects or those who "pass." Transition belonged to what Fernando called "in-between migrants" whose ways of life did not reflect their ascribed identities, but who were too disadvantaged to claim cosmopolitan or global belonging. They thus appeared to onlookers within localized racial forms, and their political attitudes were difficult if not impossible to parse because their very survival relied upon being identified as ethnically authentic. Like Maniam, Fernando saw transition as a hidden but shared cultural practice, one that belongs both to the writer "crossing over" for a wider perspective, as well as to characters like Sally in Fernando's *Scorpion Orchid*, a service worker of ambiguous racial history and sexual orientation, who goes as Sally Yu (Chinese) and Salmah (Malay).

For both Maniam and Fernando, cultures of transition were condemned to remain unrecognized, to fade away struggling against a colonial pluralist discourse where transition was unthinkable. Within a world of borders, nations, and pluralist conceptions of identity, these "chameleons" appear as already established identity types. But their practices of transition provide an alternative politics of identity from the vantage point of Southeast Asian colonial history, where identity can bring both a sense of community and belonging, as well as the implicit demand to close off cultural borders. By exposing how identities have been produced through imperial encounter and the demand for surplus labor, these narratives encourage migrants not to reject such identities, but to manage them with a broader vision of belonging that allows for cultural, spiritual, and political crossover. They urge us to see identity as a process of unceasing transitions that shifts with every new context—a process that can be controlled, reimagined, and, with enough savvy, made pleasurable.

To read the motif of transition across multiple contexts, I dub this unceasing process "transitive culture" to mean a set of shifting cultural practices tactically mobilized in contexts where identity is defined as fixed and authentic. I implicitly invoke Paulo Freire's notion of "transitive consciousness" as a state between fighting for survival and political agency, wherein subjects gain an awareness that enables them to perceive and respond to themes and myths that stretch over histories and nations. To be transitive for Freire is to be aware of the broader situation even when not recognized politically. Yet, one can still foster "a permanently critical attitude" to "become integrated with the spirit of the time" (5).[5] "Transitive" calls not upon the aggression of the tiger, but upon the chameleon's ability to perceive of imperial culture as "the result of men's labor, of their efforts to create and re-create" (Freire 41). "Transitive" invokes its Latinate sense of "to go" (*itus*) "across" (*trans*), and its dominant sense "to pass into another condition" (*OED*). Transitive culture, like a transitive verb, positions the migrant between one subject (himself or herself) and infinite conditions or possibilities, acknowledging ever-evolving, complex histories, and selves re-created through drift, detour, and difference.[6]

This book asks how transition can be recognized as a sustainable cultural form that maneuvers through, rather than directly against, given identities and categorizations. By emphasizing "culture," I spotlight how transition functions as a cultural practice that is engendered through contexts of pluralism and that takes advantage of recognizable aesthetic forms or genres. I am influenced here by Brent Hayes Edwards, who has written of diaspora not as a culture but as a cultural practice, a strategic cultural response to uprooting (22). As James C. Scott has similarly written, cultural practices become politicized when "open, organized, [and] political activity" is seen as "dangerous, if not suicidal" (*Weapons of the Weak* xv). In the context of Southeast Asia, where authoritarian regimes have made populations legible through immobilization, Scott stresses the importance of local knowledge, informal processes, and improvised tactics, which allow groups to remain mobile and illegible (*Seeing Like a State* 6). Tactics are learned through practice and experience, and reveal forms of difference that cannot be adequately understood from an objective, schematic point of view. Such tactics emerge as tactile knowledge, what Scott calls *metis*, from the Greek for cunning or "cunning intelligence"; the knowledge of riding a bicycle, of living in one's own body.[7] Though Scott deals with rural migrants and itinerant communities, I follow his insights in formulating transitive cultures not as organized social actions, but as the shared cultural practices that underwrite the complexity of identity.

In *Bodies That Matter* Judith Butler invokes the term "transitive" to describe when an identity, in being named, also inaugurates the subject into a norm that she is expected to routinely recite and reproduce (6). Naming a newborn baby a "girl" is "transitive" when it "initiates the process by which a certain 'girling' is compelled" (232). This process, though embedded in culture and language, is not absolute. One is "compelled," as Butler writes, to perform gender, sexuality, race, and nation, but this development is susceptible to an array of disruptions: queer sexual desires; critical, violent, and intimate encounters with others; inhabitations of "abnormal" bodies; and witnessing the reiteration of state, colonial, and imperial forms of governance. Indeed, today the term "transition" in the United States invokes a spectrum of queer political discourses, where "to transition" is to elide normative definitions of gender. But as others have argued, this critical edge of transition becomes lost in its reiterations as an authenticating label for one's "true self": a "transwoman," a "transman."[8] As witnessed in talk shows and celebrity transitions, the impetus of witnessing transition—racial, gendered, sexual, or other—is to rename such individuals into recognizable and celebratory identity types.[9] Transitive culture broadens the idea of transition beyond that of a new identity to be recognized for one's "true self," to an understanding of shared tactics and techniques for dexterously crossing gendered, racialized, and sexualized borders, for being, as RuPaul stated, "not real," but "everything and nothing at all."

Like Butler's and Freire's conceptions of "transitive," transitive cultures suggest some awareness of the varied processes of identity-making, which are often revealed through experiences of exile, migrancy, mobility, and critical encounters with colonial histories and contemporary imperial violence. Transitive cultures thus respond to major and minor instances of being uprooted from one's given identity, of feeling estranged from or indifferent toward one's given culture, community, gender, sexuality, and nation. Such expressions do not easily register within the tactics of North American liberal politics. They come not through manifestos or political speeches, but through connotative signs of metaphor, symbols, gestures, performances, and tone. Their refusal to seek public recognition for their "true selves" reveals how identity is practiced in the everyday within contexts of plural governance, what are usually called "multicultural societies."

MULTICULTURALISM AND THE 1960S

> If the cultural basis of colonialism is racism, . . . then the cultural basis of neocolonialism is multiculturalism.
> —Chen Kuan-Hsing, *Asia as Method*

In the United States, the 2007–2008 economic crisis spurred a discursive sea change, whereby American multiculturalist values of tolerance and diversity were put radically into question. As Gayatri Spivak put it, the limitations of such values were exposed as the white middle class feared themselves becoming "sub-alternized," of losing access to healthcare, education, welfare, and housing (Gai-rola). Succeeding years have seen greater crises in the American racial imaginary. From the victimization of racial minorities through the U.S. subprime mortgage crisis; to the #BlackLivesMatter protests that erupted over the deaths of Trayvon Martin (2012), Michael Brown (2014), and Eric Gardner (2014), and the subse-quent acquittals and refusals to indict their killers; to the election of a president endorsed by the leaders of the KKK, whose efforts to galvanize the Republi-can base included the dehumanization of Mexican immigrants as rapists, drug addicts, and thieves. These events are counterdiscourses to a dominant percep-tion of America as a multicultural nation. The election of Barack Obama (2008), the appointment of Sonia Sotomayor to the Supreme Court (2009), as well as the Supreme Court decision to allow same-sex marriage (2015) have all been deployed as evidence that the long project of the American civil rights move-ment has reached into the highest governmental offices. What if, however, we saw these two discourses of race as part of the same general ideology? What if we saw both series of events as mutually reinforcing the panoptic gaze of the state, which makes positive representations of empowered racial minorities hypervisible? Can we be living in an age where both class and race are at their most unequal, while at the same time, we are also the most equal that we have ever been?

These two discourses, one of racial crisis and the other of racial progress, have drawn lines in the sand across the academy, dividing those who wish to defend multicultural institutions, and those demanding to dismantle them in exchange for more intersectional and antiracist coalitions.[10] The former have come to the defense of ethnic studies and identity-based projects in universities and public life, while the latter, represented best by critical ethnic studies scholars, have con-tinued to explore how American tolerance has been casually invoked to bolster support for imperial expansion, and has produced new "Others" in those deemed racist, sexist, fundamentally religious, or otherwise intolerant.[11] For these schol-ars, the difficulty in parsing the American political crisis as a racial crisis lies in the sacrosanct history of civil rights, perceived as a bottom-up 1960s movement. Though the most recognized speakers about civil rights politics, Martin Luther King Jr. and Malcolm X, rarely used the terms "multiculturalism," "diversity," or even "tolerance," contemporary racial discourse invests heavily in these thinkers in marking its own origin as a domestic American product, and its most value-laden ideological export. In turn, American racial histories have cast the United States as a morally superior power, one of "multicultural exceptionalism" that legitimates imperial and capitalist projects abroad. The separation of civil rights history from a revolutionary anti-imperial politics has made the contemporary American context a particularly difficult minefield to navigate through. Despite flagrantly racist social structures, from its prison system and its anti-Hispanic immigration policies, to its racially skewed poverty and its targeting of Islamic "terrorists" at home and overseas, the American project of multiculturalism has continued to provide the talking points for antiracist politics.

It is through this contemporary fissure that we need to take a broader historical and spatial view to consider how contemporary racial governance can be traced back to the challenge of racial management that emerged within American and British colonies in Southeast Asia. As Shu-mei Shih and many others have pointed out, racial discourses in America have continued to presume that the values associated with civil rights (diversity, tolerance, multiculturalism) are a Western and American construct, thus serving to "safeguard the primacy of the West as the source of methodological and theoretical paradigms" (Shih, "Toward an Ethics" 92). Understanding the American racial crisis means decentering America from its own invented history of global multiculturalism, and to instead construct an alternative genealogy that traces contemporary racial formations to sites in Southeast Asia, where pluralism was deployed as an imperial strategy. In the everyday multiculturalist exceptionalism of the United States, one easily forgets that "American" is not the only nationalist symbol naming a multiracial populace. The terms "Malaysian," "Singaporean," and "Filipino" all refer to diversities of people that rival that of the United States in varieties of language and ethnicity. While the 1960s are seen as the time of the birth of multiculturalism in the United States, in the former colonies within Southeast Asia, the 1960s mark a series of crises where riots and repression unmasked the ideals of diversity and tolerance.

With the protest-driven end of British rule after the Second World War, postindependence Malaysia and Singapore suffered their own crises in multicultural ideals. First envisioned as a multiracial nation, the Federation of Malaysia broke down only a year after Singapore's inclusion, when during the 1964 Maulud (Prophet Muhammad's birthday) celebration, fights between Malay Muslims and Chinese Singaporeans culminated in race riots that resulted in twenty-two deaths and hundreds of injuries. Although this crisis is often blamed for the separation (or abandonment) of Singapore from Malaysia, it also signals a crisis in how multiracialism was imagined within a postcolonial context, where racial differences had been identified as a potential source of violence and upheaval, thus necessitating a strong state power (the British) to "keep watch" over ethic factions. Before the end of the decade, the ideals of multiculturalism were torn asunder by the 1969 race riots that occurred throughout Malaysia, causing the state to forgo multiracialism in its "New Economic Policy" that produced Malay hegemony and prompted the exile of many Chinese and Indians. Meanwhile, Singapore continued its narrative of racial harmony through a state as strong-handed as Britain's before it. Under the ideals of a militant multiculturalism, Singapore was able to legitimate one-party rule and to enforce the draconian Sedition Act of 1948 by restricting freedom of speech and prohibiting "seditious" gatherings and protests.

In America's former colony of the Philippines, the election of Ferdinand Marcos in 1965 contradicted the ideals of a multiethnic Filipino/a populace through twenty years of repressive rule, nine of those years under martial law. "Filipino" was previously imagined by revolutionaries as a conglomerate of distinct ethno-linguistic groups, but American colonizers later emulated the British in Malaya by recasting the diverse Filipina/o populace as potentially violent and thus in need of colonial management. Post-independence saw the contestation of Filipino identity until Marcos's rule, when those of religious, linguistic, and ethnic difference were repressed and branded as enemies of the state. A new multiracial crisis under Marcos culminated in the 1968 Jabidah massacre, when Filipino armed forces killed dozens of Filipino Muslim (Moro) recruits attempting to desert. The massacre sparked an insurgency for Islamic autonomy in the Philippine South that has continued to this day, and helped prompt Marcos's nine years of martial law. During Marcos's rule, the "multiethnic" Philippines would be ideologically replaced by the concept of "Filipino" as Catholic (in the anti-Muslim sentiment) and as Tagalog-speaking. With the fervent religious differences between Catholics in Luzon and the Visayas and Muslims in Mindanao, as well as cultural and linguistic differences between groups, the Philippines is, as E. San Juan calls it, "vibrant with differences—at the price of the suffering of the majority of its citizens" ("Paradox of Multiculturalism" 2).

In both the former colonies of the Philippines and Malaysia/Singapore, the 1960s crises caused a fundamental recasting of racial, religious, and ethnic differences into political factions. In all three cases, the ideals of multiracialism were not defeated so much as deferred into the future, thus rationalizing the presence of a repressive state to manage factions. This history offers the 1960s as a conjunctural moment in the formation of American multiculturalism, not of its origin-point, but of its migration from the colonies to the imperial center. It enables us to separate multiculturalism from its sacrosanct history, and causes us to find historical corollaries in the present moment that avoid, as Vijay Mishra has put it, the "tendency to read multiculturalism as a purely Western phenomenon" ("Multiculturalism" 199). In a context where racist structures pervade every aspect of American life, in education, incarceration, police violence, poverty, and consumerism, the view from Southeast Asia allows us to reframe our understanding of multiculturalism as well as its critiques.

MULTICULTURALISM AS DISCOURSE

> For the intellectual the task, I believe, is explicitly to universalize the crisis, to give greater human scope to what a particular race or nation suffered, to associate that experience with the sufferings of others.
> —Edward W. Said, *Representations of the Intellectual*

Broadly defined, "multiculturalism" is most often conceived of as a social system that expects racial and ethnic groups to visibly and proudly express their given identities in order to be recognized politically and to be accommodated socially by state institutions such as public schools and the armed forces, as well as through positive forms of cultural and media-based representation. But as an ideological symbol, "multiculturalism" plays the role of an empty signifier wherein "culture" need not signify race or history.[12] In the United States, multiculturalism emerged in the interwar period, when, despite the past racial "diversity" of North America (indigenous, African Americans, and Chinese), it wasn't until the "New Immigration" of Jews, Eastern Europeans, and Southern Europeans in the late nineteenth and early twentieth century that notions of cultural pluralism began to flourish. Following the work of William James, the political philosophers Horace Meyer Kallen (1882–1974) and Randolph Silliman Bourne (1886–1918) defended cultural pluralism during and after World War I, when American xenophobia was at an all-time high, and later culminated in the restrictive Immigration Act of 1924. In his 1915 essay "Democracy versus the Melting Pot," Kallen argued against "melting pot" models of assimilation, and advocated instead for a cultural pluralism model defined as "multiplicity in a unity [and] an orchestration of mankind."[13] Alain Locke later expanded on the advantages of cultural pluralism as an alternative to assimilation, yet the concept rarely migrated from the realm of political philosophy, as Kallen himself noted. It wasn't until the post–World War II era that cultural pluralism became a rallying cry for American patriotism and imperial power.[14]

Critics of institutionalized multiculturalism in the United States have seen it as a state and capitalist co-optation of civil rights discourse that commodifies and depoliticizes difference. This counterdiscourse points to how state and corporate power have produced, in the broadest sense, Asian Americans as highly skilled "model minorities," Latin Americans as service and farm laborers, and African Americans as trapped within a "culture of poverty" (Lisa Lowe; Dylan Rodríguez).[15] Since the War on Terror, critical ethnic studies scholars have focused on multiculturalism's role in giving moral justification to U.S. imperial practices worldwide. Jodi Melamed calls this form "neoliberal multiculturalism," and defines it as "the contemporary incorporation of U.S. multiculturalism into the legitimating and operating procedures of neoliberalism," including counterterrorism ("Spirit of Neoliberalism" 15). Melamed's work considers how the era of multiculturalism and the era of neoliberalism do not merely coincide, but act as co-constituting ideological forces that organize conceptions of difference by recognizing racial identities as labor classes and as targets of state repression.

I expand upon Melamed's work by refusing to confine critiques of multiculturalism within a nationalist perspective (whether Canadian, Australian, or American). The genesis of the term "multiculturalism" in fact speaks to its emergence not as a characterization of the United States populace, but of the United States in contrast to its overseas enemies, who were cast as "monocultural." "Multiculturalism," as far as I can trace it, was first used in the novel

Lance: A Novel about Multicultural Men (1941) to characterize people ("men") who could transcend nationalist languages and culture. The novel's subsequent review in the *New York Herald-Tribune* in July 1941 used the term "multicultural" to mark the United States and its allies as morally and ethically superior to the racial nationalism of the Axis powers, comparing the "national prejudice" of the Japanese and Germans to America's "'multicultural' way of life." Even in its genesis, multiculturalism had little need to be defined—its function was simply to provide an exceptional characteristic that projected racial prejudice onto others. Confined by this nationalist lens, multiculturalism continues to celebrate racial diversity to give value to U.S. empire, allowing the United States to embody "the universal, so that U.S. government and military actions are to be understood as being for a supranational good" (Melamed, "Spirit of Neoliberalism" 16). In the context of the U.S. War on Terror, to see multicultural ideology as disseminating from the United States to the global "rest" allows America to make "monoculturalism" and religious fundamentalism a category of stigma that justifies torture (ibid.). World War II can thus be seen as the catalyst that brought pluralist values to the forefront after the racist violence characteristic of Nazi Germany, Fascist Italy, Imperial Japan, and later communist Russia and China, all of which were depicted as totalitarian powers that pushed for various forms of ideological, cultural, and political homogeneity, despite the fact that Soviet Russia, Imperial Japan, and Communist China all had multicultural agendas of their own (Jin). In an effort to win the ideological battle, American discourses diagnosed enemy nations as homogenous social structures, while in contrast, the United States was marked as a nation accepting of difference, with immigrant groups (and later refugees) as living proof. With the emergence of the United States as a superpower, multiculturalism was no longer an ideal that offered alternatives to overseas expansion, as Randolph Bourne had theorized a "Trans-National America." It was enshrined as the epitome of how a moral and just society was organized, a blueprint to be exported abroad.

If the Allies-led war against racial nationalism saw the invention of multiculturalism as a term, the Cold War was its moment of flourishing. The World War II narrative of a diverse America against the racist Axis powers would, during the Cold War, convert to envisioning a multiculturalist nation (the United States) against totalitarian communist states. The United States would fashion itself plural in order to cast the stigma of racial nationalism upon communist countries aligning with the Soviets and the People's Republic of China. This comparison enabled a new imperial governance that operated through "nonterritorial imperial tactics," including "economic support," "humanitarian aid," and "structural adjustment policies" (Kim 18). Domestically, the Cold War resulted in greater migrations of Asians from French Indochina, a symptom of wars in Asia that was reframed as a symbol of national diversity and compassion (Tang 86).[16] Internationally, the ideals of communism were reconstituted through depictions of communist homogeneity. Images of Han Chinese crowds saluting Mao Zedong went side-by-side with depictions of diverse American military fighting in Vietnam. [The answer to incorporating populist desires for structural equality came in claiming multiculturalism as the face of empire. With the waning of the Cold War in the 1980s and 1990s, multiculturalism became formalized in education and media representation, which coincided with the production of new "intolerable" others. The hostage crisis in Iran and the subsequent wars in Iraq, Iran, and Kuwait drew upon religious intolerance as yet another instance of homogenization, while the drug wars of the same period saw many civil rights activists and people of color incarcerated for possession charges, an injustice that flew under the radar of a culture newly saturated with multicultural concepts of "empowerment" and "identity."]

Critical ethnic studies scholars have emphasized how multiculturalism has been instrumental in creating legitimacy for institutions such as the U.S. military and the prison industrial complex, and have refused America's self-representation of multicultural exceptionalism. This crucial scholarship has worked toward building a transhistorical and comparative lens that causes us to reconceptualize multiculturalism as an ideology formed through comparisons. The "multicultural society" of 1941 has as its foil the Axis powers, while conceptions of U.S. diversity during the Cold War conflated the economic equality promised in communist states with racial and cultural homogeneity. The formalization of multicultural-ism in U.S. institutions also allowed the U.S. state to continue identifying its enemies as intolerant and racist (present-day revisions of the terms "backward" and "uncivilized").[17] Critical ethnic studies scholars have unsettled the "bottom-up" narrative of multiculturalism as an exceptional form of social belonging originating in North America. They thus leave open the question of emergence. What happens if we shift our view from one sort of Anglophone society (Australia, Canada, the United States) to the Anglophone societies within Southeast Asia, where values of tolerance, diversity, and multiculturalism are not coded as grass-roots, social justice products, but as legacies of colonialism and empire?

PLURALISM AS COLONIAL STRATEGY

> The fundamental character of the organization of a plural society as a whole is the structure of a factory, organized for production.
> —J. S. Furnivall, *Colonial Policy and Practice*

If we understand multiculturalism as a governing strategy reliant upon celebratory conceptions of diversity, tolerance, and "racial harmony," we can begin to compose a longer genealogy of multiculturalism that first emerged as an imperial form, beginning with the British and then the Americans, that took root within imperial centers. Though British and American colonial histories are often thought of as distinct, much historical work has shown how these two empires constituted each other in Southeast Asia through the sharing of infrastructure, linguistic mapping, and transportation technologies. Joint imperial projects between the United States and Britain were most clearly present in the shared governing strategies that formed a pluralistic conception of the "local" in order to manage, produce, and incorporate racialized populations. The "inter-imperial" connections, Paul Kramer writes, played a central role in building state governance throughout the colonies in terms of "organization, policy making, and legitimation," such that "the architects of colonial rule often turned to rival powers as allies, foils, mirrors, models, and exceptions" ("Power and Connection" 1316). The impetus to mark the American colonial state as pluralist emerged from the need to differentiate its "legitimate" colonial project from the "illegitimate" colonial powers also operating within Southeast Asia, particularly the British. The parading of tolerable ethnic minorities was common in both the British and American colonies, and comparisons were frequently made upon the degree of stability that the colonial governments could provide. As Kramer writes the British often legitimated their empire through exhibiting "civilized" natives, while the Americans did so by viewing themselves as an "anti-empire" or a "non-empire," educating Filipino/as through American literature, culture, and religion to guide them toward democratic independence. This process of colonial race making was meant to surveil populations and place them into hierarchies to fashion cooperation ("Power and Connection" 1319), resulting in forms of racial thinking that "had a decisive impact on American racial ideology itself" (ibid.). As America abroad fashioned itself as pluralist, America at home began to do the same. As Matthew Frye Jacobson has written, white ethnics in the United States were able to assimilate with Anglo-Saxons as Caucasians by comparing themselves to Filipino/as, on the one hand, and on the other hand by incorporating Filipino/as into the American national imaginary alongside Native Americans and African Americans, as populations who could be educated and controlled by a white supremacist managerial force (181). The inter-imperial ethical war thus reconstituted American identity itself, as both British and American colonial powers executed a managerial technique that taxonomized racial identities and made the most educated hypervisible, providing segments of peoples who were divided but not factionalized, and who were constituted as "the White Man's Burden."

The colonial history of Southeast Asia sheds light on contexts where diversity serves the interests of the state as both a governing strategy and a legitimating ideology. The ability to manage pluralist populations casts the colonial state as managerial rather than coercive—in the American context, a non-empire empire. By taxonomizing populations, colonial states also produced stratified labor classes, where one's racial identity determined one's position as a field hand, manager, or factory worker. Indeed, the concept of a "pluralist society" originated in the economist J. S. Furnivall's 1910 analysis of "Southeast Asian tropical dependencies," where Furnivall criticized pluralist strategies for employing racial difference in order to maintain cheap labor costs and to exploit resources (310). Colonial plural societies were an ideal place for fomenting capitalist investment, as they lacked a central set of cultural values, a common "social will" that would pressure economic forces to provide a living wage and better working conditions.[18] Furnivall argued against the colonial governments' depictions of themselves as civilizers, educators, and managers, and explored how this managerial class looked at social problems "not as a citizen but as a capitalist or an employer of labour" (306).[19] These plural societies were the manifestation of both multinational philosophy and capitalism in its purest form; they were societies that respected cultural values so long as common desires were directed toward economic values.

These comparisons of multiculturalism, multiracialism, and pluralism are not meant to laud some instances of racial management over others, but to pinpoint the fundamental assumptions that these formations share. Since multiculturalism's dominance as the primary antiracist politics in the United States, leftist critiques of multiculturalism have focused on particular elements and symptoms, such as "boutique multiculturalism" (Regina Lee), "official multiculturalism" (Lisa Lowe), "neoliberal multiculturalism" (Jodi Melamed), "imperial multiculturalism" (Duncan Ivison), "conciliatory multiculturalism" (Wen Jin), and "establishment multiculturalism" (E. San Juan). These concepts are meant to separate a corporate and state-sanctioned multiculturalism from the multiculturalism of cross-racial coalitions and large-scale societal transformations ("strong multiculturalism" or "critical multiculturalism") in order to reveal the inconsistencies of multiculturalist practices in the United States. Many of these critiques, however, seem to offer few alternatives, and rarely do they seek to unsettle the very fundamental optics of multiculturalism that makes it seem necessary, that is, the "identity" of identity politics.

If multiculturalism is the abstract governing strategy, identities are the particular modes through which power is enacted. But identities are not simply framed by power. They are invested with such ideological and personal intimacies that to criticize them (or those who take them on) marginalizes the personhood and agency that exists behind the optics of population and community. Suffice to say that racial identities are modes of recognition and communal belonging, and thus provide routes for marginalized peoples to earn the privileges that come with state recognition—citizenship entitlements, equality under the law, mutual respect, democratic participation, historical and cultural representation. Therefore it should elude no one as to *why* identities are claimed by minorities themselves. The power enabled by claiming identities can be marked as a strategic positioning that reflects shared memories, languages, and cultural practices, and can offer "lifestyles of empowerment" (Grewal 16). The adoption of identities is never *not* a negotiation, as their entire purpose is to conflate notions of ethnicity, race, nation, sexuality, gender, and labor, and to produce racial types that hardly reflect the individual living under its name. The critical theorist Étienne Balibar famously identified this conflation as enabling a "neoracism" that continues racist institutions and social stratification by assuming that racialized bodies are fixed into "insurmountable cultural differences" (22). But what makes neoracism racist isn't merely this conflation, but the imperial context wherein these differences are valorized only when presented as "tolerable"—a strategy of "acceptance" that divides, hierarchizes, and produces Others under consistent surveillance and repression.

Transitive Cultures departs from previous critiques of racial identity in seeing its homogenizing forms not as a problem to be resisted by naming more heterogeneous forms of identity, but as a governing strategy that is routinely being traversed, managed, and appropriated. Asian American studies has particularly contributed to the deconstruction of Asian American identity, so much so that the preoccupation with identity critique has characterized Asian American studies almost as much as the subjects it treats. "Asian American" identity itself began as a political response to the injustices of the Vietnam War and the denial of civil rights. It exists as an invented identity that emerged through the very racist optics that it sought to resist, transitioning "Orientals" into "Asian Americans." This reinvention was made possible not by accounting for unseen modes of difference, but through appropriating the state's mission to control the production and circulation of difference, with the taxonomy of identity serving as a primary means of obtaining and orchestrating this control. This disciplinary method is characteristic of what Michel Foucault called biopolitics, a strategy of governance that emerged in the nineteenth century and produced subjects who were self-regulating, productive, and passive, but who took on modes of identification (and thus subjectivity) as authentic representations of themselves. In his lectures, Foucault noted that in the era of late global capitalism, biopolitics had shifted within a neoliberal context where political power was exercised "on the principles of a market economy" (*Birth of Biopolitics* 131). He explored this contemporary form using the term "governmentality," or the "art of government," which named an "ensemble formed by the institutions, procedures, analyses and reflections" that induced an ideological order so profound as to reinvent social relations. As Furnivall too concluded, it took an ensemble of forces to produce populations who could be categorized through group identities, but who thought of themselves as individual self-regulating subjects.

This book employs the term "pluralist governmentality" to capture the varied dimensions of pluralist racial forms. The Singapore literary scholar Philip Holden has argued that governmentality can illustrate "continuity between the colonial and postcolonial states," and I would add that governmentality too reveals ideological overlap between the colonial states and the imperial centers. In the case of Southeast Asia, colonial pluralism has legible logics, rationalities, and legitimations that appear congruent with postcolonial as well as North American governments. Rather than call this racial form "multiculturalist governmentality," I find "multiculturalism" itself a tool made blunt by overuse. I hereafter retain the term "pluralist" to invoke multiculturalism's colonial heritage and to unmask its reliance on conceptions of difference rather than similarity, where even the slightest set of differences can turn a group multicultural rather than homogenous, plural rather than mono. Pluralist governmentality names an art of government that expects individuals to visibly express their difference via given group identities, and in doing so, to represent imperial state power as neutral, universal, or benevolent. In what follows, I chart a genealogy of pluralist governmentality as it has developed in Malaya, the Philippines, and Asian North America.

PLURALIST GOVERNMENTALITY IN THE TRANSPACIFIC

> To articulate what is past does not mean to recognize "how it really was." It means to take control of a memory, as it flashes in a moment of danger.
> —Walter Benjamin, *Illuminations*

Transitive Cultures follows a tradition of comparative projects from thinkers like J. S. Furnivall, Shirley Geok-lin Lim, Benedict Anderson, and others to visualize a transnational history of pluralist governmentality that has operated through imperial networks and colonial governance. Despite the pioneering work of these scholars, Southeast Asia still remains in the popular imaginary as a region too complex to be studied in any broad or comparative manner. It contains economies both high (Singapore, Taiwan) and low (Laos, Cambodia); religions that challenge their own normative conceptions (the moderate Muslims, the consumption-permitting and militant Buddhisms); and histories that belie Western understandings (the "semi-colonial" history of places like Thailand, the scattered remnants of Chinese domination and Japanese colonization). This great complexity, when read under today's pluralist common sense, is interpreted as containing "the great merit of diversity" (Reid 6). But from another point of view, this region's histories of trade, economic migrations, investment capital, militarization, and national formations in the face of great cultural, linguistic, and religious difference reveal a crucial nexus in the formation of pluralist governmentality. From the vantage point of Southeast Asia, the U.S. brand of multiculturalism, which Beng Huat Chua has referred to as "liberal multiculturalism," can be distinguished as a unique form of pluralist governmentality that "insists on the 'freedom to choose' as a basic right of an individual" ("Cost of Membership" 171). In this view, multiculturalism in the United States appears not as *the* legitimate form of racial egalitarianism, but as a unique racial formation produced through the intersection of imperial strategies and American cultural pluralism.

Pluralist governmentality has its roots far from American soil. Modern pluralist ideas that we today would recognize as American can be traced to defenses of cultural pluralism in Johann Gottfried Herder (1744–1803), who adapted the Italian philosopher Giambattista Vico's notion of multiple truths into notions of cultural difference, separating "truths" by cultures rather than historical periods (Berlin). Often regarded as the first philosophical spokesman for both nationalism and multiculturalism, Herder named the nation (*Volk*) as a sovereign cultural whole, where each contained "a centre of happiness within itself" (Herder 186).[20] Many of these philosophical ideas remained unpracticed until the Indian Mutiny in 1857, when a colonial rebellion caused the British Crown to take over governance of South Asia from the East India Company. The crisis of rebellion gave the opportunity for pluralist ideas to emerge within policies meant to manage unruly populations. In 1862, the English political scholar Lord Acton argued that multinational (pluralist) empires or confederacies were the best way to derive consent from the governed because they allowed freedom for cultural autonomy. As Acton wrote: "Where there are only two races there is the resource of slavery; but when different races inhabit the different territories of one Empire composed of several smaller States, it is of all possible combinations the most favourable to the establishment of a highly developed system of freedom" (35). Acton found the ideal progenitor of this political style in the United States, which he considered a great pluralist federal structure, so long as each state had autonomy. Acton's ideal of a multinational federation was to be field-tested in the British colony in Malaya, which in 1867 fell into the control of London's Colonial Office. As a colonial entity populated by distinctly different ethnic groups—namely Chinese, Malays, and Indians—Malaya was to be governed through a form of pluralist governmentality that permitted the freedoms of cultural and religious autonomy, while successfully extracting resources (tin, gold, rubber).

The challenge for European colonizers in governing Southeast Asian societies was the same that researchers today have in studying it: that the region seems to be divided by a regional "cultural matrix" that is far more diverse ethnically, religiously, linguistically, and culturally than its neighboring regions of India and China, making Southeast Asia seem impenetrable and unknowable.[21] This "fluid cultural matrix" has extended, in various permutations, to the present day, and is most visible in state nationalist discourses that promote varying forms of pluralism to produce a national people and to deradicalize resisting groups.[22] In the Philippines, U.S. colonialists devised a particular form of pluralist governmentality that stressed ethnic and religious difference to disintegrate factional groups and to prevent "any sense of national unity that would challenge colonial rule" (San Juan, "Paradox of Multiculturalism" 1). In Malaya, different forms of ethnic nationalisms have been put forth as alternatives to a state nationalism that manifests through education, state ritual, and the media.[23] The difficulty of comprehending Southeast Asian nations has pushed scholars to rethink these organizing forces as more akin to pluralist models that reinforce national belonging by valorizing the nation's diversity and racial harmony.

If "cultural diversity" often characterizes studies of Southeast Asia, "free market," "commerce," and "trade" make up the second major concentration, since much of Southeast Asia's "diversity" has roots in the long-distance labor migrations that have been continuous since at least the sixteenth century (Lieberman, *Strange Parallels* 45). Already established trade routes set the stage for European colonizers to mark populations by their racial difference, in effect pairing racialized bodies with particular fields of labor.[24] These racial distinctions were not confined to any colonial state, but were revised and reimagined through the vast network of colonial trade routes in French Indochina; the Dutch East Indies; British India, Burma, and Malaya; and Spanish and American Philippines. As trade was dynamic and interdependent among the colonies, race was not made and remade simply through the colonizer's will. Southeast Asian societies did not just receive trading posts and imperial market-trade, but designated ports for the purposes of hosting trading routes, hoping to take advantage of these markets. Ethnic identities, employed for colonial rule, were not purely products of colonialists themselves, but were often managed and reinterpreted by colonial subjects for their own gain. Indeed, it was in the aftermath of these race-making projects that J. S. Furnivall criticized pluralist societies for only encouraging cross-racial interactions "in the market place, in buying and selling" (313).[25] Yet despite Furnivall's warning about the racial inequality within pluralist societies, contemporary neoliberal discourses of pluralist societies often cite Furnivall to reinforce the notion of a "Furnivall-Smithian" social structure, which marries the diversity of pluralism with the "liberation" of the free market, as if, together, they form an ideal antiracist space (Young 17). This binding of pluralist values with the free market allows us to trace pluralist governmentality as a transpacific form of power, wherein the assumption that the market is an equalizing and pluralistic force seems to be the very ideological incentive—as well as the ideological veil—that has maintained imperial dominance.

If the aftermath of World War II and the Cold War notes a sea change for U.S. domestic politics in forming pluralist governmentality, it marks a seismic shift in Southeast Asia, where the Cold War marked two separate and competing pluralist structures: the Soviet communist federation and the American imperial "sphere of influence." The Cold War era was a period of cataclysmic violence in Southeast Asia, with Chinese-led communist insurgencies and coups in Cambodia, the Philippines, Vietnam, and Laos, as well as anticommunist atrocities in Indonesia, Taiwan, Singapore, Malaysia, and Thailand. These aggressions were made within imperial spheres recognized through American alignment rather than citizenship. As the scholar Chen Kuan-Hsing has rightly pointed out, the repudiation of communist states led nations like Taiwan to embrace the United States as their alternative, as U.S. alliance included a faster route to modernity, and gave partial autonomy within a pluralist imperium (166).[26] In former colonies like the Philippines, Taiwan, and Malaya, the U.S. role in World

War II allowed it to finally surpass other colonizers as the benevolent imperial power, the "savior" from the Japanese, and the protector after the abandonment of Europe. Though American prowess was disrupted in the subsequent violence in Vietnam, Cambodia, and Laos, the amount of American ethical capital shored up during World War II solidified the United States as the trusted transpacific power, ushering in neocolonial regimes across Southeast Asia that have remained in place to the present day.

This genealogy of pluralist governmentality aims to understand contemporary multiculturalism as a broader transpacific strategy that shares distinct qualities with colonial pluralism in the colonies and cultural pluralism in the United States. First, pluralist tradition is not necessarily antagonistic to nationalism, but advocates for a larger "confederation," "multinational empire," or "trans-nation" that organizes and manages cultural differences. Second, this pluralist tradition emphasizes the equalization of cultural difference despite the vast asymmetrical inequality of class, gender, and linguistic differences, splitting up populations into collectives bound not by a common "social will," but by capitalist forces that seek to produce cheaper and sell higher. Finally, as the Cold War context shows, understanding this larger history causes us not to speak of a single "multiculturalism" that affects American minority groups, but of a transpacific American imperial sphere that operates through "pluralist strategies," "pluralist discourses," and "pluralist technologies." Rather than provide a "fictive ethnicity" of the nation-state, through which the state is the main expression of a national will, the state is made to appear "neutral," an "umpire" managing different groups, whose factitious nature could at any moment turn violent. If pluralism was never about creating harmony, but managing racial conflict, then the multicultural state, by definition, is also an imperial state.

Yet to speak of America today as an empire feels like adopting a trend only surpassed by speaking of the death of the American dream. In the words of Noam Chomsky, talking about American imperialism is like talking about triangular triangles. I carefully follow Paul Kramer's use of "imperial" as an adjectival framing device for "a category of analysis, not a kind of entity" ("Power and Connection" 1350). In both theory and practice, pluralist governmentality is a form of imperial power, whose imperial subjects are cataloged to represent both the diversity and harmony of the imperium, as well as the unruly factions whose way of life threaten its cohesion. Tracing pluralist governmentality across time and space reveals its common alliances to terms like "civilization" and "progress." So too, "pluralism" and "multiculturalism" refer to utopic endpoints, so that the entity cast as "multiculturalist" is also cast as "exceptional."

TRANSITIVE CULTURES IN ANGLOPHONE LITERATURE

It is in the bedrock of pluralist governmentality where transitive cultures emerge as a transnational formation that reveals how identities compete, shift, and transition in various contexts across the transpacific.[27] To explore these cultures, this book focuses on literary narratives that consider multicultural strategies through the use of English, a distancing language that is variously coded as "neutral," "universal," or "colonial," and is seen as a lingua franca operating among diverse linguistic groups. Because Anglophone authors do not fit their national ethnic norm, their literatures have been pushed to the margins of both the nation-state and the global English audience. Their use of English can also be seen as a means of positioning themselves outside of ethnic and national identities to better grasp the function of pluralist governmentality internationally (from the Global North to the Global South) and domestically (from Manila to Cebu in the Philippines, from the Malay and Chinese majorities in Malaysia and Singapore). These literatures offer conceptual tools to understand pluralist governmentality in its multiple forms, as their very use of English marks them as imperial products.

Anglophone literature from Malaysia and Singapore has reinterpreted the region's history of diversity and free trade into a broader history of pluralist governmentality. Texts by Lloyd Fernando trace the region's diversity to prenational eras like the sixteenth century, when the Ming Empire fostered trading routes between maritime Southeast Asia and China, and Malaysian cities like Melaka were used as geographically convenient trading ports (see chapter 1). State-driven celebrations of diversity are shadowed by Anglophone texts that trace how this diversity was produced through the intrusion of various colonial powers—the Portuguese, the Dutch, the British, and the Japanese—wherein Chinese traders and Tamil laborers were imported to support the trading centers of Melaka, Penang, and Singapore.[28] Anglophone writers have thus depicted the reality of racial divides, like the Chinese in multinational factory work (Lawrence Chua's *Gold by the Inch*), intimate sexual and religious crossovers (Lee Kok Liang's *Flowers in the Sky*), the suppression of Tamil temples (K. S. Maniam's *In a Far Country*), and the resentment felt for state multicultural policies like the New Economic Policy or the Internal Security Act (Shirley Geok-lin Lim's *Joss and Gold* and *Among the White Moon Faces*). Anglophone narratives by Chinese in Singapore often resist the commodified identity of being a "trade diaspora" or speaking Mandarin (as historically most Chinese in Singapore are Hokkien), while other narratives represent both nations' race riots as an opportunity for the state to produce new forms of social control (Lloyd Fernando's *Scorpion Orchid* and *Green Is the Colour*). These texts reinterpret English from being a "neutral" language—one not ascribed to any three ethnic groups—to speaking for cross-cultural and cross-ethnic communities.

Anglophone literature in the Philippines uncovers the enormous class divisions that correspond with linguistic, cultural, and religious differences. Many Philippine novels, for example, trace the dominance of a mestizo class of Chinese, American, and Spanish mixtures back to the earliest moments of national formation (see chapter 2).[29] The prominent Filipino Anglophone writer, Nick Joaquín, famously wrote in 1988 that "the identity of the Filipino today is of a person asking what is his identity" (*Culture and History* 244). His texts characterize Filipina/o identity as a process of becoming, emphasizing "what we are at this moment." F. Sionil José's novels capture the difficulties for Ilocano and Cebuanos to integrate into Tagalog-based state nationalism, while novels by Eric Gamalinda and Ninotchka Rosca reveal how histories of economic strife and imperialism spill out of pluralist histories that promote the Philippines as a place of diversity. As is the case with Malaysia/Singapore, Anglophone literature often becomes an expressive haven to critique nationalism and state policy in times of censorship. Famously, during Martial Law, Ferdinand Marcos seemed to censor almost every expressive medium besides literature in English, believing that Filipino/as rarely read literature (English or otherwise). With even greater absence of state censorship after Marcos, the theme of transition appears in narratives concerning queer subjectivity (Bino Realuyo's *The Umbrella Country*), mestizo privilege (Miguel Syjuco's *Illustrado*), state oppression (Ty-Casper's *Awaiting Trespass*), and transnational migration (Charlson Ong's *Embarrassment of Riches*).

Since the 1980s, class strife in the Philippines has become a transnational phenomenon, propelled by the estimated eight million Filipina/os working overseas as domestic workers in places like Hong Kong, Korea, and Israel; as nurses in the United States, Canada, and the United Kingdom; and as technicians, engineers, and merchant seamen worldwide.[30] Recent Anglophone literature like José Dalisay's *Soledad's Sister* and Mia Alvar's *In the Country* critically responds to Philippine textbooks and media that parade the image of the "family-oriented" Filipina, or the "sea-faring" Filipino, which shape national identities into multicultural identities that are easily placed in global divisions of labor (McKay; R. M. Rodriguez). Philippine Anglophone literature allows us to understand how pluralist governmentality can function as an *intranational* empire that seeks to "civilize the margins," and how this intranational empire is also necessary for finding recognition through given identities that then cater to the export of commodified bodies.

Literatures in English push us to understand the motif of transition as a response to pluralist governmentality. They give us a glimpse at the methods and modes of transition, at the ability to remain invisible even within contexts of hypervisibility, and at the ways of surviving and flourishing within the identity-based optics of their (and our) time. These texts provide a critical reconceptualization of pluralism, not as the ideal end of liberal democracy, but as a form of imperial governance masked under the guise of benevolent rule over unruly racial factions. In doing so, they also give us a chance to explore how various cultures, at the dawn of multiculturalism, managed to "decorporate," not through outright resistance, but through feigning incorporation. This was by no means always a revolutionary, resistant, or even counterdiscursive act, but a means of harbor and safe haven, of keeping a community not based on race or nation, but one of colonial, imperial, and pluralist leftovers. This literature exposes a politics of marginality that eludes rather than reinforces the power of the imperial state. If we can see pluralist governmentality as a structure forged out of the need to control a "diverse" colonial populace for the purposes of providing cheap labor and of legitimating imperial power, then we can begin to see this literature itself as a type of social practice, one that develops a culture of transitioning among given identities in order to access a more critical, reflective, and ambiguous mode of being.

THE ANGLOPHONE

> I have been faithful / Only to you, / My language. I choose you / Before country.
>
> —Shirley Geok-lin Lim, "Lament" in *Modern Secrets*

I draw on Southeast Asian texts written in English to uncover responses to pluralist governmentality from groups speaking within a language deemed "inauthentic" to their ascribed identities. In lacking authentic, national, or even diasporic culture, these writers explore pluralist racial formations across the region. Their literature compels us to confront Southeast Asian history, wherein identities have been produced at the nexus of multiple imperial projects, competing postcolonial states, and various forms of multiracial governance. Southeast Asia offers a method of thinking race *ex*-centrically (as well as *eccentrically*) that forces us to shift from "diaspora" as a framework that reinstitutes national categories by seeing migrants as caught between a homeland and a host country.[31] Such conceptual models tend to reflexively equate Western cultural practices (like speaking English) with particular nation-states, creating a Western "homeland" that can only play host to its Others. But the view from Southeast Asia suggests that those models may themselves be a product of pluralist governmentality, wherein the complex political histories of "homelands" are routinely simplified and defined solely by their relationship to the Western power, marking migrancy as a progressive act ("diasporic peoples," we are told, never seek refuge *from* the United States).

Transitive Cultures reframes Asian migrant texts from diasporic texts into "transpacific Anglophone" texts that spotlight works deemed "inauthentic" to both nationalist literatures and American ethnic literatures. I see Anglophone as a way to account for marginalized literary traditions within the United States that do not fit easily into the Anglo-American literary canon, and are thus seen as foreign or minoritized. I take this gesture from Shu-mei Shih, who uses "Sinophone" to signify non-Han Chinese minorities both outside and inside the People's Republic of China, particularly those in Tibet, Inner Mongolia, Xinjiang,

Hong Kong, and Taiwan. For Shih, "Sinophone" exposes how global multiculturalism renders "national cultures of the globe," and makes visible the "new global regime of multiculturalism" by disrupting the conflation of nation and ethnicity (*Visuality and Identity* 63), and by parsing the complexity of Chineseness to make identity "difficult to consume" (ibid. 5). Shih's use of Sinophone to disrupt global multiculturalism allows us to consider how the Anglophone might also offer alternative modes of seeing Southeast Asian and Asian American cultures as employing similar responses to pluralist governmentality. Whereas the Sinophone thinks through instances of Chineseness within an American minority politics to separate "minor" Chinese cultures from the hegemonic form represented by the People's Republic, I see Anglophone as doing the opposite. That is, the Anglophone brings the political dimensions of anti-imperial politics within the former colonies to American minority politics. Rather than think in terms of majorities or minorities, the Anglophone traces how communities fluctuate among positions of power through mobility, history, and transition. Its emphasis on imperial networks spotlights Southeast Asian migrants, whose presence has been difficult to render within American minority politics, because their very bodies speak to American imperial projects, and their "success" as "model minorities" has been less visible. Their ambivalence is manifest in the multiple terms used to describe them: "Southeast Asian," "Asian Pacific Islanders," "Asian Pacific Americans," "Filipino/a," "Malays," or simply "mixed." Anglophone bypasses identities made solely based on ethnicity or race while still accounting for the marginalization present in Asian American populations. Rather than mark the migrant as tethered to the "homeland" and the "host country," or co-opt the Asian American into multiculturalist discourses of success, "Anglophone" coheres as an expression of the "inauthentic."

Transitive Cultures treats Anglophone literature of the transpacific since World War II, which includes texts from Malaysia, Singapore, and the Philippines, as well as from Southeast Asian migrants in Hawaii, Canada, and the mainland United States. By reading across the transpacific, I hope to excavate a complex imperial history of pluralist governmentality that enables us to isolate its typical logics and procedures, and to derive new means for resisting or managing its contemporary formations. Many of the texts examined here are categorized in nationalist terms as Asian American, Filipino, Malaysian, or Singaporean.[32] The racial histories of many transpacific Anglophone writers are often too mixed to meet a reader's expectations about minority literature, and their refusal to incorporate with the language and culture of their own nation also eschews national identities. This ambivalence in a pluralist social order has allowed transpacific Anglophone literature to either be ignored or marginalized as "second rate."[33] Similarly, in the American context, much of Asian American literature has been ghettoized into a "literary Chinatown" that meets a reader's expectations for "real voices," and uses marketing techniques that emphasize authenticity and exoticism (Partridge). This study follows materialist literary critics and reads these texts as refracting histories of pluralism, while also constituting alternative cultures that have operated within it.

My readings of Anglophone literature focus on Malaya, the Philippines, and its diasporas to understand how the postcolonial use of English has enabled new ways of depicting the relationship between race/identity and state/capital. As Shirley Geok-lin Lim observed in her 1993 book, *Nationalism and Literature*, Malaya and the Philippines both exhibit what N.V.M. Gonzalez called the "cross-roads syndrome," as Lim defined it, "the collision of Asian and Western cultures leading to a sense of discontinuous history and cultural hybridization" (11). Anglophone artists depict the crossroads of race and empire within a language presumed to be a "neutral," "imperial," or "cosmopolitan" mode of address. But as a non-nationalist and inauthentic language, English can easily be appropriated to evade the censorship of the state and the condemnation of nationalist audiences (Holden, "Colonialism's Goblins" 26). By being cast as a distanced and estranged language, English can stage discussions of race, identity, nation, and language itself as socially constructed categories rather than ontological ones.[34]

In Malaysia and Singapore, English has been entrenched since the British colonial policies that promoted its use in business under the East India Company (Ibid. 160). After independence, English became depicted as a necessary "neutral" medium for communicating among races. The "mother tongues" of Tamil, Chinese, and Malay contrasted English use by providing a "cultural ballast" or "moral compass" to stabilize traditional identities, keeping Malaysians and Singaporeans from being "set adrift" in the mobile language of globalization. English use contains a multicultural/neoliberal double-effect because it not only implies a society wherein no one group is dominant, but also functions as a world language that gives access to an international business class (S. G. Lim, *Writing S.E./Asia in English* 39). As the Singaporean poet Edwin Thumboo wrote in his preface to *Perceiving Other Worlds*, many Anglophone writers turned to English in order to recognize histories of imperialism, migration, and racial mixture, which nationalist narratives had sought to diminish. English literature, rather than English administration, has been a project of reexamining English to better discover what had been "over-looked, neglected, or suppressed as a colonial language" (xvii).

The use of English to analyze colonial discourse and to build interethnic coalitions harks back to the use of English during the colonial period as a cross-racial lingua franca. Shirley Geok-lin Lim's devotion to English "before [her] country" expresses an allegiance to English that carries historical roots within her Peranakan background. The first non-British English language journal of the Straits, *The Straits Chinese Magazine*, launched in 1897, provided an outlet for Straits Chinese (and Peranakans) to communicate among various southern Chinese dialects. This use of English also gave Straits Chinese writers the chance to engage in political discussions and to experiment with Western literary forms, producing stories that sought to inspire social change (Keong 41). English use, then, became seen as a main vector that could shape new communal identities opposed to the racial categories proffered by the nation-state.

In the Philippines, Anglophone writing emerged out of American colonial education, where the linguistic diversity of the Philippines was reimagined by American schools as a "linguistic 'chaos,'" and English provided a practical solution as "the bearer of cultural value and moral authority" (Wesling 11). In effect, English grew to encompass so much of the territory that the Philippines has now become the third largest English-speaking country in the world, a surprising fact considering that its literary contributions have nowhere near the recognition of Anglophone nations like Canada, Ireland, or India. From the beginning of American colonization, the English language was thought to be a civilizer on its own,[35] and attempts to educate Filipino/as in English resulted in a very quick cultural shift, so that by the 1930s more Filipino/as spoke English than Tagalog, and Manila's Anglophone publishing scene far outshone that of anywhere else in the region (Holden, "Colonialism's Goblins" 161). After independence, English was still kept as an official language used in education, and remained as an elite, mestizo medium until the 1960s, when Tagalog-language texts emerged from the renewed sense of Filipino/a nationalism. Even still, many writers continued to prefer English as both a national and a global lingua franca. As in Singapore and Malaysia, English in the Philippines was labeled as "neutral," but was often associated with imperial interests, mestizoness, and upper-class cosmopolitanism. As F. Sionil José has written, Anglophone literature had the potential to bring Filipino/as "closer to our colonizers so we could understand them, and also curse them—to repeat, curse them in the language they handed down to us" (21).

Indeed, English's immediate distancing allowed a critique of sensitive social norms and strongly held nationalist ties. The ideology of English as a tool to communicate among ethnic groups has placed the Anglophone writer in the position of a cultural interlocutor, where English can symbolize a discursive space that allows the individual to be both "inside and outside" of a racial identity. Topics deemed sensitive or silenced are often mediated through English as a way of exploring racial issues in a speculative, estranged discourse. Thus English use can avoid the language of the nation-state, while still maintaining colloquial idioms and code-switching.

Across Southeast Asia, English use has become a highly valued skill, and it cannot be separated from its imperial heritage or the desire to be published by Western presses. However, to cast all cases of English as mimicry reinforces the notion that the English language is owned by the colonizers (who never had to learn it in schools), and that it is really only for Anglo-Saxon people. In some parts of the Visayas, Ilocos, and Mindanao in the Philippines, English is used as an alternative to Tagalog, which can seem like an arbitrary national tongue. National languages too have a history of effectively marginalizing other linguistic groups, leading many writers to side with English over their given national identity (Lim, *Writing S.E./Asia in English* 47). In his essays on English writing, Lloyd Fernando saw Anglophone texts as "deserv[ing] study because they explore intercultural problems under compulsion" (*Cultures in Conflict* 124). Indeed, such writers have attempted to build new cultural form through owning English as a discursive space to manage and reinterpret racial categories.

I group Asian American literature into the transpacific Anglophone as a means of emphasizing a text's ambivalence toward Asian American identity projects. Scholars have already pointed out that labeling a text as an "Asian American novel" has become increasingly problematic, especially for novels that take place outside of the United States (*Book of Salt, Dream Jungle, Turning Japanese*) or novels that feature protagonists who identify as migrant or transnational (*Salt Fish Girl, Brazil-Maru*). Novels from Southeast Asian diasporic writers, such as Jessica Hagedorn's *Dream Jungle,* Le Thi Diem Thuy's *The Gangster We Are All Looking For,* and Viet Thanh Nguyen's *The Sympathizer,* depict the struggle to be liberated from given cultural identities, Asian American included. Despite these limitations, Asian American scholars continue to insist that "Asian American literature is American literature," a characterization that promotes the multicultural mythos of America, and limits these texts and authors within national epistemologies and commitments (Ho 128). This book reads them as neither Asian nor American, but as transpacific Anglophone, a category that stresses encounter and exchange.

As identity categories in the United States are commonly seen within cemented histories of struggle, transpacific Anglophone literature in the United States appears less as an aggressive, explicit critique of pluralism, and more as an implicit critique that can be exposed by reading against realist and autobiographical tendencies. Rather than "denationalize" Asian American politics, these texts, when read outside the logics of pluralism, can work to undermine multiculturalist myths. Many of the novels treated here gesture toward the creative freedom of "inauthenticity" by developing styles of antirealism through myth, irony, absurdity, and speculation. They operate as "antihistories" that deviate from the sentimental and romantic genres through which nationalist myths are so often mediated. Absurdity and play make history appear more as speculation, shoring up a seemingly infinite variety of ethnic identities to account for suppressed (or "intolerable") cultural practices. For Asian American scholars like Tina Chen, Jeffrey Partridge, and Betsy Huang, Asian American literary production and criticism has long assumed an "autobiographic imperative" that casts "all Asian American fiction as forms of life writing" (Huang, *Contesting Genres* 7). Anglophone thus not only names an archive, but a method of reading that deviates from reading for typical tropes of "minority literature": identity construction, empowerment, marginalized histories, autobiography, and ethnic authenticity. Anglophone readings include and expand upon the sarcasm, the satire, the play, the wearing of different masks, and all the carnivalesque elements that constitute a creative project.[36]

In "Stranger in the Village," James Baldwin's brief visit to a remote village in Switzerland sparks an epiphany about his own black identity. American history, he realizes, can be seen as repeated efforts to protect, dignify, and valorize white identity. And this imperative has characterized nonwhite identities, including Baldwin's own, by their persistent need to stabilize and justify their own belonging within America.[37] Likewise, the identities enabled and empowered through American ethnic literature are modes of recognition that respond to American whiteness—white forms of masculinity and femininity, white presumptions to civilization as a European product. Transpacific Anglophone literature, in one sense, reveals how American minority politics has always relied upon whiteness as its major constituting force. Anglophone literature opens new comparisons from across the array of cities, nations, and identities within the transpacific. It contrasts forms of imperial power and domination that exist in America as well as in China, the Philippines, and Malaya. The impetus of Anglophone literature dares us to ask of ourselves: Who are "we," if we need not compare ourselves to American whiteness, to American heterosexuality, and to American patriarchy? Who are we without these comparisons, and who are our Others?

CHAPTER OVERVIEW

In order to study transpacific Anglophone texts without losing historical and local specificities, the chapters of this book flow through the transpacific, from Malaya to North America, as well as through history, from the 1960s to today. Each chapter uses a comparative mode of analysis that juxtaposes authors of various genders, nationalities, and diasporas, to compare histories and perspectives. Similar to Edward W. Said's "contrapuntal analysis," I analyze texts from different positions and contexts simultaneously to contrast how different groups respond to pluralist governmentality, and to understand how these texts create allegiances by imagining new forms of crossover (*Culture and Imperialism*). I rely not on comparing the imperial center to its Others, but on comparisons of Others to Others, where those who appear victims from the U.S. vantage point can be seen as colonizers from a different view. These comparisons attempt to understand how cultural tactics emerge as strategies for confronting transnational forms of domination by disrupting binaries between "the perpetrators" and "the victims," the "dominant" and the "marginalized." Each chapter thus compares texts to foster what Said has called an "exile perspective," wherein "an idea or experience is always counter-posed with another, therefore making them both appear in a sometimes new and unpredictable light" (*Culture and Imperialism* 60). To think comparatively is to think like an exile, which is to think critically. By refusing to focus on one nation, one event, one author, we are compelled to broaden our view by seeing things "not simply as they are, but as they have come to be that way" (ibid.).

Part I: "Histories," investigates the tactics and affordances that emerge in Southeast Asian contexts of pluralist governmentally. I read metahistorical novels that juxtapose colonial histories with postnational race riots, revolution, and state repression. Chapter 1 treats Lloyd Fernando's *Scorpion Orchid* (1975) and Su-Chen Christine Lim's *Fistful of Colours* (1993) to consider how these two canonized literary texts represent the region's "communitarian multiculturalism" as a reiteration of British colonial pluralist strategies. Both novels follow "multiracial clans" rather than individuals to meditate upon histories of violent and intimate racial crossover. Chapter 2 reads two Philippine Anglophone novels, Alfred Yuson's *Great Philippine Jungle Energy Café* (1988) and Ninotchka Rosca's novel *State of War* (1988). Both novels reveal ways in which ethnic, racial, and tribal identities can be made excessive to the cultural practices encouraged by state and capitalist actors, and both interrupt realist representations of 1980s state repression with absurd historical narratives that parody the multiple revisions of racial identities over Philippine revolutionary history. Both chapters explore how transpacific texts eschew official state histories of diversity and racial harmony through genealogies of transition.

Part II: "Mobilities," explores novels of transpacific travel to ponder how radical shifts in locality can conjure new racial, gendered, and sexual identities, while also revealing the everyday presumptions about identity back at home and abroad. I conjure the term "global imaginary" within these chapters to understand how pluralist governmentality functions not merely through nation-states and governments, but through metropolitan cities, global capital, and symbols of belonging that reappear in transit. Chapter 3 treats two novels where travel across the Pacific invokes comparisons that see North American spaces as ideally liberal and tolerant. In Peter Bacho's *Cebu* (1991), a Filipino American priest travels to the Philippines to cast Filipino/as as "intolerable" migrants branded by loose sexual norms and violent tendencies, while in Lydia Kwa's *This Place Called Absence* (2003), a lesbian Singaporean psychologist living in Vancouver, Canada, reimagines the homeland as a place of patriarchal violence and homophobia. These narratives reveal how pluralist governmentality constructs North American cities as liberal and tolerant, while spaces outside North America, like the Philippines and Singapore, are constructed as bastions of historical trauma, violence, patriarchy, and perverse sexuality. My fourth chapter extends this inquiry by reading texts of queer brown migrancy, beginning with Lawrence Chua's 1998 novel, *Gold by the Inch*, which follows a gay young migrant of Thai, Malay, and Chinese heritage as he travels through Thailand and Malaysia. I compare Chua's text with R. Zamora Linmark's 2011 novel, *Leche*, which follows Vicente De Los Reyes, a queer Filipino Hawaiian migrant who travels to the Philippines, only to be "boxed in" as a foreigner or *balikbayan*. Both novels consider queer of color travel as a rejection of American senses of brownness and homonormativity. In Southeast Asia, brownness becomes an ambiguous and illegible racial form that offers opportunities for transition.

Part III: "Genres," explores the aesthetic forms of transpacific Anglophone texts, focusing on how these texts transgress racial, gendered, and sexual identities through nonrealist (speculative) genres. Here I expand upon previous reflections about how literary form, tone, and style challenge representations of diversity, tolerance, and racial harmony. Chapter 5 draws from Hwee Hwee Tan's *Mammon Inc.* (2001) and Han Ong's *Fixer Chao* (2001) to consider how both novels use styles of cynical distancing (like chick lit) to represent Southeast Asian migrants who form new communities based on their shared roles in service work. Chapter 6 considers the antirealist elements of the texts treated in this book, and explores the rise of speculative fiction in contemporary online Anglophone writing. I trace my own experiences as a fiction writer writing under the name "Kawika Guillermo" to ask how aesthetic strategies can reframe our understandings of pluralism and transition. In my conclusion, I return to the concept of transitive culture as a means of building new coalitions and collectivities against contemporary forms of pluralist governmentality.

This transdisciplinary genealogical project highlights transpacific Anglophone literature as an all-too-ignored literary tradition, and explores how crossing national, racial, and gendered borders can reveal new ways of seeing pluralist governmentality in its various forms. My purpose in taking a more critical stance toward diversity, tolerance, and multiculturalism is not to claim these values as insincere or failed, or to progress them into a new phase, but to ask what has been done—and continues to be done—in their name. Any project of supranational, queer, or antiracist solidarity must also take into account how such values can cater to nationalist exceptionalisms, with often catastrophic results for those then presumed worthless, villainous, or fake.

PART I

HISTORIES

Racism first develops with colonization, in other words, with colonizing genocide. If you are functioning in the biopower mode, how can you justify the need to kill people, to kill populations, and to kill civilizations? By using the themes of evolutionism, by appealing to a racism.

—Michel Foucault, *Society Must Be Defended*

Wherever in Asia one is geographically positioned, a syllogism is emerging: Asia is becoming the center of the world and we are the center of Asia, so we are the center of the world. This is where history comes in. Contrary to the now-fashionable claim that we have entered the postcolonial era, the mood of triumphalism, which is a clear reaction to colonialism, indicates that we still operate within the boundaries of colonial history.

—Chen Kuan-Hsing, *Asia as Method*

1 · MULTIRACIAL CLANS IN COLORFUL MALAYA

It's not a single society, really ... thank God, the British are here. The Malays are in their kampongs, the Chinese own all the business, and the Indians are in the rubber estates. And the Eurasians ... sit in their cricket club and imitate us, rather poorly actually. You see, they have nothing in common. If we left tomorrow, there'd be such a lovely bit of mayhem that we'd have to come back and keep the peace. No, I'm afraid we have to grin and bear it—the white man's burden, I mean. (Fernando, *Scorpion Orchid*, 89)

So says Ethel, a British university professor from Lloyd Fernando's 1976 novel *Scorpion Orchid*, who hopes to convince another English professor, Ellman, that British rule is legitimate not merely because of the greatness of British literature (that's a given), but because of the colonial state's necessary management of other races. Ethel's hopes to sustain the British Empire are vanquished when the British are cast out, yet her confidence in a racial hierarchy managed by a strong state is prophetic for the future of the region. Though the legacy of pluralism in Malaya would shift from the "multinational empire," its pluralist structure would remain.[1]

Ethel's imperial defense is directed not at the protestors who seek to expel the British, but at Ellman, whom she has just had sex with, and who has also just admitted to impregnating a young South Asian woman, Neela. For Ethel, such mixture goes too far in unsettling the pluralist categorization of racial types. British managerial power implicitly demands that there be no shared intimacy between racial groups, that they be kept separate. This demand, justified by "the white man's burden," appears in Neela's family as well. In the novel's first chapter, her family shames her for her pregnancy, and attempt to domesticate her by tasking her brother, Santinathan, to keep watch over her. Both Ethel and

Neela's family fear the dangers of intimacy to upset the stable distancing of pluralism. Where pluralist governmentality abstracts relations into stable identities, intimacy suggests the danger of "crossover contamination" that may disrupt the social harmony of a pluralist society.[2]

Scorpion Orchid delineates the anxieties of pluralist governmentality through the friendship of four university students of different racial backgrounds, who each represent the CMIO (Chinese, Malay, Indian, Other) pluralism of postcolonial Singapore and Malaysia. Sabran is Malay, Guan Kheng is Chinese, Santinathan is Indian, and Peter D'Almeida is Eurasian. Their friendship, forged by the privileges of higher education and the English language, becomes tested by the surges of political, economic, and racial violence that characterized the 1950s and 1960s, when the Federation of Malaya ceased being a British colony and integrated Singapore in 1963, only to exclude it in the aftermath of the 1964 race riots. The boys' broken ideal of cross-racial friendship provokes questions about how racial harmony can exist alongside extreme inequality and repressive state violence. Contrasting with these four "diverse" college boys is the waitress and sex worker Sally, who transitions as Sally Yu (Chinese) and Salmah (Malay) to mix with whoever her clients happen to be. Sally offers an abrasive response to pluralist governmentality as a formal structure that, in the 1960s, posited traditional ethnic communities as the only recognized communal spaces, wherein straying from one's ascribed community was condemned as Western individualism.

As one of the first postcolonial Anglophone novels from Malaya, *Scorpion Orchid* established a countertradition to hegemonic ways of seeing and representing the CMIO multiracial system. Few novels seem to better extend *Scorpion Orchid*'s critiques of pluralism than Suchen Christine Lim's 1993 novel, *Fistful of Colours*, which won the inaugural Singapore Literature Prize. Lim's novel follows a similar multiracial form that establishes modes of narration from multiple races and genders, providing a "three-dimensional perception" that revolves around a "fluid group" of multiracial literati, the "Saturday Group" (Nazareth). Like Fernando's multiracial college students, the Saturday Group consists of four main members: Suwen, a Chinese painter who is sexually assaulted by her stepfather; Mark Campbell, her teacher from the U.K. and love interest; Zul Hussein, a Malay journalist writing for the *Straits Herald* and their main spokeswoman and organizer; and Nica Sivalingam, a sculptor of Baba (Chinese) and South Asian descent (23). The multiracial and economically diverse members of the Saturday Group break through their imposed racial distance by collectively attempting to surpass their "inner barrier" of ethnic orientation—a break made possible through intimate relationships with others.

For both *Fistful of Colours* and *Scorpion Orchid*, the attempt to reimagine multiracial grouping requires inventing counternarratives to official Malayan history. In *Scorpion Orchid*, the main contemporary narrative of the four university students is consistently interrupted by italicized excerpts from myths, travel logs, official British histories, fictionalized histories written by university students, and unpunctuated stream-of-consciousness vignettes. Each excerpt comments upon and undermines the events of the main narrative by juxtaposing the violence and racial tensions of postcolonial Malaya with metahistorical narratives of crossover (Holden, "Colonialism's Goblins" 163). In these excerpts, the violence, censorship, and pluralist strategies of the two states are juxtaposed with the similar strategies of past colonial powers: the Japanese, the British, the Portuguese, the Chinese, and the Malay Sultanates. At the same time, the hopes of building alliances among racially diverse communities are set alongside romantic myths of racial mixture and permeable religious beliefs. While the main narrative of the four university students comments on the racial tension of the period, the novel's synthesis of the Western-style bildungsroman with mythological and historical narratives of mixture and transition imagines alternative forms of cultural representation and practice.

In *Fistful of Colours*, the artists and intellectuals of the Saturday Group strive to reject official histories and art forms that are managed and censored by the historical and cultural "lobotomies" of the Singapore state. To do so, the novel's protagonist Suwen visits historical sites of riots, labor strikes, and sexual abuses, hoping to understand how forms of violence have continued to exist and are even reproduced through an otherwise ideal and progressive multiracialism. The contemporary narrative of *Fistful of Colours* is interrupted by alternative histories; yet unlike those in *Scorpion Orchid*, these histories are not myths or magical realist fictions, but are intimate stories of mixture, including histories of Chinese coolies, Malay waiters, and Indian soldiers, all told by the family's descendants who make up the Saturday Group. Through reflection on their complex genealogies, the members of the Saturday Group refuse to act as the mechanisms for racial reproduction, by either marrying outside their ethnic group, or like Suwen, by remaining virginal.

As two of the most critically examined texts from Malaya, *Scorpion Orchid* and *Fistful of Colours* are often cast within nationalist canons, despite the transnational histories and characters they depict. As one of the "first-generation" Anglophone writers who began writing in the 1950s and 1960s,[3] Lloyd Fernando was raised in a culture of British formal education (Raihanah 56), and thus his novel is often read as nostalgic for an imagined Malayan multiracialism that emerged among the Anglophone elite in the 1950s and was later shattered by the pro-Malay litigation following the race riots of the 1960s.[4] Similarly, Lim's text has been interpreted as a plea for a more diverse conception of Singaporean identity that stresses intimacy over the distanced cross-racial interaction of the marketplace. Yet this intimacy is still limited to a state multiracial project that re-creates Singapore identity (Nazareth). This chapter broadens the scope of both *Scorpion Orchid* and *Fistful of Colours* by reinterpreting their critiques of state multiracialism as responses to a regional history of pluralist governmentality. Rather than idealize multiracialism in the colonial past (Fernando) or as a new nationalist identity (Lim), these novels conceive of a regional Southeast Asian history that emphasizes mixture and transition through their "three-dimensional" group-based narratives. Their representations of the intimate crossover of segregated groups express how racialized subjects appropriate and refashion such ascribed identities.

I first explore how contemporary global manifestations of multiculturalism can be traced to British pluralist governmentality in British Malaya (as Malaya was known before the Malayan Union in 1946), by considering how both novels trace pluralist discourses that emerged from British colonial politics, but reappear in independence and after the 1960s race riots. Second, I consider how these novels fit within a tradition of Anglophone writing that has produced counternarratives to official histories, foregrounding how the Malaysian and Singaporean states have managed racial identities to sustain social hierarchies and to repress political dissent. Fernando's essays on English writing help us conceive of "in-between migrants" not as particular racial identities but as beings who recognize multiple historical narratives and take on new identities as a cultural practice as well as a strategy for survival. In Fernando's text, transition is represented by the racially ambiguous sex worker Sally, a migrant who is defined by her ability to transition between recognizable cultural forms, but only as a byproduct of her subjugation and labor. Similarly, *Fistful of Colours* contrasts the intellectual distance between races encouraged by the state with its multiple intimate crossovers: Suwen and Mark (Chinese and Scots-English), Nica and Robert (mixed Chinese-Indian and Chinese), and Janice and Zul (Chinese and Malay). Their intimate connections enact a cultural form that is derived neither from the racial types of pluralism, nor from the cosmopolitan types of the empire. The novel instead depicts transition as a deeply personal and intimate connection that challenges one's position within a single collective historical past.

PLURALISM AND MULTICULTURAL EMERGENCE IN MALAYA

The legacy of colonial pluralism in Malaya emerged from an already "diverse" region. The Strait of Malacca had been an important passage for traders from India, China, Thailand, and the Indonesian Archipelago, so when sixteenth-century Europeans first arrived, they discovered a dynamic world of cross-cultural influences driven by networks of traders, religious profligates, and the collaboration of small states.[5] These native Indo-Malay cultures were in themselves diverse and permeable, as they incorporated other cultural practices and beliefs (Islam among them). During British rule, the labor burden of tin mining and rubber farming was solved by importing migrants from China and India to keep the Malay sultanates from resisting colonial rule, and later these migrants found positions working for the British military forces and as merchants. By the early 1920s, Chinese outnumbered Malays in places like Malacca, Singapore, and Penang, and Indians grew to a substantial presence. Pluralist governance strategies emphasized spatial segregation over cultural assimilation, and colonies like Singapore were segregated into Chinatowns, Little Indias, and Malay *kampungs* (Gudeman 141; Nam 170). Though many had migrated as individuals, the narrative of migrancy focused on family connections, framing migrants as both homogenized and alienated diasporic extensions of a mother country. Thus Chinese were marked as commercial middlemen, Malays as indigenous peasant smallholders, and imported Indians as municipal and plantation laborers (Holden and Goh, "Introduction" 5). This mode of pluralism was instituted geographically, socially, and economically across British Malaya.

Separations based on origins encouraged Chinese and Indians to see themselves as part of an overseas diaspora, which marked them as temporary residents or guests without legitimate claim to Malaya as a homeland, nor to English as a tongue (Bernards 314). Even the mixed Chinese and Malay Peranakans (Baba-Nyonya), who had settled and creolized in Malaya over hundreds of years, were simply marked as Chinese. As Shirley Geok-lin Lim puts it in her 1997 memoir *Among the White Moon Faces*, the "language of the South Chinese people [Hokkien] will always be an ambivalent language for me, calling into question the notion of a mother tongue tied to a racial origin" (27). Lim's memoir details the struggles of growing up Peranakan and speaking Malay and English instead of her presumed mother tongue, which "had never been a language of familiarity, affection, and home for me" (28). Though Lim's family had remained in Malacca for generations, the remaking of Chineseness as diasporic marked her as an outsider, which in turn, solidified Malay identity as indigenous, even as many were also of migrant heritages. By tethering Malays to Islam, the British bound Malays not only to labor, but to religion and land (as aboriginals or *bumiputera*) (Bernards 314). This lasted well after independence, when the legacy of British segregation influenced the architects of the new nation-state to inherit pluralist categories and even to recognize them in the constitution (Gudeman 141).

Though British pluralism had suffocated notions of national identity, the three main groups (Chinese, Indians, and Malays) were able to oust the British through an interethnic anticolonial alliance. The stagnant trading economy, the poverty, and the recent memory of British abandonment during the Japanese Occupation created public sympathy for a multiracial upsurge of protests that eventually led to violent confrontation with British colonial powers.[6] After independence, the state attempted to capitalize on these interethnic coalitions. Singapore's leader Lee Kuan Yew called for a "Malaysian Malaysia," a desegregated nation-state where all citizens were seen as "Malaysians" rather than as Indians, Malays, and Chinese.[7] But with the end of the British presence also came the end of cross-cultural alliances against a common enemy, and soon enough the "transethnic" forms of solidarity were marginalized within the memory of postcolonial history (Mandal, "Boundaries and Beyond"). Shirley Geok-lin Lim's memoir captures the feeling of the period, as she writes that the Japanese massacres of three million Chinese in Malaya were almost immediately suppressed as decolonization became credited to the Malay majority (*Among the White Moon Faces* 68). Interethnic coalitions soon broke down in suspicions against Malaya's Chinese, who were marked as communist insurgents or as British sympathizers.[8] A series of guerilla wars dubbed "The Emergency" (1948–1960) resulted in laws restricting individual freedoms, paving the way for a limited democracy that has resulted in one of the longest running ruling parties in the world, the United Malays National Organisation (UMNO). The legacies of the "divide and rule" governance that fostered interethnic conflict came to violent upheaval in the 1964 race riots in Singapore, and in 1969's May 13 riots in Malaysia. In the aftermath of these riots, Singapore, being 75 percent Chinese, became associated with its Chinese majority. The leader of Singapore's dominant political party, Lee Kuan Yew, now called for a "Singaporean Singapore," envisioning the city-state as a more equal and ideal pluralist society "to be ideologically reconstituted as the 'citizenry' of the new nation" (B. H. Chua, "Being Chinese" 240).

Both Malaysia and Singapore posited themselves (their party), as the new colonial power tasked with managing disparate racial groups. In Singapore's case, pluralism reinforced economic growth by shifting racial stereotypes to symbols of multiracial acceptance that stressed hard work, entrepreneurship, and a commitment to nationalism that ignored acts of state repression (censorship, brutal punitive measures, surveillance). Echoing the function of Lord Acton's "multinational empire," the Singapore state posited itself as structurally above the interests of any one racial group, what Chua Beng Huat has called a "neutral umpire that allocates resources and adjudicates disputes among the races" ("Cultural Logic" 345). This neutrality was produced through "neutral" signifiers, foremost in its use of English as a language of bureaucracy and business rather than as a language of art, literature, or cultural belonging (ibid.). In the 1970s and 1980s, the discourse of the Singapore state as neutral solidified the idea of the nation's ethnic groups as trapped by cultural and religious interest, thus justifying the new regime as an "umpire" necessary in maintaining racial harmony. After the death of Chairman Mao and the opening of Chinese markets, Lee Kuan Yew started the "Speak Mandarin" campaign, seeking to recognize Chinese heritage by requiring all Chinese children to learn Mandarin, despite the fact that most Chinese in Singapore spoke Hokkien, Hakka, Cantonese, or Teochew. Mandarin had the double effect of both satisfying the multicultural commitment and producing an international business class of bilingual speakers. Similarly, keeping Malays tied to Islam had the double effect of serving the multicultural commitment while repressing political dissent among Malay unions and political organizations, who were regulated by special courts bound to Sharia law. South Asian migrants from Sri Lanka, Burma, and West Bengal were reduced to a national identity as "Indians," their identities pinned to a homeland to which they were implicitly expected to return. South Asians were integral in supporting a narrative of racial harmony, since without them the nation would be seen as one racial group (the Chinese) economically dominating another (the Malays). Like Asian American "model minorities," South Asians validated the nation through their "success."

In Malaysia, the afterlife of colonial pluralism and the race riots resulted not in attempts to depoliticize race, but to give privileged status to *bumiputeras* or Malay Muslims.[9] Malaysia's May 13, 1969, race riots between Chinese and Malays became an opportunity to reestablish pluralism, with a strong Malay state replacing the British colonial apparatus.[10] The result of the riots was the New Economic Policy (NEP), which greatly enhanced rights and privileges of the Malays while criminalizing challenges to the NEP as "a seditious criminal offence" (Ganesen 143). As Shirley Geok-lin Lim writes in her memoir, policies like the NEP reversed the unifying effect of the term "Malaysia": "More and more, the term 'Malay' appeared where 'British' once stood. The 'Malaysian,' that new promise of citizenship composed of the best traditions from among Malays, Chinese, Tamiles, Eurasians, Dayaks, and so forth, seemed more and more to be a vacuous political fiction, a public relations performance like those put on for Western tourists at state-run cultural centers" (*Among the White Moon Faces* 188–189). The race riots of the 1960s in both Malaysia and Singapore led to a climate where in-depth discussions about racial relations were substituted by superficial representations of racial types that were "assigned an official culture, and that culture [was] expected to be 'preserved'" (Philip 108). By depoliticizing racial communities, both the People's Action Party (PAP) and the UMNO have maintained one-party rule, and repressive measures such as Singapore's and Malaysia's Internal Security Acts (ISA) have been excused as the necessary evils of a benevolent "umpire." The homogenization of racial identities has rendered, according to the writer Eddie Tay, "the nuances of ethnic identities and languages ... invisible" (*Colony, Nation* 13). These conditions have also helped produce populations of surplus labor for Malaysia's special economic zones, and have increased Singapore's reputation as a multiracial utopia fitting for investment capital. Race here is thus conceived as a perpetual crisis, with the state as its dependable umpire.

SCORPION ORCHID: THE COLORED KALEIDOSCOPE

It is in the 1970s context of emerging postcolonial pluralism that Lloyd Fernando wrote most of his essays and his first novel, *Scorpion Orchid*. His standing as "unquestionably one of Malaysia's most important Anglophone writers" has been engrained in Malaysian literary scholarship, yet his position within the Singapore Anglophone canon has often been veiled due to his prominence as a Malaysian artist.[11] Fernando's essays, his two edited anthologies of Malaysian writing in English (*Twenty-two Malaysian Short Stories* in 1968 and *Malaysian Short Stories* in 1981), and his two novels (*Scorpion Orchid* in 1976 and *Green Is the Colour* in 1993) are essential to any discussion of Anglophone writing in the region. Likewise, his novels contrast with the 1980s Singapore poetry scene, which was dominated by an aesthetic ideology of art inherited from British imperial culture (S. G. Lim, *Nationalism and Literature* 17).[12] In contrast, English novels in Malaya took politics as their main influence and inspiration, *Scorpion Orchid* being the first among them, with writers like K. S. Maniam and Shirley Geok-lin Lim following.[13] *Scorpion Orchid* captures Singapore's early history of riots: the Sino-Malay riots in the 1950s, which occurred while Fernando attended Singapore's University of Malaya in 1959; and Singapore's 1964 riots, which occurred while Fernando pursued his doctorate at the University of Leeds. Fernando later returned to a Singapore of heightened racial tensions where being "Malaysian," after the separation of Malaysia and Singapore, now meant he was no longer "Singaporean."[14] As a Singhalese (Sri Lankan) migrant, Fernando was never really a target of the 1950s and 1960s riots in Malaya, and his outsider position gave him a point of view that exceeded state narratives of "racial harmony" (Ng, "Nation and Religion" 115).

Scorpion Orchid follows four college-aged men in 1950s Singapore, Santinathan, Sabran, Guan Kheng, and Peter, whose racial identities reflect Singapore's CMIO system (Chinese, Malay, Indians, and Others). The four boys foster male comradeship in the University of Malaya (then in Singapore) by exerting dominance over college freshman, mocking each other's ascribed cultural traditions, and gazing upon the waitress Sally, whom Sabran refers to as "the pole around which they had been magnetized all unawares" (103). The novel's narrative is distinctly multiracial, as it attempts to share the first-person narration among all four boys, establishing a shared communal gaze. The novel introduces the four boys as they observe a procession, which the reader might mistake for an aestheticized multicultural parade. They "watched the Chinese, Indians, and Malays jostle out of the ground, it seemed unendingly.... Banners of white cloth in English, Malay, and Chinese crudely written in red and black ink began to unfurl and were held aloft on poles at each end" (11). Though this event is revealed as a protest march by cooperative unions, the four boys collectively suspect that it "might have been football partisans returning after a rousing game." The boys' gaze, collectivized in the shared narrative of the novel, identifies the protest as an idealized (and depoliticized) form of multiracial belonging, and even the union speeches seem to celebrate diversity over their collective struggle, as each speech is translated by students, first in Mandarin, then into English, then into Malay.

The novel abandons realist conventions by making the purposes and dates for its protest marches ambiguous, as the 1950s was a period where labor struggles and anti-British protest often merged together to create interethnic alliances. The ambiguity concerning the time and place of the procession is underscored by the confusion of the protest's participants, who begin to feud as each translated speech emphasizes different purposes (12). This antirealist style allows Fernando to renarrate the racial riots as symptomatic of colonial pluralism's afterlife. As Andrew Ng notes, the novel employs a type of speculative fiction that dehistoricizes the 1969 riots in order to avoid censorship and to mark the riots as a real social and ethical problem that cannot be blamed on either the Chinese or the Malays ("Vision of Hospitality"). The novel's fragmented version of the riots make them irreducible to racial difference. At times, the riots seem to reflect the religious extremism of the Maria Hertogh Riot in 1950, but then considering the union-busting present in the novel, the riots also seem to reflect the later 1950s labor revolts. And then again, the riots are accompanied by the racist rhetoric that one might expect in the 1964 and 1969 riots, which were seen as anti-Chinese or anti-Malay. The superimposing of one riot for another stresses the continuous anxiety brewing beneath an otherwise multiracial glaze.

Though the interethnic procession might be read as a means of idealizing multiracial values, Fernando's antirealist depiction parodies even the anticolonial form of pluralism. The text focuses on the symbols of mixed colors, as the different races jostle together in multicolored lights, and a wheel rolls "in a vast circle while the coloured lights played on [the four men] like a kaleidoscope continually changing the colour of their faces . . . so that they looked like refugees in flight" (15). These playing lights reflect the boys' symbolic identities, and as each color shifts back and forth among their faces, each of the boys' auras seems placed onto the others, suggesting a playful attitude toward racial identity that augurs the idealism of independence. The four boys' naïveté borders on insulting when Santinathan dares his friends to bet him ten dollars to join the Tamils in their religious ritual by wearing a *kavadi*, a large necklace lined with needles to pierce the skin. Their idealism, seen as playful, naïve, and disrespectful, is later depicted as hypocritical when the four boys are among their own traditional households, and their attitudes about race dramatically shift to more conservative attitudes that reproduce their respective cultural traditions, especially toward women. Though Santinathan finds humor in the *kavadi*, he refuses to let his sister, Neela, take a similar attitude when he catches her smoking a cigarette that "didn't go with her shabby sari, nor with their way of life" (45). Despite his own attempts to distance himself from his ethnicity, Santinathan seeks to domesticate his sister as an ethnic Indian woman, and later berates her for her pregnancy by Professor Ellman. Here the ideals of the four boys appear less idealized (or made "nostalgic"), but are rather depicted by Fernando as a naïve and depoliticized notion of going "beyond" one's racial identity.

While the public streets are presented as a kaleidoscope of colors, the alleyways are obscured with massive amounts of black smoke, a darkness that conceals the city's "derelicts'" and "hawkers' burrows" (15). The four boys' idealistic multiracialism parallels this growing darkness, as their idealism feeds on their privilege as Anglophone male university students. Guan Kheng comes from a well-to-do family, while the middle-class Peter D'Almeida continues to sympathize with the British. It is not until the riots, halfway through the novel, that both Guan and Peter are forced to face their own privilege, when Guan abandons Sally to an enraged mob and Peter is beaten and lynched. In contrast, the friendship between Sabran and Santinathan becomes more substantial after the riots, as their differing backgrounds find shared experiences in their resistance to institutionalized conventions and British power. The intellectual maverick Santinathan is expelled from the university for disrupting lectures and meetings, and is forced to find work as a shipyard day laborer. Similarly, after participating in union strikes, Sabran is arrested and detained for his activities. Their shared experiences became a microcosm of the interethnic coalitions formed against the British, as Sabran and Santinathan find "an indescribable way, not simply through language, of making their differing backgrounds respond to each other in mutual sympathy. It was like being attuned, words were no longer always necessary" (52). Their racial backgrounds seem not to separate them into tense competitors, but act as a means of becoming "attuned" through self-reflection upon their shared struggle. Guan Kheng and Peter, on the other hand, carry heavier investments in a state-condoned multiracialism, as it helps sustain their European and Chinese privilege. So long as these alignments are held, the "harmony" of their friendship remains as superficial as a rotating color wheel.

Supporting the mixed naïveté of the group is the waitress Sally, who moves among the four boys "as with old friends" (19). But while the four boys seem playfully distanced from ethnic identity, Sally survives by being seen as "authentic," relying on her abilities to speak both Cantonese and Malay fluently, and to transition into the Chinese "Sally Yu" or the Malay "Salmah." She performs authenticity based on her audience, changing "her name and her language according to her customers" (160). Sally escaped abuse at the hands of her elderly husband in the rural *kampongs*, and has migrated to Singapore in order to escape her conscripted identity. Yet her labor as a waitress and sex worker, alongside her lack of formal education, does not allow her the same ethnic distance as the four university boys, even as she provides them emotional and physical solace. Indeed, the boys' distance from racial identities does not seem to critique and reflect upon racial differences so much as mark them as superior to racialized Others, as part of a multiracial "e/umpire" supported by higher education, by their use of English as a "neutral" language, and by contrasting themselves to Sally, their female and lower-class Other.

PREFERENTIAL AND COMMUNITARIAN
MULTICULTURALISM

> He loved the orchid whose stems flower, curving free away from the sup-
> porting posts, but feared the scorpion which lurked among the roots hidden
> in the rich soil.
>
> —Lloyd Fernando, *Scorpion Orchid*

The ideal multiculturalism depicted in *Scorpion Orchid* is symbolized by the orchid, a flower that seems to have no "supporting posts" (read: structural under-pinnings), and the scorpion, the poisonous creature lurking "among the roots." For Fernando, the state-ordained CMIO system advocated for a multiracial society deracinated from the "rich soil" of both precolonial and colonial Malaya, legitimating rule by positing itself as a racially egalitarian power. The model of colonial pluralism appears to have few similarities with the cultural pluralism conceived in the United States during and after World War I, which kept to a liberal, individualist framework, and marked identity as more adopted than con-scripted (one could, it was promised, always assimilate). For the theorist Chua Beng Huat, this ability to adopt an identity reflects a "preferential multicultural-ism," "an ideology that defends the co-presence of groups that are constituted by and through freely chosen cultural preferences" ("Cost of Membership" 171). The liberal individualist model of multiculturalism in the 1960s and 1970s in Austra-lia, Canada, and the United States saw identity as a preliminary, inessential social construct that one can freely escape through given liberalist assumptions: the valuation of individualism over community, the emphasis on individual rather than group rights, and the conceptualization of culture as "an ongoing acquisi-tion, subject to addition and deletion according to an individual's freedom to choose" (ibid. 173). Though skin color makes this preferential multiculturalism far more difficult for people of color, it is also reflected in racial identities, such as during the early years of Asian American movements, when "Asian American" was adopted as a pan-ethnic banner under which heterogeneous groups could rally against white supremacy and overseas imperialism.

In contrast to the U.S. style of "preferential multiculturalism," Chua sees Sin-gapore and Malaysia as representing a "communitarian multiculturalism," where "exit" from a community is not a conceivable option, and where "cultural mem-bership cannot be simply rejected when the balance sheet of gains and losses are not in an individual's favor" ("Cost of Membership" 175). Here Chua con-ceives of identity in Singapore as connoting a shared duty respective to mono-lithic racial histories, rather than an acquisition of individual cultural practices and tastes. This construct also forecloses possible critiques brought through hybridity and mixed race, since the Malaysian and Singaporean states have both set in place policies that ascribe the father's race to the child at birth (ibid. 183).

As regulations based on race are typical in government policies—even housing quotas are organized by race—the stable functioning of the state thus relies heavily on racial categories remaining monolithic and unchanging. "Communitarian multiculturalism" is perhaps best exemplified in how the Malaysian state yokes race and religion together in categorizing Malay identity as Muslim (Ng, "Vision of Hospitality" 173). This synthesis of traits as an identity guarantees a privileged status through the NEP, with the goal that Malays (*bumiputeras*) should hold 30 percent of the national wealth. Yet native status is not given to non-Muslim indigenous communities like the Iban and Kadazan, who do not fit into the state's conflation of religion and race. To renounce Islam, for Malays, would be to renounce NEP privileges such as scholarships, quotas in ownership of company stock, and welfare.

Fernando's *Scorpion Orchid* traces the emergence of communitarian multiculturalism as a form of pluralism reanimated through the postcolonial state's desire to surveil and control racialized populations. The novel depicts the four university boys as true believers in the multiracial ideal, an ideal exposed as glossy "orchids" that ignore real social inequalities. Peter and Guan become so tantalized by the ideals of diversity that they become complicit in silencing social struggle and unionization (14). Guan Kheng imagines that "he and Sabran and Santinathan and Peter seemed in microcosm a presage of a new society, a world of new people who would utterly confound the old European racialist way of thinking" (67). "Old European" racism is traced throughout the novel as a residual state formation that was reemerging in the Singapore and Malaysia states as if it were completely new and entirely non-Western. As Chua writes, communitarian multiculturalism had to appear as a "counter discourse to liberalism, not a reformist one" ("Cost of Membership" 180). It is in this sense that we can see notions of "racial harmony" in Singapore or the recent "1Malaysia" campaign in Malaysia as distinguishing "Asian values" from "Western values" while still invoking a shared mode of pluralist governmentality. Communitarian multiculturalism envisions itself as a break with Western colonization and "the old European racialist way of thinking" while still maintaining its structures of dominance. If American multiculturalism can be seen as a revision rather than a rejection of cultural assimilation (as I will argue in chapter 4), then multiracialism in Malaya can be seen as a type of pluralist assimilation, where one is assimilated into one distinct category of the CMIO system, with each racial identity naturalized as authentic.

As soon as "the bond of their young manhood" seems at its most ideal, the four young men of *Scorpion Orchid* are torn apart by the racial, class, and religious differences that were exposed in Singapore's early race riots. The riots leave the ideal of a colorful multiculturalism burned to black ash, as the boys each become disillusioned with their own friendship. Santi witnesses a Malay mob burning a Eurasian man in the streets because "he wanted to be European" (66).

Guan Kheng's idealism shatters as he retreats into "a tacit acknowledgement that they were living in a kind of capsule" (70). This "capsule" is a state of suspension, from which they can ignore the tides of history that seemed, for Guan, to push them in different directions. He describes his inclusion in the group as a "jettison" from his own cultural background, and feels that "he must look to conserving, however inadequately in his own life, the stabilizing sense of his own past" (71). The playful attitudes that Guan, Santi, Sabran, and Peter inhabit together perishes in the violence of the riots, and their university years appear "suddenly to be too paltry an excuse for their continuing friendship," as if those years belonged "to people they did not know" (73). The novel ends with the four friends feeling estranged from each other as they retreat to their respective social groups—Guan to the business class, Sabran to union work, Santinathan to teach children on the rubber estates in Labis, and Peter to Essex to become a schoolteacher. The crisis of the riot results in each character following the ascribed racial categories of the CMIO discourse and remaining within their own group. Only Peter later returns to Singapore as his "home," hoping still to overcome "the true blight of the colonial era" (68).

FISTFUL OF COLOURS: THE INTIMACY OF COLOR

Lloyd Fernando's 1976 novel *Scorpion Orchid* apprehended the pluralist transformation of race as a superficial ideal (among the four boys), a coalition against colonial and capitalist power (in Sabran and Santi), and as a dormant threat propagated by state narratives. In 1993, Suchen Christine Lim's *Fistful of Colours* captured a more intimate and rooted vision of racial histories that responded to the normalization of homogenizing policies like Singapore's "Speak Mandarin" campaign, Malaysia's New Economic Policy, and the fear disseminated through both states' Internal Security Acts. Like Fernando's novel, Lim's follows a CMIO group: Suwen (Chinese), Nica (Chinese-Indian mixture), Zul Hussein (Malay), and Mark Campbell (British and Other). Unlike Fernando's college-aged boys, these four are older, in their thirties and forties, and have already established careers that range from journalism (Zul), English teaching (Suwen and Mark), and professional artistry (Nica). Fernando's four characters ponder the history of their nation, but Lim's characters are bound to their immediate family backgrounds, which appear as multitudinous and mixed as their perspectives. Suwen comes from an unknown heritage of migrant bondmaids and prostitutes; Nica is identified as Indian because of Singapore's patriarchal identity system (though her mother is Chinese and Mandarin is her native tongue); Malay Zul is marrying Janice, a Christian Chinese woman; and Mark identifies as Scottish rather than British. If Fernando's four characters speak from a position of an imagined neutral "e/umpire," Lim's Saturday Group members speak from a historically grounded position of crossover that is reflected in their collective devotion to art and politics. As "the one who held the group together" (31), Nica is the voice of the group's politics. She encourages them to defy ethnic expectations, to "reach beyond your ethnic group."

Written nearly twenty years after *Scorpion Orchid*, Lim's novel traces the reemergence of pluralism within a neoliberal context, where racial identities are not only indicators of labor and citizenship, but also commodified unique "essences" that can be exchanged in a global market.[15] The racial distancing that the characters witness is not merely political or economic, but restricts the spiritual and personal journeys of creativity and self-invention. Despite Nica's own rejection of her strictly Indian heritage, she is able to transition into her Indian ethnic identity to invest her image with artistic authority. As Suwen describes her, "When she got up to speak in front of an audience, she became like an animated piece of art. . . . Her heavy bangles of Indian silver, carved ivory and tortoise shell with coloured stones caught the light as she moved. Her scarves and necklaces draped about her neck created a tension of colours, fabrics, and stones" (65). For Nica, identity is art itself, with skin as palette and the pluralist imagination as genre, so that even "heavy bangles" can make her appear "animated." While Nica performs as an exotic Indian artist, Suwen chooses color itself as her medium. Attempting to go beyond the commodification of racial identities, she reinterprets metaphors of color, reading them instead as hybrid histories and peoples unrecognized by the state. She describes the Saturday Group as "the strands of different histories and cultures woven into this modern fabric of many hues and textures" (124). These "hues" come in "shifting patterns," that depict being "Chinese and yet not Chinese; Indian and yet not Indian . . . yet, here they were, the new Asians" (125). Suwen's solemn use of color expresses her own anxiety as a victim of molestation from her stepfather, and as a woman within the Chinese diaspora. In the novel's opening, Suwen's mother berates her for being molested as a child because she left her bedroom door open, as if to invite her stepfather in. While her mother rants, Suwen "stir[s] her paint pots vigorously, mixing colours and feelings" (13). She "paint[s] as she was feeling and feeling what she was painting, filling huge abstract spaces with colours" (15).

Fistful of Colours captures the concerns of artists in the early 1990s, when many were pressured by the censorship, intimidation, and imprisonment that the Singapore state had imposed upon artists in the 1980s. After an era of cracking down on artist-dissenters, in the early 1990s, the Singapore state began to invest heavily in art projects, imposing an understanding of culture that was chiefly industrial, commercial, and national (Wee, "Creating High Culture" 84). Artists at the time had to choose either to abandon their art, or to produce sterile art celebrating Singapore as a global multiracial city. Suwen's choice of color as her medium is an attempt to strip away these commercial modes of art, and to tear color from its discourse within the CMIO system (where Chinese are yellow, Malays are brown, Indians are black, and Others are white). Indeed, the narrative invokes racial discourses of color to invoke gendered depictions of race, as when Suwen's mother considers suitors for Suwen: "Brown, white or black, it would not bother her at all" (166). The metaphor of colors structures the book into separate parts, where "Part 4: Yellow, White, and Brown Reveries," is a nostalgic look at Suwen's relationship with Janice and Nica, while the last section, "Part 8: Paint . . . Scarlet / Painted . . . Red" analogizes reddish colors with the Singapore Art community's view of Suwen as "cheap" and her painting as "porn." Color here is not a mere identity that one can play with, as Fernando's four boys would understand it. Rather, colors are internal, "shading into one another, mixing and merging, so that for an instance, one whole uncomplicated and integrated individual, the artist, had painted in total control" (15). The novel considers how art itself, as a social practice, can effort control over the constitution of color and race as "mixing and merging."

In choosing to remain silent about her rape, Suwen expresses her rage through controlling the colors on the canvas.[16] The novel begins and ends on the day after Suwen's controversial painting is unveiled at a Singapore art gallery (302). The painting depicts two people of different races, later revealed as Nica and Mark, nude and engaged in passionate love-making. Rather than appear playful or distancing, the colors "dominated and filled the entire wall," portraying the Indian woman's breasts with five shades of brown, "hanging like ripe fruits of brown, cinnamon, russet and auburn, shading into deep chocolate before the greedy white mouths reaching up to suck them" (304). The strokes are bold, with "vibrant colours" that "throb with such life and energy. Such abandon!" (304). After Suwen's exhibition, Singapore art critics blame her eroticism on Westernization, and read the use of colors as a betrayal of Asian values, of a "person devoid of a sense of her own ancestral roots and history" (19). Suwen finds this ironic, since her attempt in the painting is to represent the history of her Saturday Group, hoping to represent "this island's forefathers and its myriad histories" (19). Her mission to "paint the past for what it was," "unadorned by political myths" (19), ends with her moving to the provinces of Malaysia in order "to start her life anew" (18).

Both Nica's and Suwen's attempts to control and manage their modes of self-expression, whether through performance or painting, gives them a measure of control over historical violence. Nica's upbringing in the Malaysian town of Alor Star "was like a prison," and her mixed heritage was ignored by both her community and her state, as she is punished for "picking up her amah's Cantonese," and pressured to deny her mixed heritage (69). Her father, once open-minded enough to marry a Chinese woman, changes after Malaysian independence to become "so proud of his Indian heritage that he was determined that his five daughters should be brought up as Proper Indian girls and nothing else" (69). Similarly, Suwen's upbringing by her mother, the mistress to a rich Chinese man, leaves her vulnerable to her stepfather's sexual assault. Plagued with guilt after her molestation, she sees her silent suffering as the duties of a Chinese daughter, since "only the West relishes sordid confessions" (257). Her cultural muffling is analogized to the symbol of the fist, the eponymous symbol of *Fistful of Colours*. After her stepfather molests her, Suwen hides in the locked bathroom. She "shoved a clenched fist into her mouth and bit hard. She would not cry. She refused to cry" (16). The fist, as a form of self-censorship, extends throughout the novel as a symbol of silence in refusing the burden of racial reproduction. Later, when Suwen imagines the concubine Sia Liew's rape by her stepfather's father, she writes: "She clenched her fists and thrust them into her mouth when he rammed into her. She bit hard. Inside her head, she was screaming over and over again" (58). The transhistorical and transethnic experiences of sexual abuse are here expressed as a psychological violence reproduced through the burden of racial reproduction. For these women, it is not the mixture of races that seems threatening, but their continued stability. When their voices are muffled by "the fist," they express this violence with vibrant, shifting colors.

ANGLOPHONE AS DISCURSIVE SPACE

Despite the critical achievement of Fernando's *Scorpion Orchid*, it received little attention upon its release, and remained out of print until 2011. This is perhaps due to its exposure of racial tensions, a topic deemed sensitive by the Malaysian state, which prefers works that deflect attention from political issues (Morse 95). Because the novel is written in English, it also cannot be placed within the realm of "nationalist literature," a state-mandated policy that Fernando himself lauded, as he advocated for bilingual education (Mandal, "Reconsidering" 1004). Only recently has the novel become part of the nationalist narrative. In 2011 it was reprinted as part of the Singapore Classics series by the Singaporean publisher Epigram, and gained popularity as a novel that crossed nationalist canons. By the time Lim's *Fistful of Colours* saw publication in 1991, a tradition of English writing was well embedded in Singapore. Their rejection and acceptance bookend the historical shift of English from a "non-nationalist" language to a global, cosmopolitan one.

In both Malaysia and Singapore, English has functioned as a language of utility, marking Asian "mother tongues"—Mandarin Chinese, Malay, and Tamil—as languages of values and tradition. In Shirley Geok-lin Lim's memoir she remembers the alienation imposed by learning English in the 1960s, as she was encouraged not to become too intimate with the language. "Depriving us of Chinese or Malay or Hindi," she writes, "British teachers reminded us nonetheless that English was only on loan, a borrowed tongue which we could only garble" (*Among the White Moon Faces* 187). Similarly, in his essays written in the 1970s, Fernando observed how English was seen as a second tongue used only as a language of public administration, commerce, and industry. But for Fernando, English literature, unlike

English political administration, had the potential to counteract "the conventions of silence" that were the norm in both Malaysia and Singapore when discussing race ("Truth in Fiction" 225). Although producing the first Malaysian novel in English, Fernando himself was haunted by the implied violence and prejudice of writing about other races, saying that "I explained to myself—very earnestly, I remember—that I was not a racist" ("Truth in Fiction" 222).[17]

As an inherited language, English provided a discursive space to explore assigned racial identities. In their devotion to English as a culture rather than a simple language, writers like Shirley Geok-lin Lim and Ee Tiang Hong went into self-exile after Malaysia began to restrict English through the increased enforcement of the National Language Act, which defined the national language as Malay (Washima and Norita 155). This privileged Malay writers alone to be involved in "the construction of the identity of a new nation" (ibid.), while Anglophone and Sinophone writers were left out.[18] English writers went into self-exile in Singapore, Australia, or the United States, while Chinese writers migrated to Hong Kong and Taiwan (Bernards 316). Lim, who migrated to Singapore and then the United States, called the Language Act "a more effective silencer than tanks and barbed-wire" (*Writing S.E./Asia in English* 299). The act was seen as a final blow to Anglophone communities, and stranded writers in what poet Wong Phui Nam called "a naked and orphaned psyche" (175). These "second-generation" Malaysian writers in English felt associated with a soulless language, and were marked as "inauthentic" within any cultural tradition. Yet this inability to participate in national literature also had the effect of positioning English as a discursive space from which writers could reflect upon "nationalism" and "authenticity." As the fiction writer K. S. Maniam pointed out, authors writing in Malay rarely handled the "multicultural reality" and tended to highlight ethnocentric issues "that are seemingly exclusive to the Malay community" (Washima and Norita 162). Anglophone writers, on the other hand, tended to emphasize racial conflict, drawing "inspiration from problems arising from within a multicultural society" (ibid.).

Since independence, Singapore has seemed far more hospitable toward Anglophone writers, as it has adopted the path of pan-racial, enterprise-based, economic nationalism. But this hospitality smuggled along with it expectations for Anglophone writers to represent official narratives of Singapore citizenship and history (Quayum, "Editor's Introduction" 23). As the writer and politician Philip Jeyaretnam put it, "Singapore literature, like all Singapore art, assumes a confinement of the soul from which only memory or exile can free the soul" (164). Unlike in Malaysia, Singapore Anglophone writers were not ignored by the state, but their use of a global language made their texts heavily susceptible to censorship. Anglophone writing has been "accommodated" only insofar as it allows advancements in commerce, business, and education, and continues to be seen as a global language (Mandal, "Reconsidering Cultural Globalization"

1005). As in Malaysia, Singapore Anglophone writers must navigate through a global language that is marked as spiritually defunct.

Both *Scorpion Orchid* and *Fistful of Colours* explore the potential of English through the novel's bilingual characters, who refuse to use language in its official form as a system of classification and administration. In *Scorpion Orchid*, the "neutrality" of the English language is mocked by the novel's historical accounts, where a realist history of contact between Europeans and Malays is later revealed as a "bogus history" invented by a cynical university student (147). Similarly, in Lim's *Fistful of Colours*, Suwen and Nica are cast as only "half Chinese" and "half Indian," as they dream and think in English rather than their official mother tongues, as if their culture has corroded through too much intimate contact with English. Nica blames Suwen's self-perception of being "half" as part of the state's "cultural lobotomy" that rewrites histories of Chinese and Indian dialects to "Think Mandarin" and "to sculpt a new kind of Singapore Chink" (79). Both the playful mockery of Fernando's text and Lim's depiction of feeling "half-Chinese" reframes English as an alternative to rigidly defined racial identifiers.

NOT MASKS, BUT FACES

Ee Tiang Hong's 1960 poetry collection, *I of the Many Faces*, expresses feeling "guilty and penitent" for having "many faces." In a context where race was emerging as a subject to be feared, and those who sought to hybridize were the new victims of race riots, English provided a space to problematize and reinterpret racial identity. But for whom does one reinterpret identity? Who are "the people," and who "the government"? As *Scorpion Orchid* and *Fistful of Colours* both stress, the focus on family genealogy present in Tamil, Chinese, and Malay reinforces the notion that subjects cannot simply choose to "escape" or "think outside" their filial designation without embarking on a type of social suicide, and being irrecoverably lost to history. This commitment to the unit means that identification with a single ethnic heritage turns community into ideology. Rather than attempt to alienate subjects from communities, pluralist governmentality casts individuals into groups who must be assisted, organized, and managed by a benevolent power. It has thus been the "burden" of many postcolonial states to conceptualize racial groups as coherent cultural units, as communities.

The importance of filial communities has displaced English into a language ideologically divested of its cultural and historical dimensions, and utilized to reposition the postcolonial state as a "neutral" umpire. *Scorpion Orchid*'s fusion of a bildungsroman with excerpts from regional and imperial histories that are mythical or fake traces cross-racial communities based on this characterization of transitioning among, rather than transcending from (or beyond) normative racial types. The complexity of these histories, read together, produces a cultural form that can fall on many intersecting scales: intra-national, inter-national, regional, or transpacific. In *Fistful of Colours*, Nica's family history of Straits Chinese and Tamil Indian mixture belies her official "Indian" identity, while Zul Hussein's family history, intertwined with Mark Campbell's own, reveals a hybridity unaccounted for by the CMIO system. Rather than insist on the individual as the main alternative to multicultural identities, in Lim's novel the family unit itself undergoes a revisionist process, wherein the uniformed markings of the state are exposed as arbitrary given the family's hybrid genealogies.

Lloyd Fernando's essays, written between the 1969 race riot and the release of *Scorpion Orchid* in 1976, give us a window into an Anglophone cultural form. In 1971 Fernando called the emerging culture of migrants "in-between migrants" who refused to perform either the national culture or the homeland culture, and who lived "in a state of suspension, by believing that the tide of history has another alternative, by hoping that another set of conditions will prevail" (*Cultures in Conflict* 142–143). Fernando's dismissive tone reveals the ideological boundaries of nationalist narratives within Malaya, where concepts of cultural belonging outside of nationalist paradigms were positions of exile to history's "waiting room" (Chakrabarty). In a 1975 essay, Fernando shifted from this dismissive tone to further develop the concept of "in-between culture" as a psychosocial symptom, one induced by the trauma of migration and the alienation of living through monolithic racial identities. Fernando named this state of mind "detribalization anxiety," a condition wherein the migrant experienced "complex stresses and strains resulting from the fear of losing his identity on the one hand, and on the other the fear that he may not succeed in achieving the new identity which he seeks to assume" (*Cultures in Conflict* 13–14). Because neither choice here is presented as authentic, Fernando indicates that neither the "homeland culture" nor the "national culture" come naturally, but must be "assumed" by the migrant. Detribalization anxiety is a symptom created by the fear "of completely valueless or undifferentiated existence" (ibid.). The value of "in-between culture" emerges through its own shifts, in functioning as "part of an unceasing process" that is "capable of continuing as if in infinite series, with every stage of the series having no lasting validity" (ibid.). Fernando saw this "infinite series" of cultural transitions as able to reverse the logics of race and identity, but he doubted that it would ever be accepted in a world structured by nation-states and racial belonging. In 1975, it seemed clear that to build a national "folk," the migrant had to assume one of his given identities, no matter how "inauthentic" it would feel.

Fernando's theories of racial identity allow us to separate the act of transitioning among racial groups from the individualism of "self-fashioning." Rather, we can see transition as a reaction to imposed racial identities that forcibly thrust the migrant "into the no-man's land between cultures" where "colonial history in particular has left an indelible mark" (*Cultures in Conflict* 122). Transition then emerges as a shared cultural practice that assigns participation within a cross-racial formation. As members of an Anglophone culture forcibly thrust into a "no-man's land" (of pluralist governmentality), transition assumes identities not as masks, as Ee Tiang Hong writes, but as an "I of the many faces"—as intimate engagements with a recognizable cultural form and its underlying histories of mixture.

TRANSITION IN *SCORPION ORCHID*

Scorpion Orchid explores transition as a meaningful reinterpretation of identity through its juxtaposition of historical narratives with its main narrative, and through three characters: Peter, the hybrid Eurasian; Tok Said, the mysterious spiritual leader; and Sally, the racially ambiguous waitress. Unlike Guan, Santi, and Sabran, who each return to their given cultural communities, Tok Said, Peter, and Sally represent identities repressed by pluralist governmentality, and have no "home" to return to. Peter is mixed race and marked as "inauthentic"; Tok Said holds a radical commitment to his culture, one that cannot conform to that of a multicultural society; and Sally occupies an impossible position of mixture. Peter D'Almeida's identity as a Eurasian, an Other in the CMIO construct, alienates him from participating in the new postcolonial nation. When Sabran suggests that he try to fit into Singapore society by learning Malay, Peter responds that he was born speaking Portuguese in Malacca, and then when "the British had ousted the Dutch, I learnt English and forgot my Portuguese. It was like taking out the parts and organs of my body and replacing them with others. Then the Japs came and we were told to forget English, learn Japanese. So once more I began taking out parts and putting in new ones—unlearning my language and learning another" (132). Peter compares language with "parts and organs," marking his separation from his three friends through being a "colonial creature." He speaks here for a complex Eurasian history of transitioning from one forced cultural type to another, a continued experience that has "gone deep enough for it to hurt to try to remove it" (132). His body acts as a historical archive, a "record of colonial influence" (Chiu 53). Peter invokes themes of transition as a historical byproduct of colonial encounter, where the need to shift identities has changed from an imperial command to a necessary tactic.

If Peter emphasizes transition as a violent historical process, the elusive Tok Said, a religious leader targeted by the Malaysian government, transitions to inspire others to new political and spiritual communities. Labeled as a communist threat, Tok Said conjures the 1950s Emergency period, when the Commonwealth forces and the Federation of Malaya fought a guerilla war against the Malaya Communist Party. Tok Said appears in rumors, each depicting him as a different racial persona. Santinathan claims he is a Malay *bomoh* (shaman), Guan Kheng claims he is Eurasian, Sabran claims he is a Chinese geomancer, while Sally claims he is an "Indian man with a greying beard . . . [and] he only wore a sarong" (25). Each character sees him as an Other who eludes pluralist categories. His ability to transition gives him a mythical quality that inspires awe in the populace, while his reputation as a religious radical gives the state an easy scapegoat for the upsurge in racial violence.[19] Just as the Malaysian and Singaporean governments blamed religious fundamentalism for much of the violence in the 1950s and 1960s, in *Scorpion Orchid*, racial unrest is blamed on Tok Said's mythical influence, thus legitimating acts of repression. But when the young characters meet Tok Said, they realize that the threat is not his religious extremism, but his pan-racial, ecumenical spiritualism, which could endanger the CMIO system, as it would inspire other racial groups to convert to religions separate from their assigned identities. Pluralist racial types would be made irrelevant by Tok Said's ecumenical construct, because his spirituality might speak more to an individual's "true nature" than racial or familial communities. Like Peter, Tok Said refuses to stay within the boundaries of his own race and religion, and rather maintains different racial markers depending upon context and audience—in this case, he is always an Other. His seductiveness, both as a revolutionary and a profligate, is in inviting the subject into a shared interracial cultural space.

Sally, as the "the pole around which they had been magnetized all unawares," is perhaps the most unsettling character of the novel (45). Like Peter and Tok Said, her alienation starts with her racial ambiguity, yet unlike them, it is not her privilege or reputation that allows her to be racially ambiguous, but her subjugation as a migrant female sex worker whose transition is necessary for survival. Her racial ambiguity gives her appeal as an exotic and allusive sex object, but also makes her invisible to the pluralist optics of the state. During the riots, Sally is abandoned by Guan Kheng to endure a "multiracial rape," an act committed by four men who reflect the same racial identities as the four protagonists (114). At the hospital, Sally's racial anonymity confounds the police and nurses, as she looks Chinese but her identity documents describe her as "Sally Yu alias Salmah binte Yub" (119). Her language also offers no racial clues, since "she speaks both Malay and Cantonese fluently" (ibid.). The state hospital staff relies on the racial categories marked by accent, name, and skin color, and they cannot determine whether or not to treat her as a subject of Sharia law. If the three racialized protagonists represent nationalist cultures formed to map and control populations, Sally is a subaltern figure who represents those made unrecognizable to multiculturalist state institutions, but who are also essential as service workers. Rather than confound the populace like Tok Said, Sally is subjugated and silenced for her ambiguity.

Sally's story is useful in exploring the gendered dimensions of multicultural belonging, where men (the four boys) can feel "playful" and "resistant" with their assumed identities, while women are made to bear the burden of racial performance. Since women are defined as homemakers with the ability to reproduce their race, their "authenticity" is even more rigidly policed. Sally's backstory takes the form of a sentimental tragedy, of a woman who escaped abuse at the hands of her elderly husband in the rural *kampongs* by fleeing to Singapore. Her first scene in the novel is immediately juxtaposed with an excerpt from the *Hikayat Abdullah* that features Singapore founder Sir Stamford Raffles espousing his well-known aversion to sex slavery. A reporter tells Raffles that "the majority of the female slaves were Balinese and Bugis. They were bought up by men of all races, Chinese, Indians, Malays, who took them to wife and whose numerous progeny are here to the present day" (21). Sally's story of service work and sex work is tethered to this history of sexual labor in service to the "stability" of racial harmony. As she says while at the hospital: "Malays, Chinese, Indians, Eurasians, I give them rest, I know they are confused, they talk bad of one another sometimes—sometimes even they get very angry. But when they are with me they become calm, they don't argue, they don't talk. Why shouldn't this be called love, too?" (111). After the riots, it is only a fellow subaltern, a homeless vagrant named Arokiam, who comes to her aid. Though Guan Kheng and Sabran both visit her in the hospital, Sally only remembers Arokiam's act of kindness, as she now perceives the group's "self-centered agenda" (27).

Sally's rape, in its brutality and violence, disrupts the notion that "diversity" in itself can be ideal by associating it with the patriarchal violence that eludes race-based social justice. The investigator Adnan Hamid blames the rapists' multiples races as the reason for ending the case, as he could not "tell the pattern" from a mixed-race group because there were no "race habits" to follow (114). It is not despite, but *because* of their diversity that the four rapists go unpunished. Sally's accent and poverty contribute to her remaining invisible to the CMIO system, as her poor English skills and poor education further separates her from the privilege of the four boys (24). Her plight contrasts with that of Santinathan's sister Neela, who is impregnated by the British professor Ellman. As she carries with her the privileges of money and education, Neela is able to overturn gendered cultural expectations to reject both her family and Ellman's belated offer of marriage (100). While Sally is unable to escape the burden of cultural authenticity, Neela appears hopeful and heroic as she sets out in search of a new life with her unborn child, "casting about for a new orientation" (55).

Though Sally's ability to transition among ethnic types is wrought from experiences of brutality and oppression, we can also see her racial ambiguity as a refusal of the patriarchal presumptions that are embedded in racial identities, where racial "purity" defines the boundaries of female reproduction. In the hospital, when Sabran discovers Sally's Malay name, he suddenly "felt protective towards her" (118). Believing he has some intimate knowledge of Sally due to her discovered "Malayness," Sabran calls her "adik," his younger sister. But like Neela's refusal of her brother's advice, Sally shuns those seeking to subjugate her as their kin, and refuses to see him again, telling him that "You think because we speak Malay together better than all of them you alone are responsible for my life.... [Y]ou simply wanted to take me out of their hands to put your own chains on me" (121). To accept Sabran's recognition would result in living in a private, traditional community where she would "cook and sweep—put up with the gossip about my life—[and] put up with old men's ogling stares" (121). Her racial ambiguity thus acts as an alternative to the familial commitments of communitarian multiculturalism. By the end of the novel, Sally vanishes from the hospital, retreating into Singapore's underground economy.

Fernando's representation of Sally deserves pause, as it speaks to our current climate where marginalized networks of domestic laborers are subsumed under racial types, and service work has become a means of fetishizing "ethnic" workers who are presumed to be "authentic" but in fact transition among recognized identities. As this book will explore in later chapters, this gendered critique emerges in much transpacific Anglophone literature alongside themes of transition. For now, we should keep in mind that Sally's refusal to identify as a racial type is not so much a political gesture to discover her "true self" beyond identity categories, but a way to obtain access to a wide range of potential clients, many of whom, like Sabran, Guan, Santi and Peter, embody ideals of racial harmony and capitalist success. Sally's story expresses how gendered labor and sexual objectification are the *necessary preconditions* for the multiracial idealism expressed through the four boys. It is thus not merely the riots that disrupt the boys' multiculturalist idealism, but Sally's departure from their lives.

TRANSITIONAL INTIMACIES

> As long as we mix and mingle in the comfortable confines of the marketplace, all is well; move beyond that into the personal and the intimate areas, then the hub quivers and shakes like a machine into which one has accidentally poured water instead of oil.
> —Zul Hussein in *Fistful of Colours*

Scorpion Orchid's three characters of transition may represent specific communities: the ex-colonials occupying fluid positions of privilege and power (Peter), the "Othered" cross-ethnic spiritual communities (Tok Said), and the communities of ambiguous affective laborers (Sally). In *Fistful of Colours*, the narrative focus is less on the individuals as representatives of transition, but on the transitions within intimate bonds and collectives. Like Sally and Neela, the women of Lim's novel—Nica, Suwen, and Janice—are burdened with the responsibility of racial and cultural reproduction. And similarly too, all three characters defy this role: Nica lives unwed with her wealthy Chinese partner; the Christian Chinese woman Janice decides to marry the Malay Muslim Zul; Suwen decides to remain adamantly asexual, a virgin in her late thirties. These women's refusal to perform reproductive labor exposes the bind between the ideologically separated discourses of race and reproduction, where one can discuss "multiculturalism" or "multiracialism" in isolation of gender and sexuality. To expose this conceptual unit of pluralist governmentality, Alys Weinbaum has traced the bind between race and reproduction that constitutes national and ethnic belonging, as Weinbaum calls it: "the inextricability of the connection between race and reproduction—the fact that these phenomena ought not to be thought of as distinct, though they have all too often been analytically separated" (5).

The female characters in Lim's novel provide an intimate depiction of the race/reproduction bind. We meet Janice and Zul Hussein in the midst of their engagement, when Janice has been disowned by her father for marrying a Muslim. She recalls sleeping in her father's house during his abuse to her mother, "unable to sleep because of her mother's muffled cries in the next room" (153). Her father's cruelty does not seem to represent traditional Chinese patriarchy, as his anger is roused by Janice's abandoning her Christian faith, to which he himself had converted before marrying. While her father and fiancé are both able to cross religions and races without incident, Janice herself must continue to act as "a Chinese seeking to safeguard her cultural self from change" (155). Her struggle influences the Saturday Group to inhabit a more critical mindset, one that combines understandings of racial mixture with intimate transitions. Through Janice's intimacy with Zul, Suwen discovers her own racial biases, as their relationship "open[s] up a whole new social world for her" (148). Zul, as a writer for the *Straits Times*, gains a wider perception on the transnational and transhistorical pattern of pluralist governmentality, as he remembers his great-grandfather was a chief in Penang who resisted the British, while his father gained an education through the help of a white British colonial. While Fernando's characters transition to cope with new contexts of power, Lim's characters, like Janice, throw themselves into racial intimacies "heart, body, and soul." Janice decides to marry Zul, take classes on Islam, and learn Malay, while Nica chooses to have a "live-in" relationship with Robert Lim, who comes from a wealthy Chinese family and helps Nica with his business connections. Nica's ability to transition both in appearance and in mind translates into her artistic philosophy, as she encourages Suwen to "ferret things out from other people . . . other races," claiming that to become a great artist she must reach beyond her ethnic group (246–247). Nica labels the advice she gives as "sermons" (247), and displays a measure of control over how she envisions her own racialized body, as she "held out her hands in a theatrical gesture and intoned like a priest delivering a sermon" (247). Having maintained the struggle against identity through reobtaining control, she influences Suwen to do the same. "We can change our lives, you know," Nica tells her along a beachside. "Our lives are for us to mould into whatever shapes we want" (115).

Nica's determination to throw off the burden of racial reproduction becomes a political project fueled by her desire for vengeance against all forms of patriarchy, which she finds embedded in the "cultural lobotomies" of the Singapore state.

Whereas Suwen seeks to paint Singapore history, Nica seeks to "sculpt the male form. In all its ugliness." Her critique eschews both the performativity of a racial identity, and the pull of a cosmopolitan freedom from identity, a male vision of transcendence that Nica thoroughly rejects. Her father, once cosmopolitan himself in his marriage to a Chinese and his fluency in English, represents a patriarchal tradition of a different sort, one characterized by the desire to be free of ethnicity while managing and identifying others (in this case his daughters). Nica's desire to sculpt her own life seems time and again driven by her antipatriarchal politics. Her performance as an exotic Indian woman allows her to seduce Mark Campbell, Suwen's crush. She asks him to pose nude, then depicts his naked body as a "grotesque" white man with "loose skin." Nica refers to this as "Art as Vengeance" for the history of whites exploiting Asian women, and despite Mark's public humiliation and shame, Nica feels "no harm in doing it" (293).

If Nica comes to represent a determined political force, Suwen seems reflective and pondering. Yet like Nica, Suwen's desire to break from racial identities is driven by a violent past. Her devotion to English begins in the schools of Malaysia, when after the 1969 riots, Malay was made the language of instruction, and Suwen came to Singapore because she "got A's for English" (184). By her thirties, Suwen's adoption of English left her with an urge to understand and become like other racial groups. As an "avid reader," Suwen's isolating personality leads her to investigate Singapore's various family histories, seeking to represent them in her own art (83), especially the Malay, Chinese, and Indian workers, who she feels "are sojourners like my poor self here, but a good deal worse off" (122). Suwen's desire to connect to others is not merely a way to escape her racial identity, but to take control of her own past, and to understand the histories that led to her being blamed for her own rape. Her desire to intimately know others then turns into a more radical critique of Singapore state historiography. As Nica tells her, "our history academics are competing to see who can write the most boring inoffensive history of Singapore." Nica rouses Suwen to produce an alternative narrative that captures her place as an artist in constructing history as a historiography.[20] By taking control of historical narrative, Suwen challenges state narrative. Yet her provocations against state history remain superficial until Nica exposes Mark's nude body, an event that leaves Suwen so upset that her internal barrier is broken as she paints (Nazareth 905). The potency of the act transforms to a radical potency that enables Suwen to critique the state on a more substantial level, sparking controversy in the Singapore art world for her painting's graphic depictions of interracial sex.

In Fernando's *Scorpion Orchid*, transition is made a naïve ideal for the four boys, but a harsh reality for Sally. But in *Fistful of Colours*, transition is felt as a group effort, one that similarly is rooted in the need for survival, but that carries with it the hope and solidarity that emerges in the collective. Although the group's members strive to intimately understand other races, they are also unable to find themselves free of ethnic self-perceptions. As Suwen thinks, "She could never go to bed with a white man ... she was too much of a Chink.... She simply could not see herself locked in copulation with a white hairy body" (125). Lim's characters explore transition as a viable group practice, one that does not necessarily need to be "above" ethnic perceptions, but one that takes on a life-long project of racial crossover. Lim's novel captures a response to pluralist governmentality that goes beyond the self-enriching clans of cosmopolitanism or colonial mimicry, but one that seeks understanding, intimacy, and refuge.

TO BE SOUTHEAST ASIAN

In experiencing the struggle of cross-racial intimacy, Lim's Saturday Group begins to see themselves within social relationships across Southeast Asia that include all the people and histories they feel intimate connections with. As Southeast Asians, Lim's characters position themselves within a non-nationalist, nonracial form gathered around mixture, heterogeneity, and colonial history. Janice finds herself "prepared to become more of a Southeast Asian," and immerses herself in Southeast Asian history, choosing not to envision home as a distant homeland, but home as where she is now. She has "already sunk her roots here" (187). Suwen, by the novel's end, returns to the provinces of Malaysia, seeking her "roots" away from her designated homeland of China as well as from her once fetishized ideal of Britain. Rather, she finds home among the mixed working class of Malays, Indians, and Chinese, her fellow "sojourners." Finally, Nica decides to be "neither Indian nor Chinese," but maintains that no "person, however highly educated, could forget his colour and his language" (337).

   Both *Scorpion Orchid* and *Fistful of Colours* express the possibility of a regional identity not merely through their characters, but through their revised narratives of Southeast Asian history. In *Fistful of Colours*, Suwen's meditations on history appear as a secondary narrative interspersed throughout the novel. Each meditation captures a moment of ideological frisson from pluralist governmentality, moments when identity barriers separating races were ruptured by political, social, and gendered prejudices. Zul's history of his father's support by a white colonial tells of the 1950s and 1960s riots, while Nica's history of her great-granduncle's work as a translator for the Singapore police takes place during the 1915 Singapore mutiny, when Indian *sepoys* (soldiers) revolted for independence. These historical narratives capture the oscillation between revolution and antirevolution, as every disruptor of pluralist discourse is met with a greater determination to solidify racial identities by the state and family. During the Rickshaw Strikes, Suwen's steprelative, Ong Ah Buck, watches his friend torn apart by a mob, and learns "the spirit of hate and violence, in the name of fighting for the honour of one's motherland" (99). Yet Ong Ah Buck teaches his forebears to treasure their Chinese heritage all the same, and ends up reproducing much of the patriarchy and violence that Ong himself witnessed. In concluding each narrative with a member of the Saturday Group, each narrative portrays the burdens of the "spores" of the diaspora that are meant to be near-perfect reproductions of the original. As Nica opines when hearing of Suwen's story, this burden is especially difficult for women whose bodies can "carry the fruit" (61).

Like Lim's novel, Fernando's *Scorpion Orchid* features a double narrative that juxtaposes history to the novel's main narrative, which features historical excerpts in fourteen italicized vignettes, most of which are taken from two texts: the precolonial mythical chronicle *Sejarah Melayu* (Malay Annals), and the *Hikayat Abdullah*, the personal memoir of the nineteenth-century Malay scholar Munshi Abdullah (d. 1854).[21] These texts, covering hundreds of years of Malayan history from the spread of Islam to incoming merchants from China and elsewhere, are often used to reinforce a *bumiputera* (Malay indigenous) narrative of nationalism. However, the extracts in *Scorpion Orchid* highlight moments of racial mixture rather than purity. After Guan Kheng abandons Sally during the riots, an excerpt appears from the *Sejarah Melayu* of "Princess Hang Liu, daughter of the Raja of China" and her Chinese ministers who fathered "five hundred sons," their descendants the contemporary "Chinese yeomen" (70). This excerpt interprets Guan's abandonment of Sally as a betrayal of Guan's own mythic history. Rather than restrict marriage within a social group, as national myths often do, this myth idealizes miscegenation and racial mixture through its mythic founding of Malay/Chinese relations, and shows the permeability of Chinese identity in converting to Islam. Juxtaposed with Guan Kheng's betrayal, the story of Sultan Mansur makes the race riots seem unnatural rather than inevitable, an event more symptomatic of colonial history than of racial differences.

The fourteen interspersed passages layer *Scorpion Orchid* with a dreamlike quality that mirrors the novel's main narrative. Time and space are constantly made ambiguous. The excerpts resonate thematically, and develop an associative rather than a strictly chronological narrative (Chiu 50). Perhaps the most revealing of these excerpts is the very first, taken from the *Hikayat Abdullah*, which gives us a scene of ambiguous state torture: "A man came forward and struck him ten or twenty times with a bamboo cane. Then he was asked, 'Do you want to join this society or not?' But the man remained silent. . . . Then the master ordered him to be thrown face on the ground, while two men flogged him on the back with bamboo canes until he shrieked in agony" (Fernando, *Scorpion Orchid* 10). Though this excerpt is from the *Hikayat Abdullah*, Fernando leaves the violent state power ambiguous, as well as the racial body being punished. The question "Do you want to join this society or not?" bookends the novel, reappearing at the very end in a fictionalized history of the Japanese Occupation, where Peter's uncle is tortured by Japanese soldiers who pump water into his stomach and then stomp on his bloated belly, repeating the question "Do you want to join this society or not?" (142). But in the novel's end, Fernando switches the abstract power to a specific power, the Japanese, and a more familiar subject, Peter's uncle. The moral ambiguity of the novel's first excerpt is made all too explicit in the moral impunity of the final one. Here the presage of a new multicultural society functions as a social construct to produce consent despite the state's threat of violence and repression. The question "Do you want to join this society or not?" interrogates the executioner and the audience more than the subject being asked. It implies that the nation allows the subject the freedom to choose, yet punishes those who do not make the choice that benefits the state.

The historical excerpts from *Scorpion Orchid* and *Fistful of Colours* offer the possibilities of managing an identity that allows for new bonds and new histories: Southeast Asian. To be Southeast Asian, for these novels, takes intimate connections and reinterpretations of given histories to emphasize transition and racial mixing, rather than social segregation and the fear of race as a potentially violent source of conflict. The insertion of these secondary narratives disaggregates history from hegemonic state narratives of pluralism and racial harmony. It insists instead on narratives that might produce an entirely different imagined community. In *Scorpion Orchid*, these scattered histories give us a greater understanding of the "racial crisis" as it is interpreted by the state. It is only after the riots that the four boys can define themselves as "colonial creatures," as they see the riots within a series of traumatic events, each resulting in histories of mixture and transition being replaced by myths of racial purity and homelands. But without these other histories, Peter feels that they will be doomed to relive the violence "again and again and again. And for no bloody reason" (130).

2 · SO THAT THE SPARKS THAT FLY WILL FLY IN ALL DIRECTIONS

Pluralism and Revolution in the Philippines

In the last chapter of Alfred Yuson's 1988 novel, *Great Philippine Jungle Energy Café*, the Cebuano revolutionary, Leon Kilat, is assassinated during the Cebu rebellion in 1898, only to magically reappear in a jungle with a "mysterious aura of grand polish," a place "where heroes are headed" (203). After passing a circular foyer made of seashells and a plaque that reads "GREAT PHILIPPINE JUNGLE ENERGY CAFÉ" (204), Kilat finds himself "in the company of stalwarts toasting each other in particularly raucous corners":

> There was ... James Dean across the table in red denim jacket listening to daily columnist Teodoro Valencia holding forth on the constitutional provision of inviolate separation of Church and State, to which Mr. [Nick] Joaquin snarled contemptuously, "What are you, crazy? Darling, don't you think he's crazy?" and Princess Urduja of Pangasinan quickly came to the Batangueno gentleman columnist's defense by pressing another cup of coffee upon his hand, and ... some proud mandarin says quickly: "I, Lim Ah Hong, say that Church and State should marry and be one, for only in one is the Tao."

In this imagined afterlife cafe, Filipina/o artists and writers converse with the American icon James Dean, the legendary warrior princess Urduja, and the sixteenth-century Chinese pirate who invaded Manila, Lim Ah Hong. The language Yuson employs in this passage depicts these romanticized figures through their interactions (their opinions on the separation of Church and State) rather than through their heroic mythos. These characters, brought together from separate histories, are only relevant as voices adding to a critical discourse.

The jungle café is an imagined space encompassing the cultural history of the Philippines as a nation characterized by revolutionary change. The appearance of legendary and historical figures all conversing in English adds to the café's fantastic nature. Figures of revolution, from James Dean (the "rebel without a cause") to John Lennon and Mao, suggest a commentary on how revolution can be imagined. The inclusion of Chinese pirates alongside Hollywood figures, princesses, and Filipino/a Anglophone writers can be read as an attempt to project what scholar Caroline Hau refers to as the Philippine nation's "excess," the nation's heterogeneous elements "that inform, but also exceed, nationalist attempts to grasp, intellectually and politically, the complex realities at work in Philippine society" (*Necessary Fictions* 6). As a nationalism first imagined by mestizo elites to gather disparate peoples to rebel against Spanish colonialists, Philippine nationalism has been necessarily reimagined and reevaluated throughout the twentieth century through revolutionary struggle. Since the late nineteenth century when Filipino *ilustrados* like José Rizal and revolutionary groups like Andrés Bonifacio's Katipunan led a mass revolt against Spanish colonizers, the Philippines has gone through varied transitions of power—from the Spanish to the Americans to the Japanese, and to state imperial regimes like the ones headed by Ferdinand Marcos and the Aquinos.

As scholars like Reynaldo Ileto, Vicente Rafael, and E. San Juan have stressed, Philippine history reflects a series of revolutions and antirevolutions, each rupture of power producing the aftereffects of war, with shifting identities, histories, and languages. Despite these transitions, class, racial, and linguistic hierarchies have remained rooted, reproducing the form and hierarchical structure of the previous regime even while the symbolic content of "the enemy" and "the resistance" are in constant flux. Anglophone literary artists have attempted to subvert the recurring pattern of revolution and antirevolution by accounting for its shared strategies of repression, including its hypervisible military presence, its enunciation of Filipino/a identity, and its revision of official discourses that produce historical amnesia. In Yuson's novel, the imagined afterlife of a jungle café reimagines the nation not as postrevolutionary or postcolonial, but as a cycle of revolutionary and antirevolutionary tides. Similarly, the author-activist Ninotchka Rosca's novel *State of War*, also published in 1988, traces these revolutionary histories, focusing on how they have enabled transitions among racial and cultural identities. Rosca, who was illegally imprisoned under the Marcos regime and later self-exiled to the United States, characterizes Philippine history as a constant state of war where identities, histories, and languages are routinely transformed in order to obfuscate the structures of imperial power. The post-independence hierarchies that favor lighter skin, American-inflected English, and elite family connections speak to a sustained upper class that acts in turn for American imperial interests, revealing just how little has really changed (Tope 6).

This chapter reads two Philippine novels produced in the late 1980s, Rosca's *State of War* and Yuson's *Great Philippine Jungle Energy Café*, that explore how pluralist governmentality has reiterated and reproduced in and through revolution. As both novels were published in 1988, their intersection occurs just after the EDSA revolutions that overturned martial law. Their narratives expose the Marcos years (1965–1986) as an extension of colonial pluralism, wherein national identity was reconstituted as hybrid, multicultural, and mixed, but within an implicit hierarchy that privileged a mestizo upper class as figurative stand-ins for previous colonial regimes. Like the British in Malaya, the Spanish and Americans stressed racial differences in order to keep colonial subjects from armed revolution, and the ruling classes in both Singapore and the Philippines similarly sought to assign themselves to a "position beyond and above community/nation" that effectively separated narratives of the nation and the state (Tope 3). While racial identities in Singapore were primarily state induced, in the Philippines, identities were constructed upon a hierarchy of hybridity, wherein those most hybrid—most mixed, most cosmopolitan, and those closest to the colonizer's body-type and language—have continued to reign from one revolutionary moment to another. Taking lessons from the British, Americans instituted a colonial pluralist mode of governance that saw Philippine tribes as distinct racial types, and English as the lingua franca, believing that a common language was necessary for regional governance (Mabalon 34). Like the British Empire in colonial Malaya, American colonial rule was legitimized as a universalist "umpire" managing the particular interests of racialized bodies. Since independence in 1946, the Philippines has continued to import foreign products in the model of free-market capitalism, and continued to be economically dependent upon its exported labor force. While English education added to the skillset of overseas Filipina/o workers, homogenizing their identity also made them easily incorporable into a global division of labor, a global multiculturalism wherein nationalism is only recognized as a cultural "type" within the global marketplace (Shih, "Global Literature" 23).

Rosca's *State of War* and Yuson's *Great Philippine Jungle Energy Café* expose the hierarchies and governing strategies that have remained in place despite fluctuations between revolution and antirevolution. First, both novels explore how transitive cultures respond to conflicts between imperial disciplinary power and the governed by reinvesting in identities that eschew state and capitalist deployment. These texts thus depict transition as an anti-imperial social practice that can expose the recurrence of an imperial state reliant upon pluralist governmentality as a transhistorical form of power. In Rosca's *State of War*, pluralist identities are produced and reinforced through various experts whose authority stretches back to colonial anthropologists. Seeking to disrupt this historical chain, Rosca's characters develop an art of transitioning that allows them to negotiate identity based upon their own desires and political alignments. Both novels see transition within its political and social potentialities: as a tactic to instigate and conceal, as a creative parody of imperial discourse, and as a means of flourishing outside of one's conscripted identity type. Like Yuson's café, Rosca's carnival captures the bacchanalia of a racially mixed society as soldiers, tourists, transvestites, and insurgents all interact on an island of festival. In both novels, interethnic solidarity is torn asunder by the managerial state that positions itself as a "neutral" force interested only in protecting diverse populations from breaking out in violence, a fear that legitimates violent crackdowns, torture, and death.

Second, both novels depict the limits of revolution in creating sustainable change, where new forms of identity emerge in the wake of excessive violence and repression, yet these identities, once cemented, reproduce a war whose only positions are revolution or antirevolution. Both novels expose these reiterations by reimagining revolutionary history as absurd—absurd in its various reiterations meant to provide legitimacy to every new regime. Transition exposes the absurdity of multiculturalist identities, as they are performed in excess of the cultural practices encouraged by the state. In a time when the Marcos regime had attempted to revise Filipino/a history to make the state appear as a natural extension of national will, these novels retell Philippine revolutionary history as a farcical repetition, where new identities repeatedly reconceive of the nation as a collection of diverse bodies who require an "umpire" to civilize and manage them. Both novels thus warn of the post-Marcos era as a possible reiteration of pluralist governance. In Yuson's novel, the protagonist Leon Kilat leaps from 1897 into 1984 Manila and charges through the presidential palace (Malacañang Palace), only to demand that the "dictator"—Ferdinand Marcos—sign a decree declaring an all-night rock concert. Though it may seem a dismissive historical slight, this depiction sets the stage for multiple modes of revolutionary performance, which culminate in the EDSA revolution that ousts Marcos two years later. The rock concert brings feelings of "liberation and reconciliation," yet the later discourse of EDSA would forget such impromptu solidarities to instead idealize religious and purified revolutionary figures.[1] In placing various revolutionary histories into dialogue, these novels imagine the multiple and excessive forms of revolutionary practice.

Third, as transpacific Anglophone texts, both novels account for the imperial history of English, while also making a case for a wider readership of Philippine Anglophone novels as transpacific texts that engage with, respond to, and reflect upon transnational modes of governance. Philippine literature has often been seen as a catalyst for political involvement, whether it is written in Spanish (José Rizal), Tagalog, or English. Yet each of these languages have also, at one time or another, been used to track peoples into linguistic hierarchies. As E. San Juan points out, anyone engaged in a critical commentary on Philippine culture and society "is always a participant in the arena of ongoing political and ideological antagonisms encompassing two polities, the United States and the Philippines" (*Philippine Temptation* 254). Any study of Philippine literature in English must then attend to these ambiguous relations to power, as they become associated with class and intellectual elitism, but are also "seen as a vehicle of connection with other Anglophone publics" (Ponce 18). Both Rosca's and Yuson's novels meditate on the position of the Anglophone Filipino/a as one distanced from nationalist identity. Their Anglophone characters must revaluate and reinterpret their own imperial identities in order to critique and expose the powers that have allowed their privilege. As Martin Joseph Ponce argues, Philippine Anglophone texts make it possible to "articulate[ ] connections to and critiques of both U.S. and Philippine formations," and to direct "critiques of race, ethnicity, gender, and sexuality toward several audiences at once" (20). As is the case with Malayan literatures in English, this requirement for self-reflexivity and the open critique of imperial power allows for authors to "speak in different registers, as if one's identity were overlaid and occupied by other possible ones" (Tupas). I thus begin by asking how these novels portray anti-imperial transnational formations, wherein transition can be envisioned as a cultural practice.

THE HYBRID FILIPINO/A

Rosca's *State of War* follows a group of "hybrid" Filipina/o friends on the fictional island K at a festival similar to the annual Mardi Gras celebration on Panay Island (Mendible). The festival stages Filipino/a identity as an amalgam of Chinese, Malay, Spanish, Arab, and American cultures. Since "the first celebration went beyond the memory of the grandfather of the grandfather of the oldest grandfather," the festival is not ascribed to a particular ethnic group, and intersects with "no one's and yet everyone's personal history" (*State of War* 15). Over a quarter of a million people join in: locals, city folk, tourists, and military alike. While the festival's ribaldry brings feelings of pleasure and whimsy, the hypervisible presence of state surveillance condones the festival as a temporary and exceptional space, ensuring its participants execute no sustainable re-creation of identity. Indeed, though the festival might appear "postmodern" or "heteroglossic," its facade is shred by the controlled presence of soldiers led by Colonel Amor and the landowning family the Banyagas, who are invested in broadening the island's tourist market.[2] The mixture of identities within this festival zone is permitted so long as the space is identified as a space of exception, a holiday to counterbalance the otherwise daily norms of identity. Ethnicity in the festival is thus converted to signs. No one knows how it got started, so no one owns it. Even as it has the potential to transgress state narrative, the festival makes identity into a symbol, not a political practice. The festival is thus where identity is ideologically naturalized by enclosing excess and aberrance within an exceptional space.

Where the festival offers identity as a personal, individual choice, its temporary, topsy-turvy status contrasts with the natural given identities that will remain long after the festival ends. The festival can thus be seen as itself a revolutionary moment, a time of mixture and shifting that allows pluralist governmentality to reformulate and harden.

In celebrating mixture, the festival represents difference in the apolitical, as Stuart Hall might call it, "a kind of difference that doesn't make a difference of any kind" ("What Is This 'Black'? 23). If Malayan history can be understood as resulting in a kind of "communitarian multiculturalism," the Philippines can be seen in terms of a hybrid multiculturalism that reinstitutes hierarchies based upon mixedness, wealth, and mobility. Hybridity, as Homi Bhabha coined the term, disrupts and disavows the fetishization of colonial Others by revealing the mixtures inherent in mimicry, migrancy, and mixed race histories.[3] Yet, as postcolonial scholars like Arif Dirlik have argued, hybridity itself is always in relation to the colonizer, not other postcolonial states, and therefore can become just as essentialized and incorporated into neocolonial hierarchies.[4] Certainly, this has been the case in the Philippines. The representation of diversity in the festival can be read as a refraction of Filipino/a identity, since within Spanish and American colonial history, the hybrid conception of Filipino/as was employed to produce a hierarchy of mestizoness.

Hybrid hierarchies began to emerge in the period of Spanish colonization, from the sixteenth century to the late nineteenth century, when the Philippines was "doubly colonized," first through its administration by Spanish friars and state officials, and again from the landowning mestizo class who owned its agricultural exports, which incorporated the Philippines into a vast geographical capitalist system (Rafael, *White Love* 5). The Spanish integration of the Spanish language, Catholic religion, and Hispanic culture helped to produce a mestizo middle class who would, by the late nineteenth century, create a new nationalist identity centered upon revolution, while taking advantage of changes in power to acquire more land and wealth (Reid 37). These elites sought to shift the term "Filipino" from a diasporic identity of those born outside of Spain into a nationalist identity within the archipelago (Reynolds 427). Since the Philippines was a polyglot of Arab, Chinese, Malay, and Spanish ethnicities, the emerging Filipino/a identity carried with it a hybridity that enabled mestizoness to be privileged above those who seemed otherwise immobile. As an identity both multicultural (in including various "tribes") and hybrid (in its mixed race, mestizo classes), Filipino/a identity could be employed to reinstitute hierarchies based on language, education, religion, race, gender, and sexuality, while still including peoples of all varieties under a nationalist rubric. This enabled a landowning mestizo class to remain in power despite revolutionary changes, from the American and Japanese Occupation, to the Marcos dictatorship in the 1970s and 1980s and even after the two EDSA "People's Power" revolutions in the 1980s and 2000s. This ongoing history of revolution and counterrevolution has formed "one of the most enduring motifs in Philippine history," wherein the egalitarian desire to level the social hierarchy has alternated with the reestablishment of social hierarchy by incorporating (and homogenizing) revolutionary politics (Rafael, *White Love* 12). Seeing this revolutionary history as a "motif" underlines its absurdity, in the sense of the existential *absurd*, as the continuous encounter with the desire for an impossible outcome, where attempts for social leveling seem destined to continually meet its own impossibility.

Hybrid understandings of Filipino/a identity center upon the historical narrative of the first Philippine Revolution, recognized as the foundational event of Philippine history and so emphasized in political rhetoric and education that "without a collective memory of the first war, the present nation-state would have no meaning to its citizens" (Ileto, "Philippine" 217). The overthrow of the Spanish in 1896 was led by mestizo *ilustrados* ("enlightened ones") like General Emilio Aguinaldo, a leader who symbolized Filipino revolutionary identity, but who was also the son of a wealthy landowner. By the early twentieth century, the Philippines had become an Asian model for anti-imperial nationalism that would influence revolutionaries like Sun Yat-sen (Reid 25). Revolutionary identity therein functioned, as Elmo Gonzaga has put it, as "an oversimplified mask of subaltern identity that was opposed to the identity of the colonizer" (25). Indeed, despite the egalitarian status of this emergent identity, without the colonizer to act as the oppositional force, being "Filipino" operated within a hybrid hierarchy of mestizoness. Chief among these revolutionaries was the Katipunan, a group that emerged in 1892, and stressed the new Filipino/a identity as one of individual self-cultivation (Hau, *Necessary Fictions* 25), offering an alternative identity that both united the nation and implied a hierarchy of belonging based on a heightened level of needs and desires (Gonzaga 26). While leaders like Aguinaldo sought to contain the more radical and egalitarian aspirations of the revolution by emphasizing this Filipino/a figure as *ilustrado* and mixed (Rafael, *White Love* 10), Katipunan cofounder Andrés Bonifacio emphasized an opposing type of revolutionary practice (Ileto, "Philippine" 222). As the leader of a large peasant movement that advocated armed struggle, Bonifacio has been engrained into historical memory as a martyr (killed in 1897 by order of Aguinaldo) and working-class organizer. Both Aguinaldo and Bonifacio have continued to shape Filipino/a national identity, and are often used in both state and antistate rhetoric.[5]

American colonization of the Philippines co-opted the new revolutionary discourse of the Filipino/a by reframing "tribal" categories as "racial" and centering the colonial project on helping Filipino/as achieve a "civilized" independence. Having learned from their colonial experiences with Native Americans and from the British experience in Malaya, American-style colonial pluralism co-opted revolutionary attitudes while continuing the pluralist project of fostering differences among colonial subjects (Kramer, "Power and Connection" 1319). Aguinaldo and many mestizo revolutionaries collaborated with Americans, retaining their position atop the social hierarchy by reducing the heterogeneous multitude into a pluralist social hierarchy. Meanwhile, those at the bottom who did not speak Spanish (or English), who were pagan or Muslim, or who were not ethnically mestizo, were now incomprehensible to colonialist discourse. This hierarchy produced peoples in excess to the greater Filipino/a populace, such as Chinese Filipino/as, who were made noncitizens and became easy scapegoats to deflect Filipino/a economic anxieties (Hau, *Necessary Fictions* 135). Rather than repress the historical memory of the Philippine Revolution, American colonial pluralism emphasized the success of revolutionary leaders like Aguinaldo as proof that the American imperium was exceptional to the rapacious colonialism practiced by the Spanish (Ileto, "Philippine" 217).

Drawing heavily from the hierarchies of the Spanish and Filipino elites, the Americans depicted the Philippines as childlike and disobedient, yet stressed that mestizos and the upper class were less childlike than others, modeling Filipino identity according to their potential for colonial advancement. Census surveys conducted in 1899, 1901, and 1903 ossified this hierarchy by producing new racial, linguistic, and religious categories that valued peoples upon "taxonomic grids that demarcated boundaries and relationships" (Baldoz 24). The surveys organized Filipino/as into Malays, Indonesians, and Negritos, and then divided these "races" into eighty-four tribal groups ordered by "degree of civilization" (Baldoz 35). As was the case of Singapore and Malaysian identity management, taxonomizing racial types marked many racial groups as diasporic: Malays came from mainland Southeast Asia, Indonesians came from Indonesia, and Negritos came from Africa. Rather than a nation of unified people, the Philippines was depicted as "a tabula rasa settled by successive waves of colonizers" (Rafael, *White Love* 36). While the hybrid mestizos were held up as examples of civility, the Negrito and provincial villagers were typified as having uncontrollable tendencies to "run amok" and commit indiscriminate homicidal violence (as the British had said of Malays) (Baldoz 37). Using the census, American colonizers' shaped "good" revolutionary identities as mestizo and "bad" revolutionary identities as "wild" and "uncivilized."[6]

Since American colonization, memories of the revolution have continued to be used both to co-opt radical movements and to inspire resistance against the state and capitalist actors. The first People's Power rebellion (the EDSA revolution), which overturned Ferdinand Marcos, seemed to set the stage for an egalitarian nation that would finally see the social hierarchies instituted by the Spanish and Americans as a thing of the past. In retrospect, these revolutionary shifts seem now to fit into the revolution/counterrevolution motif of Philippine history, where Filipino/a nationalism has functioned to "reify identities, freeze the past, and encourage the commodification of ethnicity that situates

Filipinos abroad in a touristic—that is to say, neocolonial—relationship with the Filipinos at home" (Rafael, *White Love* 13–14). The hybrid hierarchies of the Philippines can be seen as a form of pluralist governmentality that stresses Filipino hybrid identity as a managerial class above a national populace of diverse identities separated by race as well as location, language, and "tribe." E. San Juan similarly has seen contemporary multiculturalism in the Philippines as hiding a "stratified pluralism" that reproduces inequality while "notions of cultural equality play a role as a great equalizer" ("Paradox of Multiculturalism"). Hybridity here is not an exception to pluralism, but its very modus operandi, as the very conditions of possibility for a new state-condoned form of pluralist governmentality.

Pluralism in the Philippines has not had the same advantages of positing "the indigenous" against "the diasporic," as is the case in Singapore and Malaysia. One finds the nation's "Other" also in the Muslim groups living in the southern region of the Philippines, Mindanao, a space virtually untouched by Spanish colonizers, but one that abounds in resources (rubber, pineapple, cacao, coffee, lead, zinc, iron, copper, gold). Separatist groups establishing Muslim nationality have been fighting secessionist wars since independence, represented in the Moro National Liberation Front (MNLF) in the 1960s–1980s, and the Moro Islamic Liberation Front (MILF) from 1987 onward. For E. San Juan, the situation of the south is "exemplary of the problematic nature of the plural society," as Muslims are marked as an intolerant/insurgent minority seeking to destroy the "pluralist" state ("Paradox of Multiculturalism"). The battle against the "intolerant" Moros has become a moral duty for the state to prove itself as the greater pluralist power. With the Muslims in the South as the Other to the nation-state, the Philippine collective identity has continued despite the absence of a colonial power like the United States, and despite such mixed racial histories. Revolutionary histories have cemented identity around the revolutionary Filipino/a hero, who, according to the narrative, was Catholic, Tagalog-speaking, and part of a mestizo hierarchy. This identity dismissed groups whose political participation was overshadowed by the hypervisible mestizo organizers, and who are thus relegated as mere foot soldiers on the revolutionary march of history. It marks Chinese as irrelevant, Muslim insurgents as antirevolutionary, women as "mothers" or "caregivers," and the non-Tagalog-speaking provinces as subservient.

By calling attention to hybrid and mobile Anglophone peoples, both Yuson's and Rosca's novels indirectly comment upon the ongoing civil war in the Philippines between Moros and the state.[7] The war against the Moros has been a civil war reminiscent of the long conflict interior to pluralist governmentality, wherein the pluralist and hybrid populace is set apart from the ethno-nation pleading for autonomy. To name the nation as hybrid and to showcase its history helps dismantle ahistorical cultural identities, yet does not displace the exceptionalism placed on the "neutral" state as maintaining racial stability.[8]

Indeed, when the dominant narratives of pluralism are momentarily displaced by discourses of hybridity, pluralist governmentality incorporates hybridity, but increases the scale. Zoomed in, the Philippines is a nation of separate ethnicities, races, languages, etcetera. Zoomed out, the Philippines is a nation of hybrid peoples, "the Filipinos," who are racially tolerant and modern, while the nation's Others—the Islamic Moros in the South, the indigenous villagers—are non-Filipino, *in*tolerant, and must be managed by a militaristic state. Hybridity, as these texts reveal, casts light onto that which it excludes: the intolerant, the monocultural, and the immobile.

In the next section, I look at how Yuson's and Rosca's novels focus not on hybridity as a counterform to pluralist governmentality, but on parody, absurdity, and transition. Transition offers an interpretation of neocolonial subjectivity that contrasts with the hybrid form imagined by Homi Bhabha. If hybridity names a state of mixture in postcolonial contexts, transition is a strategy employed by subaltern groups who are presumed to be authentic, hybrid, or strange. Here transition operates as not merely masquerade, passing, facade, and disguise, but includes a far more intimate process and openness involving risk and a willingness to "contaminate" oneself with the culture, experiences, histories, and beliefs of the Other. It is the ability to perform various identities not as masks but as separate parts of oneself that ensure their means of survival within an otherwise oppressive system of identity conscription.

STATE OF WAR

Ninotchka Rosca's *State of War* rethinks the freezing of a revolutionary past by juxtaposing its main narrative of a hybrid festival that lacks historical knowledge with a genealogical narrative of the Villaverde family that begins with the early Spanish friars and lasts to 1970s martial law. This genealogical history reinvests identities against official revolutionary histories, allowing the reader to return to the contemporary narrative with new understandings of each character's desires and pressures. Like in *Scorpion Orchid*, the historical breaks take on a magical realist style, and like *Fistful of Colours* these histories divulge a family lineage. These histories thus bear witness to the constant fluctuations in regime change, where shifts in languages, official histories, and identities mark the new imperial power as exceptional to the last one, though each one reiterates a similar governing form.

The genealogical narrative begins during Spanish colonization with Maya, a *babaylan* (priestess) and the mistress to a Spanish friar, who witnesses American colonizers changing the names of Manila's streets. She observes, "It was a kind of sin, certainly, to forget—but it was not easy to remember, especially when names changed, languages changed. A century-old name held that century; when replaced, a hundred years were wiped out at one stroke. Amnesia set it; reality itself, being metamorphic, was affected" (*State of War* 186). The theme of historical amnesia makes the recurrence of events seem both tragic and comic. We see in both the magical realist past and in the social realist present that the anti-contraceptive policies of the Catholic Church as well as the lack of equal development creates a seemingly never-ending recruitment pool for the revolution. In the novel's contemporary narrative, the revolutionary Rafael offers to recruit the child of a fisherman. The child's father agrees since "Even here, there is danger. He could drown anytime" (109), and because "each year [the children] increased both in number and in needs" (110). Then in the historical narrative, Luis Carlos joins the guerillas during the Japanese Occupation for the same reasons, since "There's more danger here for me" (288). These repetitions from past to present turn tragedy into farce, as when Carlos Lucas encounters anti-American revolutionaries, and sees that they took the sights off their rifles because "they made us cross-eyed"; "They were doomed," Carlos thinks, "Doomed by their own passion and ignorance" (175). Carlos later sees the ignorance of the guerillas as revealing their lack of an educated leadership, as Carlos thinks, "The leaders fought for one reason; the foot soldiers for another" (175). The fighters here represent a movement abandoned by the educated upper class, a theme that recurs throughout the novel, as during World War II, when Mayang and her son, Luis Carlos, fight for the insurgency:

> "But where are your rifle sights?" Mayang asked.
> "Took 'em off," said one of the men. "They made us cross-eyed."
> "Holy bananas," Luis Carlos muttered. (268)

This juxtaposition of revolutionary moments marks the continuous state of war as itself absurd. Though Luis Carlos cannot see the absurd repetition of events that his father witnessed, the reader can. Repetition occurs again during the American War, when Carlos Lucas pleads to his maids: "Pray for the men . . . and see that you all get pregnant. As quickly as possible. We will lose a lot of human beings" (177). The words are repeated by his wife, Mayang, during the Japanese Occupation, who tells her maids: "Pray, then—everyone. And see that you all get pregnant. We'll lose many, many good men" (242). The absurdity of these reiterations mark war as simply a measure of time, such as when Mayang's daughter Clara dies of fever, and Mayang wears black "until the next war" (246).

The historical amnesia that haunts the novel is traced to governing methods disseminated by American colonial education, and is explicitly represented through "Mad" Uncle Ed, an American anthropologist living in Manila during American colonization and later the Japanese Occupation. Uncle Ed seeks to use his scientific gaze to catalog ethnic identities, making distinctions among Filipino/as according to "civilized" traits—their education, their racialized appearance, their belief in magic. As the historian Paul Kramer has pointed out, anthropologists played a crucial role in forming the architecture of America's colonial racial state by designating non-Christians as heathen tribes, hierarchized by their potential to become civilized and Christianized (*Blood of Government* 212). When the Americans return to oust the Japanese, Mad Uncle Ed's knowledge of ethnic "mores" is used to rationalize a village massacre (291). Though these villagers had returned their weapons and "reverted to being peasants," Uncle Ed's undisputed knowledge of the villagers marks them as insurgents, inciting him to torture and drown a seventeen-year-old peasant. Uncle Ed then uses his anthropological knowledge of "spirits, honor, and monsters" to hang the young man with a dead bat on his chest at a crossroads "where four village roads converged" (293) in order to frighten the villagers and thus lower their defenses.

The imperial process of naming, whether of streets or of identities, forgets colonial histories and manages populations by marking identities as empowered and hypervisible. Back in the contemporary narrative of the festival, Maya's great-granddaughter, Anna Villaverde, recalls being tortured by Colonel Amor, head of the state police and an expert on "the human psyche." Like Uncle Ed, Amor relies on seemingly natural identities produced through American anthropology and state torture records. All Colonel Amor needs is "a face (faces), a name (names), a body (bodies) of flesh and blood. An identity (identities) he could hook his claws into and dissect into information" (349). Indeed, Amor's fascination with psyches is reinforced by his ability to document emerging forms of resistance and to compare them to a colonial archive passed down from different imperial powers. As Amor says:

> If there's anything at all I've learned in my years as—well, as an expert on con-spiracies—it is the living nature of resistance. It exists in a constant flux, changing, breeding, metastasizing.... From time to time, in the complexity of its growth, the resistance evolves into a structure similar to predecessors we have in the files. Then, it's easier to piece together its modus operandi. Not exactly the same but close enough. Of course, the traitors don't do that. We do that. For some reason, they can't seem to go beyond their experience—like they're caught in a time warp. (55)

Amor and Mad Uncle Ed are similar in tone, humor, and cruelty, but most importantly in their strategies. Mad Uncle Ed produces knowledge of pluralist identities, and Amor compares such identities across an era of revolution and counterrevolution. Both actively participate in how these identities are reimagined and renarrated back to the populace hopeful of change. For Amor, those in the resistance are unable to duplicate this strategy, as their histories are rewritten, erased, and obfuscated. The continuous revolutionary moments that seem to be ineffective in bringing structural change also mark revolution as a historical motif, repeated in indefinite absurdity.

ENGLISH LITERARY CULTURE IN YUSON'S *GREAT PHILIPPINE JUNGLE ENERGY CAFÉ*

In Rosca's *State of War*, the modus operandi of the imperial state is to subject its populace to revised narratives of histories and identities, made to seem exceptional or new by fluctuations in power. In Alfred Yuson's *Great Philippine Jungle Energy Café*, revolution too appears as a recurring motif that creates new forms of Filipino/a identity. As with previous metahistorical novels by Fernando, Lim, and Rosca, *Great Philippine Jungle Energy Café* juxtaposes a contemporary narrative with a historical revision; the years of the EDSA revolution that overthrew the Marcos dictatorship are compared with the final years of Spanish colonization and revolution. The novel begins with the revolutionary hero, Leon Kilat, growing up on the island Negroes in the late 1880s, then leaps to the Anglophone writer Robert Aguinaldo's narrative in 1975 Manila, and then back and forth between these two narratives, leading up to both the Philippine Revolution in 1898 and the ESDA People Power revolution in 1986. This whirlwind back-and-forth experience of absurd revolutionary history positions the text against more romantic and realist traditions of Philippine Anglophone literature. Shirley Geok-lin Lim has described these traditions as achieving a national stance through "an ideology of cultural nationalism," which strives for social realist histories with a didactic slant (*Nationalism and Literature* 27). A proponent of this cultural nationalist tradition, the literary scholar Maria Martinez-Sicat criticized Yuson's novel for using an elitist medium, English, to distort, trivialize, and misrepresent revolutionary history (3). Sicat sees the novel's absurd tone as "the squandering of an opportunity," and "a grave loss to Philippine literature" (116).

Scholars such as Elmo Gonzaga and Jordana Luna Pison have seen Yuson's text as indeed deviating from the cultural nationalist tradition, which replicates state narratives. The cultural nationalist tradition critiques imperialism primarily through the authentic and subalternized ethnic subject, while Yuson's novel (as well as Rosca's) reflects upon the very identity structure that produces concepts of complicity, privilege, and authenticity by making revolutionary histories magical, parodic, and farcical. In Nick Joaquín's introduction to Yuson's novel, he calls Yuson's unique perspective of history "the light of eternity," which flattens time so that "side by side occur the Revolution of '96, the demos against Marcos in the '80s, and banditry in the boondocks" (xii). The Filipino/a here does not emerge from any one revolutionary moment, nor in the subaltern identities produced through revolutionary fervor, but is expressed as "the mind [and] the memory, that shuttles back and forth across the narrative" (xii). This view recasts the various excessive identities within the Filipino/a, turning the identity, as Joaquín says, into "the sum of all our contradictions, divorces and anachronisms … that's why our meeting place is called the Great Philippine Jungle Energy Café." The café, where the various heroes of history meet to continue engaging with revolutionary discourse, seems an apt symbol of the diverse modes and attitudes of revolutionary practice.

Yuson's novel attempts to both lampoon and criticize revolutionary practice through the Anglophone writer Robert Aguinaldo, who seeks to uncover and reimagine the history of the Cebuano revolutionary hero Leon Kilat in the hopes of selling a biographical script about him. Like Emilio Aguinaldo, Robert Aguinaldo is a mestizo who seeks to forward revolutionary history and rhetoric while also furthering his own career. The novel's historical narrative follows Kilat in the 1890s as he exploits magical powers given to him by a "banana charm." Then, in the contemporary narrative, Aguinaldo becomes interested in "the ethnohistory of legend making," when he comes upon the story of Buhawi, Leon Kilat's mentor, who leads a village of pagan thieves in the mountains of Negroes (46). The novel posts Aguinaldo's own "underscored excerpts" (45) of a real essay on Buhawi and Kilat,[9] which becomes an accessible link to the history of these figures. Aguinaldo attempts to make the mythical story more "Hollywood" by stressing Buhawi's reputation as "the outlawed leader of a wandering band of rapacious rebels" (49). As he pens his script, Aguinaldo fears that "he had made it a touch experimental [because] he had bracketed the legend with his own fantasy of being the modern counterpart of the obscure hero." It becomes clear that Aguinaldo's obsession with Kilat has shaped his own behavior and political views, partaking in the "fantasy" of identifying with revolutionary identities.

Just when Aguinaldo's imagined heroism of Kilat and Buhawi seems at its most intense—and therefore its most nationalizing and problematic—the novel returns to the 1890s narrative to reveal Leon Kilat's historic first meeting with Buhawi. The novel's reimagining of this meeting disrupts Aguinaldo's own "superhero" narrative, while still taking for granted their heroic status: "Buhawi approached and Leon looked at the older man. Buhawi let loose a rollicking fart as he smiled at Leon. Leon instantly recognized him as the great leader by the manner he broke wind. Buhawi instantly recognized Leon by the degree of appreciation in the young man's face obviously marveling at the manner he, the older man, had broken wind" (60). Through the comic gesture of the fart, this scene disintegrates notions of heroic attributes built up in Aguinaldo's reimagining. The scene does not cancel out the characters' revolutionary heroics, but redefines the basis through which revolutionary heroics can be expressed. The fart is ironic but also disruptive of social norms, and phrases like "rollicking fart" and "breaking wind" lend a carnivalesque quality to the action, assigning power and agency to the disruptive act. Buhawi's and Kilat's heroics are expressed in their ability not to be restricted by repressive social impulses, as the heroes smile at each other, showing a "degree of appreciation." In this parodic act, the novel reinforces these figures as subversive heroes while breaking from the normalizing presumptions that emerge within nationalist myths. The fart marks subversion

not only to Spanish colonial powers, but also to the repression of bodily functions and the unpleasant excesses that they might generate.

The novel's juxtaposition of anti-Spanish revolution with anti-Marcos revolution follows Nick Joaquin's tradition of Anglophone literature in the Philippines even as it criticizes this tradition through Aguinaldo's privilege and
curiosity. Unlike the cultural nationalist tradition discussed earlier, Joaquín's
tradition counteracts narratives of Filipino nationalism and Tagalog hegemony
with themes of racial mixture, class struggle, and exile. As with nationalist literatures in Malaysia, Tagalog literature is often portrayed as sentimental or overtly
nationalist, while Anglophone literature has tended to explore Philippine
nationalist identity from a distance, emphasizing colonial history as a forerunner to the cultural hegemony of metro Manila. Such reflections on Filipino/a
identity as mestizo and hybrid can be traced to English narratives in the early
nineteenth century (Hau, "Filipino Novel in English" 319). Maximo Kalaw's 1930
novel *The Filipino Rebel* follows a Filipina transitioning toward American hybridity through English education, while Juan C. Laya's 1941 novel, *His Native Soil*,
explores the identity of a Filipino returnee who attempts to bring in business
models from the United States and ends up producing a laughably commodified Filipino/a identity. This Anglophone tradition reflects not just empire in the
global sense of capitalist exploitation and military intervention, but also in the
national sense of the postcolonial state creating a domestic empire (or "umpire")
by instilling colonial modes of pluralist governmentality. Even those positioned
against this tradition, like Maria Martinez-Sicat, have pointed out that these
novels seek to expose the nation as "one that accepts native oppression" (4). A
pioneer in this tradition, Nick Joaquín has delivered works that trace the overlap
between foreign and local empires. His 1961 novel, *The Woman Who Had Two
Navels*, reinterprets Filipina/o identity as one of mixture and historical complexity rather than of resistant identities. Joaquín's works contrasts with the cultural
nationalist Anglophone tradition represented in writers like N.V.M. Gonzalez
and Sionil José, whose novels acknowledge imperial mixture as integral to Filipino identity yet choose to juxtapose these "mixed" subjects against an authentic Filipino identity of rural and often illiterate farmers, to whom the "mixed"
Filipino must dedicate their cause. On the other hand, what I am calling the
"transitive" tradition, represented by writers like Nick Joaquín and Alfred Yuson,
mines the complexity of mestizoness, privilege, and imperial complicity. Even as
English marks these writers as Filipino/a strays, their novels embrace the contradictions of Anglophone writing and use it to reflect upon the myriad ways of
being Filipino/a. I read this tradition as transitive in the sense that it has sought
self-consciously to reinterpret and manage these given identities, and attends to
historical patterns where particular identities—Chinese, Muslim, queer—can
be reinvested with political importance.

The elitism of English as a language of international cultural capital is made more complex by the similar privileging of Tagalog. The Philippines has a history of attempts to institute Tagalog as a national language, though English has persisted at the top of a linguistic hierarchy (Rafael, *White Love* 9). While English still functions as an audio signifier for one's education and class background (Gonzalez 20), it has also been integrated into vernacular languages, appearing in Manila as Taglish (a combination of Tagalog and English).[10] Similar to practices in Singapore and Malaysia, English has been the interracial, interregional, and international language associated with business, academics, and politics, so that writers claiming to write nationalist texts can't help but disidentify from those at the lower, non-English-speaking rungs of the social hierarchy, even as they are critical of those on top of that hierarchy (Rafael, *White Love* 199). The distancing of English use is thus made possible by the privileged position of English itself, yet this privilege is contaminated with the colonial history of the United States. To speak of revolutionary acts in English is in a sense to admit to one's own inauthenticity.

The meeting of Leon Kilat and Buhawi in Yuson's novel speaks to the complexity of the Anglophone literary tradition in the Philippines. Robert Aguinaldo's privileged position as an English-speaking writer conflicts with his desire to speak for the Philippine masses, as well as his fantasy about "being the modern counterpart of the obscure hero" (*Great Philippine Jungle Energy Cafe* 53). Yuson acknowledges his own privilege as an English writer, even lampoons it, as Aguinaldo gets taken in by his fantasy of aligning with Kilat, even as this fantasy serves his own self-interest in becoming a famous scriptwriter. However, Aguinaldo's privilege also gives him an access to power that allows him to express revolutionary action. Only through self-conscious revaluation, reinterpretation, and management of his own imperial identity can Aguinaldo become dedicated to critiquing and exposing the structure that has allowed his own privilege.

STATE OF WAR'S THREE FORMS OF TRANSITION

Ninotchka Rosca's *State of War* follows the transitive tradition of English writing through its genealogical narrative of the Villaverde family, and through its three main characters who employ different forms of transition as a political tactic against pluralist power. In its absurd retelling of history, the novel can be read as invoking revolutionary responses to the pluralist art of government through an art of transition. In the novel's long historical narrative, we find acts of transition immediately in the family's grand matriarch, Maya, who becomes a mistress to a Spanish friar. As Maya learns how to recognize the colonial state's desire for identities invested in religious ritual, she transitions into a Filipina Virgin Mary, turning herself into a spectacle in the streets of Malolos, her "mahogany skin costumed in an extravagant embroidered blouse" as she wears "a necklace of emeralds as big as hens' eggs" (156). By appropriating a white sacred figure, Maya transitions into Mary, a sacred manifestation of ritual and religious belief that enables her to produce new cultural practices, like the tradition of self-mutilation during Lent (142). The emeralds that Maya uses for her transition become magically enhanced, and her great-granddaughter, Anna Villaverde, later uses them to magically recall her family's history. Anna's access to this history allows her to see identity transition as a tactical pattern. As she observes members of the Villaverde family appropriate identities against imperial power, she is able to see her own relationships as "merely an echo" of the past. The narrative's shift in style to magical realism is juxtaposed with the novel's realist narrative of Anna, who struggles to remember a past that has been forgotten among ever-changing names, language, and spaces.

Rosca's genealogy of the Villaverde family gives the reader a more emboldened historical perspective on the modes of power operating within the novel's present day, where Anna Villaverde acts as a revolutionary seeking to assassinate the Commander (Ferdinand Marcos) during an island festival. Although the historical patterns expressed by Mad Uncle Ed finds contemporary resemblance in Colonel Amor, who tortures Anna, the art of transition also emerges as a tactic that continues throughout Philippine history to act as a source of survival, subversion, and resistance. In the novel's contemporary realist narrative of the festival, transition is divided into three different forms that reflect each character's position, as well as his or her desire to resist, flourish, and survive. These forms appear in the novel's three main characters: Anna Villaverde, who transitions as a guerrilla tactic to resist and confuse "the enemy"; Anna's best friend Eliza Hansen, who transitions as a survival tactic, yet does so playfully, embedding her own identity performance with parody and ambiguity; and Adrian Banyaga, Anna's wealthy young lover, who transitions in order to forge an intimate relationship with Anna and to flourish beyond the limits of an otherwise self-disciplinary identity that is complicit with imperial power. These three modes of transition (as guerrilla tactic, as playful survival, and as intimate flourishing) are tested in the novel's main narrative, but are made more distinctive as historically patterned positions within the novel's genealogical narrative of the Villaverdes.

With her vast knowledge of and fascination for Philippine imperial history, Anna Villaverde carries an insurgent mindset. She is never seen laughing because she sees war in the everyday persistence of identity. She wonders "how much longer the war would go on—this elusive, almost illusory war that was everywhere and yet nowhere. . . . Somewhere, sometime, she had committed herself to what had seemed to be proper action and that was it" (23). When Anna is imprisoned by Colonel Amor and tortured with an electric battery, she learns new methods to subvert Amor's identity-based methods by creating "a mask, her other Anna" that contains "all the virtues required to survive" (75). Her use of transition to conjure another self, "her other Anna," manifests later in the festival, when she uses camouflage to elude state police. When Anna meets her revolutionary contact at the festival, Rafael, she asks, "'and what are you— here, now?' . . . She had known him as a priest, a traffic policeman, a professor, a pickpocket. 'Fisherman,' he said promptly" (21). In response to the colonial state's desire to collect identities, both Anna and the guerrilla fighters transition to camouflage themselves at the festival. They smuggle in explosives and tie them to a stage, where the Commander (Marcos) is set to give a speech. When the bomb explodes, the guerrillas attack from all sides, many of them dressed as transvestites carrying sawed-off shotguns beneath their skirts. The most elusive resistance leader, Guevarra, is the most successful in escaping Colonel Amor, in the end driving him mad, as he appears to have no recognizable identity, and no name but that of the heroic Latino revolutionary Ernesto "Che" Guevara.

If Anna's tactics as a resistance fighter employ transition as a political art, her best friend Eliza Hansen transitions in order to play upon the very conceptions of identity and the official discourses that produce it. As Adrian's friend, Eliza is "advantageous" to his family's finances, because she can use her connections to negotiate with Adrian's father, choosing "her words carefully, testing for limits" (32). Though her transitions are often for her own pleasure and self-gain, Eliza also uses her abilities for revolutionary ends when she convinces Adrian's father that Anna be allowed to smuggle a bomb into the festival, which will later kill him and cripple Colonel Amor (32). As soon as Eliza arrives at the festival, she transitions into a "Swami," a religious guru commonly seen in Southeast Asia. Calling herself "your royal Swaminess," she "held court at one end of the dance space . . . grabbing hands and peering into the palms of men and women, promising outrageous fates and fortunes. . . . by the time Eliza had metamorphosed into Rosie the Wrestler, both Anna and Adrian were red-eyed and wrung out by fatigue" (14–15). Unlike Anna's transitions, Eliza's are a form of play and parody. It contrasts with Anna's transition as a guerrilla tactic when Eliza observes transvestites, and thinks, "In such a disguise . . . man-woman, woman-man, one could live safely in illusions and avoid all confrontations" (15). Whereas Anna's transitions are predicated on eluding state optics of surveillance and control, Eliza's remain carefully detailed and hyperaware of the context, taking risks as she seduces her audience into playing along. All the while Eliza leaves herself vulnerable, attaching herself to powerful men who can at any moment turn upon her. Whereas the guerrillas disguise themselves as transvestites, Eliza skillfully elicits cooperation from the transvestite community.[11]

Eliza's transitions seem to keep no community belonging intact. While Anna has the guerrillas and Adrian his class prestige, Eliza can only understand her own political position as an outsider, hoping to survive the nightmare of war with merely her transitions. In her seduction of Batoyan, the Commander's aide-de-camp, she convinces him to share "what power he had, bringing home, so she might admire his cleverness, documents, proposals, and decrees" (98).

Her role as Batoyan's mistress enables her to weave "a bright blue comic thread through the dullness of the Commander's reign," an act of parody and satire that Eliza herself finds simply "for her own private enjoyment," but that Colonel Amor sees as dangerous, as it creates a laughter that "is *subversive*" (101, italics in original). Eliza's play upon the official histories coveted by imperial power disrupts its mechanization but leads her further away from the "safety in illusions" that she hopes to achieve. Throughout the novel, the reader receives glimpses into Eliza's impulsive anger against the ruling oligarchy: "When she was good and ready, she would hit them—really hit them, the whole asinine bunch with their courtly bows and their fluttering females" (43). Eliza's rage focuses on the misogynist plutocrats, particularly Colonel Amor, as she strives to "erase his face with her fingernails" (53), and decides that "she would have to kill him— certainly, no doubt about it" (59). Her interactions with Colonel Amor play upon his knowledge of identities and his sexual desires, keeping him guessing by "playing the game—her game" (103). When Anna's explosive detonates, it is Eliza, the unarmed seducer, who is immediately attacked by the soldiers, and it is Eliza who is kidnapped by the police like "a butchered pig, ready for flaying" (370). Eliza emerges then at the end of the novel as a news item, a deceased body washed ashore, a tribute to the festival so that normative life can carry on. Despite her ironic distance from politics, her expression of parody and satire appear to be the most threatening force against pluralist governmentality.

The third type of transition is illustrated in Adrian Banyaga, who seeks to escape his identity as a member of the landowning class. Though Adrian is heir to a corporate fortune, Rosca's language when describing him shows not a young aristocrat, but a curious mind open and engaged with others:

> A boy came running, holding up garlands of bamboo whistles on leather thongs. Adrian chose three and paid for them. . . . A laughing Japanese girl caught him in a pirouette; he danced a measure with her before she ran off. . . . A transvestite appeared, . . . and Adrian obliged by taking two swallows . . . he was nearly knocked down by a blond woman [and] he obliged her as well, carrying her toward the noise of the Festival. (29)

Adrian's open spirit of "obliging" others lacks the intimate risk of Eliza's transitions, as well as the political devotion of Anna's. Adrian seems rather more concerned with other ways of life, with appreciating the diversity of the islands and its peoples in a way that is neither distanced nor intimate, but that permits others to act upon him, "obliging" their whimsy. Adrian's openness also speaks to his disapproval of his own landowning family, who pressure him to keep within his own mestizo upper-class identity.[12] Despite his power and position, Adrian is subjected to history's cycle when he is violently conscripted by Colonel Amor into performing as a hybrid aristocrat. Amor abducts Adrian and places him upon a stage filled with objects typical of an upper-class lifestyle: "gilded plates and cups," "delicate curls of pastry," and juice "fresh squeezed from fruit flown in from Taiwan this morning" (85). Amor doses Adrian with a hallucinatory cocktail of drugs that conjures images of aristocrats in "formal evening clothes" who speak in English, Spanish, and Tagalog. All of the men and women wear "surreal makeup: demon faces, serpent skin, witches noses" (89). These hallucinations show the process of Adrian's conscription, as they turn his curiosity for others into a passive acceptance of his given role. When he awakens, he sees "the governor's daughter," who informs him that her betrothal with him "was being worked out in the dining room below, between his father and hers" (336). In the novel's end, Adrian's conscripted complicity marks him as an enemy of the resistance when he becomes a victim of the guerilla's explosive, originally aimed for the Commander. As his body is crippled, his mind is hurled "into a time warp, fixing him in a maze of words, a verbal account of four hundred years, tortured and tormenting" (380). It is within this historical "maze" that Adrian reaches his desire for a world without names, as his mind takes on various disguises of animals, plants, and rocks, seeing not names but the forms that they represent.

Together, the novel's three main characters represent a resistance to imperial power through strategies of transition, but also in their capacity to work together, and to see each other as partial to a larger project. All three characters seem aware of their own capabilities to employ linguistic and racial hierarchies.[13] In "game seeing game" fashion, all three characters are able to recognize each other's transitions, as Eliza knows instinctively that Anna's "cold" mask is a tactic to make her appear "indifferent": "[Anna would] stand there like a statue, her face a mask—but behind that, her mind was raging, pacing, tearing through one thought after another, calculating desperately" (48). In tracing three separate forms of transition, Rosca's novel targets the identity-based optics of pluralist governmentality as its most exploitable weakness. The representation of transition as marking one's relationship to power recasts apolitical, flattened notions of pluralist identities based purely on race, nation, ethnicity, and language. Instead, it exposes the identities that matter—that of allegiances to imperial violence and commitments against it.

HISTORICAL REPRESENTATION IN *GREAT PHILIPPINE JUNGLE ENERGY CAFÉ*

If Rosca's *State of War* depicts transition as a means of opening new political avenues, Yuson's *Great Philippine Jungle Energy Café* depicts it through the excessive reiteration of pluralist identities. The novel's leaps back and forth through history are leaps across different modes of expression that highlight the absurdity of regimes that produce pluralist structures. Throughout Yuson's text, the English-language writer Robert Aguinaldo cannot authentically represent Leon Kilat, since he can't read Cebuano, forcing him to embellish his script with parody and magic (115). Disregarding the impulse for authentic representation, Aguinaldo writes a metacommentary on historical narrative. When his Cebuano friend Resil—the real historian Resil Mojares—sends him archival material on Kilat, Aguinaldo finds the information "inapplicable, downright irrelevant or useless, or worse, it got in the fucking way of what he was beginning to like to call a para-genre" (115). Facts here become inconvenient for the historical truths that Aguinaldo hopes to express. While Rosca juxtaposes a realist contemporary era with a magical realist past, Yuson's "para-genre" merges genre conventions, splicing myth, speculation, and realism together to account for multifaceted types of revolutionary representation. This parodic style exposes the carnivalesque quality of revolution and shows the lineaments of revolutionary action.

Unlike Lloyd Fernando's *Scorpion Orchid*, where the more realist narrative dominates the seventeen interspersed mythic stories, Yuson's contemporary narrative is secondary to the magical history of Leon Kilat. Kilat's narrative plays upon historical events, making them magical and ironic through the reader's expectations for "authentic" depictions. Kilat himself becomes infused with the power of historical foresight after he absorbs a magical banana charm, which gives him "a sudden surge of overwhelming giddiness, then . . . clarity" (19). His gift of clairvoyance makes his own death foreseeable, and in the end, laughable. Like the emeralds that Anna Villaverde uses to see her family history, the charm is also an amulet of the Filipina/o *anting-anting* system of magic and sorcery, and provides an alternative history that has been erased by imperial and state narratives. The charm allows Kilat to laugh at his own future because "it was all open to him now, like the pages of comic books that would come years after his own passing" (19). He sees a summary of his life, of being "in the company of a traveling circus, baking bread with a Chinaman . . . falling in love with the mestizo woman in the crowd who would ultimately become his undoing." Beyond his life, Kilat sees the revolutionary cycles of the Philippines that were to come: "Rizal shot in Bagumbayan, bicycles and ice coming to his country, the Americans, Nick Joaquín, Gary Cooper, the Japanese." For Kilat, the mysteries of history become "alternating currents of laughter and rubble."

Kilat's knowledge of his own future is a form of parody that comments upon his own mythical persona in Philippine history. Kilat's voyage from the island Negroes to Cebu mythically takes place upon a sacred "silken handkerchief" that gives Kilat "lightning-like" qualities in battles against the Spaniards (Kilat's name literally means "Leon of the lightning") (19).[14] Yet in Yuson's absurd retelling, Kilat's handkerchief can only drift slowly on the waves. Since the handkerchief is paramount in Kilat's own history, he still steps upon it, but spends eight-and-a-half years waiting for the handkerchief to drift across the sea. Indeed, Kilat's foresight makes such events even more absurd, as he knows there is no historical alternative to the crossing. The novel's ironic spin on the event—that it took far longer than a voyage by boat—does not deviate from the myth so much as it deviates from the sentimental, nationalist, and romantic *genre* in which such a myth is mediated. By shifting the generic conventions of revolutionary history, the novel takes claims of magic and myth at face value, but restricts the glorifying expectations that accompany them.

The myth of Buhawi as a folk hero who trains Leon Kilat in the hills of Negroes Oriental also captures Yuson's absurd style. A figure so subversive that Spaniards forbade his stories (Pison 53), Buhawi is portrayed as the leader of a pagan spiritual group who has vast powers, a supernatural man who encourages his group to be "one with the trees and the wind" (40). Yet Yuson's Buhawi seems less concerned with subverting the Spanish than he is with *patintero*, a children's game of running past drawn grids. A significant portion of the novel is taken up tracing the logistics of this game, which is portrayed as a heated battle that bonds the group through the "camp dialectics" that emerge from after-game arguments: "He Cheated Yes He Cheated No He Didn't Yes He Did It No He Didn't He Simply Pulled A Diversion. . . . Well Let's Ask The Mountain Well The Mountain Saw It The Hell It Did Oh Well In Any Case" (71). This capitalized stream of back-and-forth altercation emphasizes the passion of the players, who become overshadowed by the argument. *Patintero* also has a revolutionary function, as it prepares the group for the battle to come by stressing "the vagaries of team effort, ésprit de corps, group swell, [and] mob movement" (71). The game takes place only a day before Buhawi and his group charge a Spanish contingent (83), and its logic transfers to battle tactics when the Spaniards are depicted as an opposing team and every man killed counts as a point: "The score at the end stood at two native Guardia Civil dead, one's neck broken by Buhawi and the other hacked to an infinitude of pieces by Fidelito" (85). "Gaming" and "play" here account for the revolutionary potential of cultural practices commonly excluded from revolutionary history.

If Kilat's reaction to historical events is to laugh, Buhawi's is to "lift his spirit" through the memories, and gain strength as "the redeemer" so he could "become a living God" (94). Buhawi's reaction thus embodies the cultural nationalist impulse to assume subjugated identities in the provinces by investing in traditional myth. Buhawi becomes a godlike "pure" Filipino, unencumbered by Spanish contamination, Christianity, or modernity. While Buhawi stays in the jungle to remain uncontaminated, Kilat leaves Negros to struggle alongside Chinese, mestizos, and Filipino/as in urban Manila, despite his foreknowledge that it will lead to his own death. The "laughter and rubble" that Kilat sees does not stop him from taking up his destiny as a revolutionary figure—in fact, his ability to laugh, and to take it in stride, allows him to continue despite the overwhelming odds against him. Like Walter Benjamin's angel of history, while others see "a chain of events," Kilat sees "one single catastrophe which keeps piling wreckage upon wreckage and hurls it in front of his feet" (257). The banana charm reveals this rubble to Kilat, but instead of feeling despair (as does the angel of history), Kilat finds joy and humor in the very pleasures of revolutionary action.

The climax in the novel's absurdity occurs when Kilat magically crosses over from Cebu in 1896 to Manila in 1984, meets Robert Aguinaldo, and storms Malacañang Palace, to force the dictator (Marcos) to sign a decree "declaring the urgent national need for an all-night rock concert atop Mendiola Bridge" (184). The irony of historical reimagining here disrupts the revolutionary imaginary of the present. For cultural nationalist writers and scholars, such a revision of revolutionary action ridicules "real" revolutionary history by reducing "human—and superhuman—dynamism to frivolity" (Martinez-Sicat 106). But we should read irony here as Roland Barthes defined it, as "a signpost [that] thereby destroys the multivalence we might expect from a quoted discourse" (44). The ironic "signpost" of the rock concert signals to the reader a vast departure from serious historical narrative, suggesting instead a metahistory, a text that flouts "all respect for origin, paternity, propriety" and operates instead as a "transgression of ownership" (ibid., 44–45). By signaling disrespect for historical "ownership" and a disobedience to the censored historical narrative, Yuson's text allows us to think through play and historical revision as themselves revolutionary acts. Similar to Buhawi's game of *patintero*, the concert sets the tone for future revolutionary action, as "everybody cheered and rocked all night long and such was liberation and reconciliation" (184). It is only after playing a pivotal role in this task that Robert Aguinaldo "step[s] aside and eventually disappear[s], never to appear again until the final party at the jungle café" (183). The fulfillment of subversive behavior, which appears to be the requirement for entry into the jungle café, is compellingly multisited, and includes various modes of revolutionary performance.

The novel's ending in the jungle café is the culmination of the power of the banana charm; it is the physical manifestation of the historical struggle that the charm allows Kilat to understand. The jungle leading to the café, as Marie Martinez-Sicat writes, connotes "a powerful metaphor for the lush authenticity of a culture untainted by the foreign" (107). For Sicat this "untainted jungle" is bankrupted of revolutionary meaning when the forest only leads to a café, which she calls a "foreign institution" that connotes "oversized, expensive, elaborate affairs" (108). Here the jungle is idealized as the place of Buhawi, where national authenticity rests on being untainted by the foreign. Yet the café, as a magical afterlife, resembles a community driven by discursive exchange, one bent on revolutionary fervor, with figures such as José Rizal, Gunnar Myrdal,[15] John Lennon, Yoko Ono, and of course, Marx and Engels. In this crowd Kilat hears voices bickering about the "constitutional right" of "peaceable assembly," "& someone else replying rapidly, 'Shit, there's no "clear and present danger of a substantive evil," is there as the Constitution says there must be before forced dispersal becomes necessary' . . . & the other earlier voice snaps right back, 'the word "inviolate" has to be defined' . . . & Leon now looking more dazed" (208). The first set of voices here takes a position on the nature of civil rights; the next assesses the constitutional applications of ideal laws ("as the Constitution says . . .") and the third seeks clarification. In the jungle society where Buhawi might reign, these multiple contestations over truth, rights, and speech would be suffocated by the authority of the self-made god, insisting upon ethnic purity (Filipinoness) over the contamination of new ideas. In the café, however, Yuson's paratactic use of ampersands rushes the dialogue, creating instant associations from one argumentative point to another, more concerned with the views of the speakers rather than their identities. The café's discourse is not isolated, but produces revolutionary politics; it is the spatial representation of the historical "magic" embodied in the banana charm. In a sense, the novel's ending feels like the magic "drop" of historical experience being transferred from the characters to the reader, empowering them with the collective knowledge of subversive histories. It is a space that sees various modes of resistance left to be adopted and reinterpreted for further revolutionary acts.

The para-genre form of *Great Philippine Jungle Energy Café* accesses different registers of revolutionary action (Pison 97). These registers of irony, absurdity, and magical realism offer ways of imagining revolutionary history without producing a normative citizen-subject that erases or marginalizes revolutionary "excess"—whether it be mestizo, Muslim, Chinese, or Anglophone. Like the café itself, the playful language and gamelike qualities of Yuson's narrative reveal its own construction and historical inauthenticity, making readers conscious of their role in determining the text's multiple meanings (Pison 97). Likewise, the conversations that occur in the jungle café seem a culmination of the historical negotiation that occurs throughout the novel. When he joins the Katipunan, Kilat witnesses the revolutionary center as a space of unending argument and contesting ideas: "'Rizal never said anything about fighting, for one.' Arnulfo looked scornfully. . . . He went on, 'Rizal is a reformist, as we all know. The fighting is Bonifacio's idea. Everyone knows that'" (159). The exchange of ideas broadens the movement by including multiple perspectives and strategies into revolutionary practice, and Kilat comes to understand that "The Movement needs dissent within its own ranks . . . so that the sparks that fly will fly in all directions" (160).

REVOLUTIONARY EXCESS AND SEXUAL DESIRE

The absurdity that characterizes Leon Kilat's revolutionary history comes most extreme in the excesses of the hero's insatiable sexual desire. When Kilat first arrives in Cebu and is employed in a Chinese bakery, the owner, Yu Cheng Co,[16] exposes Kilat to histories of revolution and resistance in China. Yu Cheng Co's part in revolutionary practice comes in a pair of pants he makes for Kilat, a powerful contribution to Kilat's heroic narrative. When Kilat receives this gift, "instantly he felt his little pearl swell to something slightly larger than a little pearl" (128). His "little pearl" is the manifestation of his machismo, his erection, which until this point in the novel has remained robust yet "little." Through Yu Cheng Co's pants, Kilat's erection is charged with a magical potency that culminates in Kilat's lovemaking to Yu Cheng Co's blind Cebuano mistress, Teresa.

I end this chapter focusing not on transition per se, but on the libidinal desires that inform and drive practices of transition, where transition can perform as not merely an intimate engagement with others, but as sexual fetish, as role-play, and as desire for the figure of political resistance, where sexual desire often precedes revolutionary commitments. In times of revolution, these desires become excesses to one's devotion or resistance to the state. Yet sexuality too provides a lens onto how everyday life and experience can be marked as an excess of the identities provided and encouraged by pluralist governmentality. Both Yuson's and Rosca's novels allow for the integration of multiple identities within the revolutionary imagination through forms of sexual desire, especially as they are expressed by revolutionary women. In Anglophone literature, Filipinas often surpass their roles as revolutionary subjects limited to a single identity. As Vicente Rafael has observed in early Filipino/a plays, women held complex positions that often personified "the beloved nation waiting to be rescued" yet also "generate[d] the conditions that make their rescue both possible and desirable" (*White Love* 49). Interpreted primarily as mother figures, these Filipinas marked the Spanish and American colonial states as "illegitimate or unacceptable fathers" (ibid., 51). Such plays also suggested "alternative roles" and an "ambiguous construction of gender categories" that arose from the instability of the patriarchal state during the revolution. As Denise Cruz has similarly pointed out, the Filipina has been idealized through her "unique ability to go above and beyond other women's abilities to provide domestic care, comfort, and cure," and even their contribution to revolution is always that of caregiver, mother, or victim (222).

In *State of War*, the drive to transition arrives just as much from sexual pleasures as from political positions. Anna Villanueva first becomes politically active through her desire for Manolo, a dissident who is abducted and seemingly killed by state police. Through creating posters with Manolo, Anna begins to see the structural hierarchies embedded in the Philippine plutocratic class: "the fifty families who control everything and anything are shown to be interrelated, by blood or marriage. They have been since the turn of the century. The whole population serves one gigantic clan" (66).[17] Wishing to avenge Manolo's death, Anna plays the part of "the widow," who "had freedom equal to a whore and more respectability." Her love for Manolo fuels her first experiences with political action, as well as her desire to seek revenge for his death. Unlike Anna, Eliza seems less concerned with cyclical histories, and is rather a "warrior of the moment," employing her femininity as an arsenal for survival and pleasure (146). According to her mother, a scandalized sex worker, Eliza is gifted with "a whore's face and a whore's body" and "if the child had any brains at all . . . she would realize soon enough that the latter were better capital for a woman than a rigid mind" (49). Indeed, Eliza's playful approach to transition makes political acts pleasurable rather than self-sacrificing. Even the sexual acts in the novel are made ambiguous, as the matriarch Maya's act of self-mutilations during Lent can be seen as a pleasurable way of transitioning into the identity of the Virgin Mary. Adrian, like Anna, also first transitions for his first love (Anna): "for her sake, Adrian painted slogans on walls, on fences, on the church belfry, and on his tennis shoes. Politics, he discovered, was simply a declaration of love" (31). Adrian's intimate transitions among political and class identities reoccurs throughout the novel through his love for Anna, who frees him from his conscripted upper-class position into one of radical freedom, until he blatantly refuses any given identity. His love for Anna makes him realize that "to love was to regain the capacity to remember a world without names, to recall . . . the unbearable fragility of mornings in this country" (33). His desire acts as a gateway to alternative histories, one free from the nation's "fragility of mornings."

In Yuson's novel, sexual desire allegorizes Leon Kilat into a figure of machismo representing the patriarchal history of the revolution. Kilat's "rod" provides a link between the censorship of Philippine myth under the Spanish, as well as the infusions of Chinese histories and genealogies in Philippine life. It is thanks to Yu Cheng Co's pants that Kilat's "little pearl" turns into an "immense rod," and his libidinal desires provide an uncontainable potency that can be read as a combination of mythical factors and sexual excess, all of which rely upon a receptive (but not necessarily passive) female body.[18] Though Kilat's desire seems typical of the Spanish "machismo," the fierceness and bravado of Spanish heroes, his "immense rod" also alludes to the fabled Chinese Monkey King, Sun Wukong, whose weapon (a phallic staff), could extend to such a length that it was used to measure the oceans. Kilat's erection too leaps into absurd elongation reminiscent of this myth: "it throbbed, high and mighty-looking, an immense instrument that now seemed to touch the very peeling ceiling itself, indeed, threaten to puncture a hole through the shop's very roof" (133). This text's allusions to Sun Wukong becomes explicit when Yu Cheng Co returns to find a hole in his roof, and recreates a kung-fu scene from Chinese Wuxia myth.[19] Kilat's sexual desire exposes the libidinal excess of the Filipino/a nation when subjected to paternal states, in Kilat's case, the Spanish state, which sought to censor tales of libidinal heroes in order to preserve for themselves the exaggerated symbols of male virility.

Kilat's libidinal excess acts also as a symbol of revolutionary power, a "veritable weapon of damning possession," that guides him closer toward his heroic destiny through various women. Kilat only encounters Buhawi because he is guided to the woods by his admiration for the woman Pintada and "her tattooed rump" (81). Similarly, in Cebu, Kilat agrees to work for Yu Cheng Co when he grows infatuated with Yu Cheng Co's blind mistress, who helps spur Kilat's "magical new member" (133). After he leaves Yu Cheng Co for the Circo Colonial de Calidad, Kilat becomes enamored by Pilar, a "mestizo of obviously high birth" (143). Only after joining the circus to be close to Pilar, Kilat learns that "the Circo Colonial de Calidad or C.C.C. was a front for the national revolutionary organization called the Katipunan or KKK," the party credited with beginning the Philippine Revolution (147).

Robert Aguinaldo's contemporary narrative of anti-Marcos protests is also punctuated with libidinal excess. The marchers "sexily filed past" while Marcos is depicted as "the poor man" who "did seem too gentle sometimes" (153). The "sexy" protestors are here contrasted with the "gentle" depiction of Marcos, a juxtaposition that relocates reproductive potency and machismo in the revolutionary crowd. The novel includes libidinal excess as a form of revolutionary power when Kilat is told the revolutionary history of "The Cause," yet Pintada "hovers above the edges of Leon's thoughts," marking revolutionary action itself as a sexually stimulating excess (163). As Kilat is told of the "economic boom in the 1860s and 70s," he can only think of "Pintada, swimming naked in the river," and imagines "Pintada squealing with delight" (171). Finally, the narrative of revolutionary history and that of libidinal excess form into the same prose, without paragraph breaks to signal change in Kilat's stream-of-consciousness voice: "Revilla's presence is confusing my sense of time zones but oh how delightfully his words are like the start and end of particularly nourishing rain like that time with Pintada but, ah, more spires and crosses rising to the skies what a lovely city.... A big problem, this cavitismo machismo … doing it with Pintada" (172). Revolutionary history merges with "that time with Pintada," overlapping Kilat's anti-imperial aggression with his masculine aggression. The "cavitismo machismo" refers to the revolutionary regional power located in Cavite, where in 1898, General Emilio Aguinaldo declared Philippine independence from Spain. Coined by the historian Renato Constantino, "cavitismo" names a regional potency and pride that was necessary in replacing the "masculine" and "paternal" Spanish state. Even while invoking its libidinal excesses, Kilat realizes that this reliance on "cavitismo" is "a big problem," as it produces a normative revolutionary subject that can "look down on the Manilenos" (those who fought in Manila), and the "peons of Bonifacio" (those who followed the revolutionary leader Andrés Bonifacio, but were excluded from becoming the revolution's ideal subjects).

While Kilat seems motivated primarily by libidinal excess, the women he chases are too depicted as active revolutionary participants who expose the limits of the "machismo." Indeed, women's role in revolutionary history bears similarities to the role of rural populations, in that their historical position is overshadowed by the increased emphasis on the "machismo" of male revolutionaries, who are narrated as the primary agents of revolutionary action. Kilat's reliance upon potency comes full circle with Pilar, the mestiza circus performer, who seduces him into her quarters to assassinate him, marking the limits of libidinal excess in the female figure who claims agency and sexual desire for herself. Similarly, in the final scenes of the jungle café, it is Pintada who appears the most engaged in revolutionary politics, as she seeks signatories for a petition that will disseminate through GABRIELA and other feminist networks. Pintada's open sexuality (she refuses monogamy) and fierce political tactics resists the identity of the global Filipina service worker, the "caring" and affective identity of domestic workers and nurses. Rather than reinstate the "collective identity" of the Filipina/o, *State of War* and *Great Philippine Jungle Energy Café* expose revolutionary action as the excess of this imagined identity—the desires, styles, and histories that spill over.

CONCLUSION: THE ENEMY AND THE RESISTANCE

Identities become depoliticized through history's revolutionary and antirevolutionary tides, bequeathing frequent shifts in names, identities, and memories. Where the state produces history, individuals become dependent upon that state for historical recognition. In *State of War*, Colonel Amor philosophizes that to maintain order "language had to be changed; names had to be changed; places had to be re-baptized; all moral and ethical signposts eradicated. Call the sun, the moon the moon, the sun and no one would be able to find his way out of confusion's labyrinth without guidance" (370). Amor epitomizes the model of identity discourse that re-creates itself in order to appear revolutionary, and to consistently reappear as history's "guide." For both *State of War* and *Great Philippine Jungle Energy Café*, the masculine "guidance" of the state is revoked only when the people take on the discourse of identity and sexuality for themselves. The separation of the state and the populace can only be a masculine/feminine separation, depicting the Philippine state under the masculinized role once performed by the Spanish and the Americans. In this construct, the feminine nation is meant to be protected from outside forces as well as from itself. In parodying and resisting discourses of identity, both novels seek to disempower this masculine role. In the final pages of *State of War*, the narrative does this by abstracting historical forces into "the resistance" and "the enemy": "The enemy saw the resistance as an irritant, a disruption in the normal conduct of its affairs. The resistance, on the other hand, saw only the enemy. . . . It absorbed its losses, withdrew its people from exposed positions, clothed itself in anonymity" (381). The forces of revolution and antirevolution here are rendered nameless, not people but historical forces. Under these terms, is Eliza part of the resistance or the enemy? Or Anna? Or Adrian? Could it be that another revolution has taken place, and those marked "the enemy" have traded places with "the resistance"? The state of war, in a sense, is the abstract invocation of historical forces without names.

The two contexts of Malaya and the Philippines show how in pluralist governmentality, identities *can* be hybrid, *can* be seen as mobile, but this mobility in itself does not necessarily upend or even disrupt its reiteration even after moments of revolution. Transition emerges as a tactic for living within these histories: to survive, to create anonymous alignments, and to fulfill oneself, even for sexual pleasure. In Part II, I extend this inquiry to explore further how mobility forms transition as a negotiated alternative within pluralist governmentality. By mobility I mean all the mobilities that come with the mobility of the body—social mobility, mobility of information and capital, and of course, the mobility of identity. Travel opens opportunities to shift identities under radically new contexts. The desire for mobility often speaks to the desire to escape one's fixed identity. But in so doing, travelers also invoke new comparisons that consider how identity functions in different contexts. Part II thus explores how mobility can offer access to new forms of identity, and illuminates transition not as a process with a particular goal, but as itself a mode of being, acting, and belonging with others.

PART II MOBILITIES

Too much can be made of homeland. Stories we tell often take their identity from a piece of soil, and the strongest stories may leave us still standing in the scene of our powerlessness.

　　　　　　　　　　　　—Shirley Geok-lin Lim, *Among the White Moon Faces*

Hindsight tells me that I could not write much fiction because fiction seems to require that one be rooted in a culture—if not the culture of one's birth, then the culture of one's adopted home. But we did not stay long in any one country. We were forever foreigners, forever strangers. On the other hand, the longer we stayed away from our country, the more distant we became. Travel writing…takes for granted that the narrator is an outsider. So I wrote enough travel essays/narratives to fill five books.

　　　　　　　　　　　　—Cristina Pantoja-Hidalgo, *Coming Home*

3 · LIBERAL TOLERANCE AND ASIAN MIGRANCY

In Peter Bacho's first novel, *Cebu* (1991), Ben Lucero, a Filipino American priest living in Seattle, makes his first trip to the Philippines to bury his deceased mother. While discovering his "roots" in Cebu and Manila, Ben witnesses surges of religious and political violence that prompt his quick retreat from the poverty and corruption of the Philippines back to the "order" and "sanctuary" of Seattle (133). Literary scholars like Elizabeth Pisares interpret Ben's retreat as an escape from his own social debt to the Philippines, that Ben "evades what he perceives as a foreign Filipino discourse represented by *utang na loob*, or reciprocal indebtedness" (80). Yet Ben's return can also be seen as a way of paying off a different social debt: his debt to the United States for providing a space of liberal tolerance. Throughout the novel, Ben shows gratitude for living in an American space where violence, corruption, and poverty are distanced into the Filipino/a homeland. But despite his imagined separation from violence, Ben returns to Seattle only to find that the Filipino migrants there have become entangled in cycles of revenge and murder. To pay off his debt to both his host country and the homeland, Ben performs as the Asian American model minority, and encourages his Filipina/o congregation to do the same by abandoning their diasporic cultural practices, which he reads as gang violence in the case of Filipinos and sexual promiscuity in the case of Filipinas. After returning from the Philippines, Ben shifts to seeing such practices, such as loyalty to one's *barkada* (peer group and community), not as empowering identity markers, but as cultural attitudes that are intolerable to the multicultural social space of the Pacific Northwest.

As murders continue to pile up in Seattle's 1980s International District and Filipinos are thrown into cycles of revenge, Ben identifies the violence as a cultural aberration of the Philippines, discovering "something in [Filipino] culture, however diluted it was by life in America, that allowed wild swings in cruelty and compassion, that ... tolerated, even glorified, violence" (149). Ben's trip to the Philippines leads him to idealize his Americanness, as he begins to see Filipino culture as promoting a level of violence that "life in America" must "dilute." When the murders and beat-downs in Seattle become so overwhelming that Ben cannot escape into his "aesthetic afternoon" at the Cascade mountain range (165), his impulse is to interpret the violence as a diasporic remnant of the Filipina/o homeland: "Ben wondered how many more would die before the killing would run its course. He feared the worst. He knew how Filipinos could nurture hatred, black and seemingly eternal, treating it like a pet sore to be scratched routinely to keep it from healing" (157). "Hatred" and "killing" here become innate characteristics of the Filipino/a "fresh off the boat" migrant, a diasporic residue that might affect other Asian Americans like Ben's childhood friend Teddy, who was "like [the Filipinos], and Ben was afraid that, at his own deepest core, he was too" (157).

Published in 1991, *Cebu* is set during a national peak in violent crime and the rapid expansion of the prison industrial complex.[1] The novel depicts an American "culture of violence" generated through police indifference, segregation, economic inequality, and the afterlife of multiple wars (the Philippine-American War, World War II, the Vietnam War), yet its protagonist, Ben, ignores these structural and political causes to instead blame the migrants themselves for choosing to retain intolerable versions of their culture. In order to continue a narrative of liberal tolerance that posits the United States as the bastion of multiculturalism, Ben must locate violence within the migrant's choice to retain a particularly intolerable cultural form, concluding at last that it is up to the individual to overcome his intolerable way of life. Bacho's portrayal of a Filipino American attempting to remain a "good boy" (or a good Asian American) provides readers with an understanding of liberal tolerance as a North American form of pluralist governmentality that stresses both the importance of a racial community as well as the distance of neoliberal responsibility.

This chapter investigates how two Asian North American texts, Peter Bacho's *Cebu* and Lydia Kwa's *This Place Called Absence*, allow us to read liberal tolerance as a form of pluralist governmentality that employs diasporic belonging to blame structural violence on migrant groups who are marked as "infected" with the intolerable cultures of their homeland. In so doing, liberal tolerance represses histories that might foster political radicalism by blaming violence on the "intolerable" individual. I see "intolerable" as imagined cultural practices that cross a "tolerance threshold," an imagined barrier between the "intolerable" and "tolerable" cultural practices that arise when migrants are no longer "kept in their place" through segregation. Rather than assert racialized spatial boundaries, "tolerance thresholds" draw cultural boundaries for what is deemed "tolerable," thus reshaping boundaries of exclusion based on cultural performance. As Étienne

Balibar defines it, tolerance thresholds "maintain 'cultural distances,' . . . in accordance with the postulate that individuals are the exclusive heirs and bearers of a single culture" (Balibar and Wallerstein 22–23). For both novels, a concept of the migrant as the representation of an "intolerable" culture compels the Asian American/Canadian protagonists to re-present an authentic homeland in contrast to the "tolerant" spaces of North America. Bacho's and Kwa's novels expose the limits of liberal tolerance by representing tolerant spaces from the point of view of the migrant subject, where social affects of reciprocity, such as guilt, shame, and debt, push the migrant to reinforce the multiculturalist exceptionalism of North America by performing the "good" and "grateful" Asian American/Canadian, while seeking to rescue "intolerable" others. Both texts consider how marking "third world" spaces and their diasporas as intolerant is characteristic of forms of liberal tolerance. In *Cebu*, Seattle's migrant Filipina/os are defined by their "choice" to continue performing an intolerable cultural form. It is this notion of choice that makes liberal tolerance unique, as Chua Beng Huat writes, because it "insists on the 'freedom to choose' as a basic right of an individual" ("Cost of Membership" 171). By continuing to consider forms of pluralist governmentality across the transpacific, I hope to see liberal tolerance in North America as a racial formation produced through the intersection of imperial biopolitical strategies in the colonies with the American tradition of cultural pluralism as expressed by John Dewey, Horace Kallen, and the antisegregationists of the civil rights movement.

Although both Bacho's and Kwa's texts are most often read as social realist texts, I will read them as social satires that expose the gaze of the liberal, tolerant reader, and that open up new ways of seeing how tolerance thresholds create imagined barriers between "intolerable" and "tolerable" cultural practices. I ask how these novels forgo notions of ethnic autobiography that continue to dominate how ethnic literature is read, and instead reveal how satire can shape ethnic identity to have subversive performative effects, and to consolidate a code of transition that registers only to audiences who are similarly positioned. This chapter considers how satire particularly can code the racial performance as performative to signal its practicality, flexibility, and ethical inconsistencies. Like performative acts in marriage ("I now pronounce you man and wife") or in birth ("It's a girl!"), these satirical styles produce an identity, but not the one it is supposed to. Or, as Sara Ahmed defines "non-performativity," they are acts that "do not do what they say."[2] In satire, performative acts take on a non-authoritative tone. They deprive the acts from their seriousness and deracinate the speaker's authority by lampooning him. Rather than connote authority, the main characters of these two novels represent deeply flawed and hypocritical individuals led by notions of gratitude and social debt to idealize North America for its liberal tolerance, marking tolerance as the standard for global belonging. The identities these novels produce will not last an eternity, but signal a stepping stone disguised as eternity. Satire, an often ignored element in Asian North American literature, reveals the temporal bind of identity.

Both *Cebu* and *This Place Called Absence* satirize their main characters by foregrounding the imperial arrogance that can emerge through mobility. In becoming mobile subjects, both protagonists believe their understandings of the homeland and host country are beyond question, though they are informed by North American imperial attitudes. Their certainty of the homeland's "intolerable" culture keeps them entangled with affects of reciprocity, such as guilt and gratitude, that pressure them to incorporate themselves as "good Asians," while abandoning the poor and marginalized. Through the point of view of the second-generation Filipino American, Bacho's *Cebu* explores how the return to the Philippines can invoke diasporic debts that homogenize the homeland as a culture of violence. Such inherited social debts drive Ben to satisfy both his debt to the homeland and his debt to the host country by "uplifting" Filipina/o migrants in Seattle. In *This Place Called Absence*, Wu Lan's migrancy to Vancouver allows her to envision Singapore as a space of intolerable patriarchy and homophobia. Despite the poverty and structural violence in Vancouver, Wu Lan continues to idealize the city as a space of liberal tolerance, while fetishizing a resistant position that can only be articulated through a tolerable and politically passive queer identity. Both novels portray how migrancy and mobility merge social debts—the debt to the homeland and the debt to the host country—by directing them toward a common goal: the development and rescue of the "intolerable" cultural other. The protagonists' certainty about the "arbitrary violence" of the homeland sees the host country—Canada or the United States—as providing the "legitimate violence" of liberal tolerance (Reddy 37–38).

THE PACIFIC NORTHWEST AND SPACES OF LIBERAL TOLERANCE

Since at least the mid-1980s, the Pacific Northwest has gained a reputation as a place of technological and corporate success, as well as a place of tolerance, progressivism, and multiculturalism. The region has become a constructed space where liberal tolerance has met its ideological ideal in both masking institutionalized racism and in positing the Northwest as a multicultural haven for middle- and upper-class migrants. The Northwest's largest urban centers, Seattle, Portland, and Vancouver, have long been seen as centers of liberal tolerance, even as the U.S. census consistently ranks Seattle and Portland as among the whitest cities in the United States.[3] This social construction characterizes a "liberal valley" zone west of the Cascades that reaches from Ashland, Eugene, and Portland, Oregon to Olympia, Tacoma, and Seattle, Washington, ending finally in Vancouver, British Columbia. Though demographically the "liberal valley" may be nearly 70 percent white, these metropolitan cities do not seem adverse to supporting people of color in prominent political and economic positions.[4] Forms of popular media have also had a hand in constructing the Pacific Northwest as a space of liberal tolerance, from the popular sketch-comedy show *Portlandia*, which lampoons white liberal subcultures, to the highly successful sitcom *Frasier* (1993–2004). Similarly, conservative pundits like Bill O'Reilly, once an anchor in Portland, have labeled the Pacific Northwest as an outpost for a "secular progressive agenda" with programs for "legalization of narcotics, euthanasia, abortion at will, [and] gay marriage" ("O'Reilly"). As the term "secular progressive" may be insulting in conservative contexts, it is celebrated in the Pacific Northwest, as the region boasts the highest number of atheists and agnostics per capita in North America.[5] To stress its economic power, the "liberal valley" has also been called "Cascadia" both by tourist campaigns and politicians who propose "Cascadia" as a transnational region unique in its environmental protection, leftist politics, and economic success (Preston).

The Pacific Northwest's association with liberal tolerance gives the region a veneer of antiracist politics, as it is often contrasted to more "racist" spaces like the American South. This narrative masks histories of racial violence and exclusion within the region, such as Oregon's exclusion laws and militant labor movements that targeted migrants. From 1847 to 1927, Oregon excluded black migrants from the state, with punishments for settlement ranging from its infamous "Lash Law" (requiring that black settlers be whipped twice a year) to forced labor (McLagan). In the late nineteenth century, anti-Chinese race riots occurred in Vancouver, Seattle and Tacoma, Washington, Oregon, and Idaho, some so violent that federal troops were brought in to suppress anti-immigrant mobs (Laurie 22). In the early twentieth century, the Asian Exclusion League, formed in 1905 from over sixty-seven labor unions, gained influence from San Francisco to Vancouver, segregating schools, advocating for Canada's exclusion laws (McMahon 23), and organizing riots against Sikhs, Hindus, and Chinese in Bellingham, Everett, and Vancouver ("Two-Day Conference"). From the 1910s through the 1960s, Seattle neighborhoods practiced overt racial segregation through whites-only clauses in property deeds, which were followed by redlining tactics from the 1960s until 2006 (Silva). While Seattle media boasts that Seattle contains the most diverse zip-code in the United States (98118), it can only do so by ignoring the long history of south Seattle segregation and poverty that has forced migrants and communities of color to live separate from the wealthier and white-dominated neighborhoods in the north (Gertsch).

The contemporary construction of the Pacific Northwest as multicultural and tolerant was formed largely in the 1980s, when multiculturalism gained credibility to signify the integration of marginalized histories, literatures, and cultures in education and popular representations. By 1980, the U.S. 1965 Immigration Act had been in effect for twelve years, and had eliminated restrictions based on national origin, but added provisions that increasingly preferred upper-class "skilled" migrants. Similarly, Canada's 1976 Immigrant Act did away with categories of people based on nationality or sexuality, and redefined "inadmissible classes" as persons who could become a burden on social welfare or health programs.[6] Both acts have allowed the post-1976 Pacific Northwest to take in highly skilled IT industry work and professionalized labor for companies like Microsoft, Amazon, Boeing, and the plethora of small software and biotech companies, making the region seem ideally multicultural and diverse, despite the underrepresentation of blacks, Latina/os, indigenous peoples, and Southeast Asians in businesses and universities.[7] This pairing of liberal tolerance with multinational corporate dominance puts the Pacific Northwest in a curious position in terms of racial politics. As multiculturalist ideals were challenged and formed in the "culture wars" of the late 1970s and 1980s, it became clear that new measures and rubrics would be needed to arbitrate what type of cultural practices would be encouraged, and which ones would be deemed too radical, violent, or unsettling. Canada's discourse of multiculturalism has risen to heights only implicitly imagined in the United States and has been described as "the most successful pluralist society on the face of our globe" (Stackhouse and Martin).[8]

The philosophical roots of North American liberal tolerance can be traced back to the political philosopher Horace Kallen's 1957 essay on Alain Locke, where Kallen articulated the form and scale of the "cultural pluralism" model he had advocated over three decades earlier. Kallen reconceptualized cultural pluralism into four phases of "toleration," beginning with *cold toleration*, signaled by a "balance of power" where individuals "stand over against each other at alert and ready to shoot"; and ending with *cooperation*, "a voluntary cooperative relationship where each, in living on, also helps, and is helped by, the others in living" (*What I Believe* 126). For Kallen, this movement toward cooperation was the basic appeal of cultural pluralism as advocated by himself and Alain Locke, two scholars who sought to overturn the restrictive 1924 Immigration Act and Jim Crow segregation (*Culture and Democracy* xxxiv). Today, the differences in degrees of tolerance seem to obscure the asymmetrical power relations implied in cultural pluralism. Rather than have a privileged majority tolerate the non–Anglo Saxon cultural practices of a disadvantaged minority, as Kallen and Locke had it, tolerance today presumes an already equal balance of power. This particularly liberal take on tolerance, as Wendy Brown points out, burdens the individual "with self-making, agency, and a relentless responsibility for itself" (17). The "subject of tolerance" here shares equal blame and responsibility for producing an atmosphere of tolerance, despite differences in class, race, gender, or other positions that leave the individual more vulnerable to social oppression.

In his 1965 essay "Repressive Tolerance," Herbert Marcuse saw the emerging post–civil rights discourse of tolerance as producing idealistic values that could be easily appropriated toward legitimating state violence and capitalist exploitation. Marcuse insisted that a state-condoned "passive toler-ance" encourages citizens to "tolerate the government, which in turn tolerates opposition within the framework determined by the constituted authorities" (34). The degrees to which a society tolerates others, for Marcuse, is decided less by the degree of difference and more on whether or not that difference "serves the cohesion of the whole on the road to affluence or more affluence." For a cultural practice or policy to be tolerated requires that it also be profitable, or otherwise incorporable into a consumable product. Similarly for Brown, discourses of tolerance have resulted in "a more general depoliticization of citi-zenship and power and retreat from political life itself" (89). In being nestled among discourses of race and market rationality, tolerance is able to mask "its own operation as a discourse of power and a technology of governance" (ibid., 19). Such tolerance can be seen as "liberal" insofar as it takes the individual as its object and emphasizes tolerance only with respect to individual liberties con-cerning economic freedoms and consumer agency.[9]

Liberal tolerance acts not as means to an end, but as the utopic endpoint to multiculturalism. Though it aims to transform social relations to end divisive conflict, it implicitly sees culture rather than politics as the domain for produc-tive transformation. Until its endpoint is reached, visible modes of inequality such as social segregation, police brutality, and a racist prison industrial complex seem like mere aberrations. Instead, what keeps tolerance from its utopic ends are "intolerable" cultural others, who make easy scapegoats, and whose presence continues to test and expose tolerance thresholds. For Chandan Reddy, where there is a presumed "true equality" among a national people, the state has "the ethical role of enforcing truly legitimate violence, of becoming the representa-tive and material expression of that violence" (11). Anti-American violence is, on the one hand, "defined as that falling outside the core value of the national people and the US state (namely, tolerance)," and on the other hand, "has the unique character of being the defining limits of what can be tolerated" (ibid.). While the "tolerable" category functions to produce cultural practices that can be commodified or made profitable, the "intolerable" is attributed to those cul-tural practices that lead to "arbitrary violence," and must be managed by the more "legitimate violence" of the state.

CEBU: SATIRE AND LIBERAL TOLERANCE

Histories of racial and class inequality in the Pacific Northwest have been masked partially through the visibility of successful minorities, particularly Asian Ameri-cans, which buttresses the narrative of liberal tolerance. As the historian Quin-tard Taylor has pointed out, the history of exclusion and segregation in the Pacific Northwest and Seattle does not exemplify the American black/white racial binary, but demonstrates a "multiracial and multiethnic" demographic pattern that includes Asian Americans, Chicanos, and Native Americans (402). In Seattle, Japanese constituted the largest racial minority until World War II, yet despite the repeated denial of Japanese citizenship and the history of Japanese internment camps in Puyallup, Portland, and Tule Lake, Japanese American and Asian American success has been emphasized within a narrative that sees racial injustices as a thing of the past (ibid., 401). In *Immigrant Acts*, Lisa Lowe investigates how model minority discourse is partially produced through a bildungsroman form, where Asian American novels make difference hypervisible, and a homogenized "ethnic tradition" becomes celebrated as a symbol of progress and multiculturalism. For Lowe, Asian American novels can also disassemble multiculturalist identities by exploring the heterogeneity of the Asian American subject, making the "'disidentification' from national forms of identity . . . crucial to the construction of new forms of solidarity" (53). Yet in a context of liberal tolerance, where Asian American identity is often crucial to presenting a space as multicultural and tolerant, we should ask how "disidentification" from the nation-state can also produce diasporic identities that are seen as "resistant," but in practice, are managed through imagined tolerance thresholds.

Against the narrative of multiculturalist exceptionalism, many Asian American scholars, teachers, and activists emphasize what Viet Thanh Nguyen has called a "resistant" or "bad subject": a character who is encouraged by "an ideological belief that Asian American is only a place of ethnic consensus and resistance to an inherently exploitative or destructive capitalism" (*Race and Resistance* 11). In practice, this occurs by valorizing Asian American characters and writers, such as John Okada, who consciously rebel against the status quo. For Nguyen, the valorization of the "bad subject" can often produce a false, idealized vision of radical change encapsulated within the diasporic ties of migrant cultures. This depiction smuggles in the assumption that by retaining parts of their homeland, the Asian American acts as a fetishized loci of antistate, anticapitalist resistance. The preoccupation with the bad subject thus evades the structurally significant role that Asian Americans play in reinforcing pluralist governmentality through the representation of Asian American success, and continues to assume that Asian American novels represent gateways to understanding (and thus managing) Asian American subjectivity. Rather than emphasize the role of Asian Americans in legitimating notions of "choice" and "self-making" inherent in liberal tolerance, the "bad subject" presumes "Asian Americanness" as a position of passive resistance, where Asian American identity becomes in itself resistant, antistate, and anticapitalist. This fetishization of Asian American identity has allowed literary scholars to speak of Asian American cultural production itself as resistant to or critical of the U.S. state, despite the fact that much Asian American cultural expression, in the form of religious, political, and diasporic media, allies with the U.S. state rather than against it, and much popular Asian American literary production is self-orientalizing.

I hope to avoid reading Asian American novels as either authentic voices or as idealizing resistant figures, and instead argue that we can and should begin to read some Asian American texts (what I am calling transpacific Anglophone texts) as social satires, wherein the protagonist is ridiculed for his or her idealism in order to reveal ideological boundaries and to provoke social change. Read as an authentic representation of Filipino American identity, Bacho's *Cebu* insists that Seattle, left to its American values, is a space of liberal tolerance, free of racial violence and oppression. If we read the text as a satire, however, Ben Lucero becomes a figure much like Voltaire's Candide, who naïvely believes that the Pacific Northwest is the "best of all possible worlds" while blaming all violence and exploitation on the cultural differences of "fresh off the boat" Filipino/a migrants. Ben's attitude toward the FOBs is integral to the satire because it reiterates the attitudes of whites toward earlier generations of Filipino/a migrants who arrived on the West Coast to replace other Asian migrants after the 1917 "Asiatic Barred Zone" Immigration Act. At the time, Filipino/as were exceptions to Asian Exclusion Acts, since as colonial subjects they were considered "nationals" and were not required to possess passports to enter the United States (Fujita-Rony 17). This did not keep them from being marked as hypersexual and violent, a stereotype that Ben Lucero incorporates in his own view of Filipino/as.[10]

The novel's ambiguous narrative style allows critiques to emerge through satirical readings, and comes strongest in its representation of the Philippines as a land of temptation that Ben must resist in order to sustain his Catholic faith. In Cebu City, where Ben's "American sense of order was offended by Cebu's chaos and pollution," Ben sees the body of a man who has crucified himself (77). Ben's shock at this event is infused with a sense of cultural superiority, as he calls Filipino/a Catholicism a "superstition passing for religion" (95). This event, which becomes the catalyst for the novel's action, satirizes the view of the Filipino American tourist, since the first one-third of the novel details the violence of World War II that has led up to this crucifixion. Unlike Ben, the reader knows that the crucified man, Carlito, does not intend to die on the cross, but only does so because his friends run from fright before he asks to be taken down. The reader also knows that Carlito's crucifixion comes from the desire to be "*mahimo man*" (to become even) with God (44). Carlito only meant to *imitate* sacrificing his own life so that his granddaughter might survive her leukemia: "[Carlito's] only comfort was that soon it would end, and his pact—his negotiation with God—would be sealed" (66). The reader also knows that the hill where Carlito crucifies himself is the same hill where he helped torture a Korean soldier who fought for the Japanese army (Carlito cut off the man's limbs in revenge for the soldier's murder of an infant). The hill is thus a symbol of the violence of World War II, a place where "so much blood was spilled it was said to have colored the ground, giving it a reddish hue that not even the monsoons nor the passage of time and the erosion of memory could erase" (46). In contrast to the novel's detailed historical account leading up to Carlito's crucifixion, Ben reacts by calling it "fundamentally antireligious" and struggles to understand "what it was within Catholicism, or maybe culture, that drove Carlito to his death" (87). Knowledgeable of a history that Ben has no access to, readers can find, through the text's dramatic irony, that Ben's comments are infused with the naïveté of a typical American tourist, one who sees cultural essentialisms instead of historical (and imperial) symptoms.

The aftermath of Carlito's crucifixion leaves Ben so disoriented in Cebu City that he retreats to Manila, a city he hopes will be more civilized. Yet like Cebu, Manila too comes to represent a land of violence, sin, and sexual trespass, as Ben quickly succumbs to the temptation of his aunt's secretary (the ex-sex worker Ellen), and then encounters violence once again in a state crackdown on a protest at the American Embassy. The protest recalls the 1970 student protests against the United States for backing the Marcos regime and for continuing an imperialist war against the Vietnamese. Such protests, known as the First Quarter Storm, led to the declaration of martial law in 1972 (Ileto, "'Unfinished Revolution'" 72). Yet in the novel, Ben sees the protests as simply confirming the violent culture of the Philippines. When the protest devolves into a riot, Ben finds "a young boy, dead," and a man shot below the rib cage (131). As Ben attempts to perform the last rites on the dying man, the man recognizes him from the hotel where he slept with Ellen, and in his last breath, the man tells Ben to go fetch "a real priest" (132). From Ben's touristic point-of-view, the violence of the Philippines—manifest through Carlito's crucifixion and the embassy protest—is not a result of historical events, but is simply innate to Filipino/a culture. Feeling corrupted by this culture, Ben flees back to the "sanctuary" of the Pacific Northwest (133).

When *Cebu* is read as satire, the sin and violence of the Philippines appears less like an ethnographic fact and more as a commentary on Ben, who is eager to distinguish himself from the Philippines and its migrants. The novel's very form seems to betray any semblance of an authentic portrayal, since the first third of the novel barely features Ben at all, but concerns Filipina/os during the Japanese Occupation, while the second third follows Ben's naïve and ahistorical interpretation of contemporary violence in the Philippines. Ben's experience at the student protest of the U.S. Embassy plays into this satire, as Ben seems to be a foil to a real-life Catholic priest, Edicio dela Torre, who was present at the protests, but, unlike Ben, was influenced by protestors' political courage to speak for the student movement, changing his political ties "from Christian reformist movements to the Communist Party" (Ileto, "'Unfinished Revolution'" 175). While Ben's position as a priest offers him the same possibilities, he instead interprets the movement in the same way the state-run Philippine media would, identifying it "with violence, pure disorder," and its participants as "gullible, immature youth" (177).

The stakes of *Cebu* as a satire become clear in the last third of the novel when Ben returns to Seattle and faces the "gang warfare" in Seattle's Chinatown. After his trip to Cebu, Ben sees gang violence as a remnant of Philippine culture rather than as something inherent in American society. Remembering the violence of his trip, Ben describes Seattle as "a sanctuary much safer than the madhouse he had entered" and longs "for Seattle's cool air, clean streets, and pronounced sense of order" (133). In Seattle, however, when violence breaks out in the International District, Ben refuses to blame the space itself, as he would have done in the Philippines. Instead he places blame on the individual Filipino/a migrants who could not overcome their own intolerant cultural practices. Whereas violence in the Philippines seems to reflect a society built upon vengeance and sin, in Seattle, violence becomes merely "arbitrary," a matter of individual choice, of Filipinos who are culturally conditioned to "nurture hatred" (157). The violence of the Philippines is definitive of the third-world space, while the violence of the Pacific Northwest is coded as exceptional to the liberal tolerant space. Seattle's violence is thus marked as a remnant of the foreign, brought by the Filipino/a migrants who have yet to relinquish "intolerable" cultural practices, and who must be disciplined by the "legitimate violence" of the state.

CEBU: MANONGS AND THE BARKADA

Cebu's last third begins with uproars of violence in Seattle that Ben seeks to explain as a cultural remnant that "fresh off the boat" Filipino/a migrants must overcome. Ben's mobility as a traveling Filipino American does not produce a humbling awareness of his own power and privilege, but creates an anxiety about the violence within "intolerable" Filipino culture that Asian American identity must transform. As Ben arrives at Sea-Tac airport, his traumatic experiences in the Philippines thrust him into his memories of the late 1960s when the Vietnam War "hit the old neighborhood hard, like a plague that swept a village" (139). His meditation on the Vietnam War recalls that Filipino/as themselves, as Oscar Campomanes wrote, continue to "bear[ ] the brand of the US Empire on his or her forehead" (29). Ben's sympathy for the Vietnam War's "choice victims" of young and poor Filipino/as conflicts with his own veiled prejudice when he returns to his post at Saint Mary's parish in Seattle's International District and finds his congregation filled with "more Filipinos, mostly recent immigrants" who are unable to "ascend" their cultural ties: "He had no experience with *recent* immigrants and spoke none of their dialects.... Ben didn't think he disliked immigrants; his mother, after all, was an immigrant." The narrator's distanced tone here marks the performative production of ethnic identity as satirical, depriving the speaker of his authority to characterize or conjure his own ethnicity. "Ben didn't think he disliked immigrants" rather than "Ben disliked immigrants," belies attempts to read Ben as an authentic representation of Filipino

American subjectivity. Rather than see what Ben thinks, the reader only sees Ben's efforts to mask himself. His emphasis on language barriers attributes his dislike for the FOBs to their inability to acquire sufficient language skills. Ben also conflates the Filipino/a migrants with the Philippines itself when he refers to Manila as "just like St. Mary's" because it was "nuts" and filled with "too many Filipinos" (144). As a Filipino American priest raised by immigrants, Ben feels that he can hold no racist attitudes toward Filipino/as, and his prejudice against them thus appears rational. The satire is particularly pointed when the narrative specifies the same vulnerable populations who were victims of the Vietnam War: "colored males, eighteen and older, poor." Those familiar with the history of Filipino/a Americans in Seattle would recognize this satirical gesture, as there is a striking similarity between the violence in the novel and Seattle's Filipino/a American violence in the early 1980s, which was sparked by political protest against the authoritarian Marcos regime in the Philippines. Ben's attitude toward intolerable migrants is reminiscent of Seattle newspapers in 1981, which claimed that the slaying of two young union leaders, Silme Domingo and Gene Viernes, was simply caused by Filipino ethnic gang violence, even as evidence showed that the murders were ordered by the U.S.-backed dictator, Ferdinand Marcos, a fact that the Washington State Court later recognized in 1989 (Fujita-Rony 202). The violence of the International District can thus be seen as a part of the same tide of political protest as the killing at the U.S. Embassy in Manila earlier in the novel. Both scenes seem based on historical events that were shaped by the protests against of the Marcos regime, and in turn, the United States, which had backed Marcos's rule.

Ben's prejudice toward Filipino migrants ironically aligns with racist attitudes against the earlier *manong* generation of Filipino migrants. The term *manong*, Ilokano for "older brother," defined a generation of Filipino migrants who arrived in the United States as "nationals" prior to the 1936 Tydings-McDuffie Act, which both declared independence for the Philippines and restricted the entry of Filipina/os to fifty immigrants per year. *Manong* writers such as Carlos Bulosan and Bienvenido Santos depicted Filipino migrants in the West as exploited laborers, as exiles, and as victims of white terrorism who were targeted particularly for their sexual intimacy with white women. At first *manong* workers were characterized by journalists and state media as politically subservient, but their reputation was soon undercut by an association with sexual deviance, as Filipinos became branded as "having a pathological attraction to white women" (Baldoz 120). Serving as the primary recruitment and departure hub for Filipinos working in Alaska, Seattle and the nearby area of Yakima County became hotbeds for racial antipathy and anti-immigrant violence (ibid. 67). The earliest recorded anti-Filipino race riots occurred in Yakima, Washington, in November 1927, "when white mobs initiated a campaign to 'deport' local Filipinos," and the violence spread statewide (ibid. 136). Like the white mobs seeking to deport Filipinos,

Ben Lucero similarly associates Filipinos with both violence and illicit sexual deviancy. As the literary scholar Allan Punzalan Isaac has argued, the Filipino *manongs* were "not excluded in terms of immigration," but by their stereotyping as barbaric and uncivilized. As Isaac points out, Filipinos were "not associated with cultures of antiquity like Japanese, Chinese, and Asian Indians," but with having savage sexual appetites (126). Ben's own "sinful" sex in the Philippines (when he loses his virginity to the ex-sex worker Ellen), can thus be read not simply as a religious trespass, but as a transition from a "good" Filipino American identity toward the traits of violence and sin that Ben associates with the homeland. Though Ben's attitude toward identity here shifts through his mobility, his reliance on American identity categories of "tolerable" and "intolerable" migrants are cemented.

Even as Ben reiterates the same racial prejudices of white mobs against the *manong* generation, in some ways his attitudes do not contradict Filipino/a American identity, which is often conceived of as the result of a long progression from the "fresh of the boat" cultures of the *manong* to successful Filipino/a Americans. In this history, the *manong* has played the role of the "bad subject" in affirming antistate and anticapitalist resistance through Filipino/a American identity even as this identity relies on distinguishing itself from "the Filipino." As E. San Juan has put it, Carlos Bulosan's depiction of the *manong* migrant provides a "metamorphic persona" that is constituted by his relationship with labor, migration, and the forms of sexualized excess that become coded as resistant ("Beyond Identity Politics" 556).[11] As a foundational Filipino American writer—and once the publicity director of Seattle's Filipino-dominated International Longshoremen's and Warehousemen's Union, Local 37—Bulosan's representations of the *manong* have represented Filipino/a Americans as "single male heroes" (Fujita-Rony 7). As Dylan Rodriguez has argued, this progressive history of Filipino/a American identity can undermine "the possibility of generating an authentically 'oppositional ideology' that positions Filipino group experience as a challenge to a white supremacist common sense" (*Suspended Apocalypse* 88). For Rodriguez, the ever-present history of Philippine engagement with the United States cannot be contained in the past or in a progressive tolerant future, but should be seen as "a relation of irreparability, illiteracy, and absolute antagonism" (ibid. 100). Similarly, Oscar Campomanes has expressed how Filipina/o American identity can often breed imperial complicity, since claiming American citizenship reaffirms one's belonging within American empire (32).

If we read *Cebu* as an authentic representation of Filipino American subjectivity, the novel reproduces liberal tolerance by depicting the post-1965 Filipino American identity as a successful progression from the earlier *manong* generation (coded as violent and sexually aggressive), to the successful Asian American, represented by Ben. This narrative of the *manong* can thus imply that Filipino/a American assimilation into the white middle class has been more or less complete, and that the violence and poverty within many Filipino/a communities can be blamed upon individual Filipino/a migrants who have yet to follow the same progression. Yet if we read *Cebu* as satire, Ben's prejudice resembles a lost opportunity to use his position as a Catholic priest to create social change through faith-based organizing (in Seattle, Saint Mary's Church has often played this role). Instead, at the novel's end, Ben rejects this possibility to instead curse a violent and hypersexual Filipino/a culture. The novel comes to a climax when a Filipino migrant boy confesses to murder in Ben's confessional. Ben offers the boy absolution only if he relinquishes his fellow Filipino/a migrants, his clan or *barkada*, and abandons his social debt to them, or his *utang*. When the boy refuses to do so, Ben condemns his soul, and the boy murders Ben in the confessional.

> The young man was crying now. "I came to you because I heard you're Filipino and you'd understand. You're hurting my feelings, Padre. You don't understand."
> "I understand," Ben said.
> "No, you don't," he argued, "not like a real Filipino. Back home, there'd be no problem."
> Ben was trying hard not to become angry. "You're not back home now," he said. "Things are different here." (201)

The boy's invocation of the homeland, "back home," prompts Ben to similarly invoke the space of liberal tolerance, where "things are different." According to Elizabeth Pisares, this climax emphasizes that Ben could never "understand the *barkada, utang na loob*, or the vengeance born out of loyalty that comprise [Filipino] culture," and in death he pays the price for his ignorance (90). Yet the very notion that these cycles of violence are caused by *utang na loob* and *barkada* extend from Ben's alignment with a narrative of liberal tolerance, where racial violence and inequality can be quickly explained as cultural aberrations. As Dorothy Fujita-Rony reminds us, the influence of the *barkada* for Filipino/as in the United States was often a response to the racism they experienced, when racial prejudice and violence encouraged Filipino/as to close ranks and to extend their kinship networks to those of "the same village, town, or region of origin" (13).

Ben's refusal to grant absolution reflects his continued presumption that Seattle's ethnic violence is perpetrated by groups of "intolerable" Filipino/as who must be individualized (give up their *barkada*) and set on a course toward a tolerable Filipino/a American identity. Ben's trip to the Philippines appears satirical insofar as he only remains aware of official versions of Philippine and Filipino/a American history, where the separation between the "intolerable" Filipino/a and the "tolerable" Filipino/a American relies upon seeing the Philippines as a space of sin and violence. While Ben sees the *barkada* as a burdensome remnant of the Philippines, the social ties of the *barkada* can actually provide a means of adapting to the structural racism within the United States. That Ben's attitude invokes

a bitterness leading to his own death causes us to reflect on the structural function of Filipino/a American identity and the myths that preserve it.

LYDIA KWA'S *THIS PLACE CALLED ABSENCE* AND RESCUING THE "SUBJECT IN NEED"

In spaces of liberal tolerance, violence and intolerance are displaced onto the
cultural defects of the migrant. Slavoj Žižek conceptualizes tolerance through an
induced "culturalization of politics," wherein political differences and economic
exploitation "are naturalized/neutralized into 'cultural' differences, different
'ways of life,' which are something given, something that cannot be overcome,
but merely tolerated" ("Tolerance" 660). Yet to say that ethnic difference
becomes "neutralized" or apolitical understands racialized subjects as merely the
roles that they portray, and misses out on the very performative effects of identification for the migrant herself. In *Cebu*, Ben constructs his Asian American
identity as a means of taking control of his marginalized racial signifiers to distinguish himself from "intolerable" Filipino/as. This distinction is predicated upon
relocating violence from Ben's Filipino/a racial heritage to the "unstable" space
of the Philippines—thus making those more connected to the Philippines also
more prone to arbitrary violence. Questions concerning methods of production,
taxation, trade, global forms of neoliberalism, and contemporary neocolonial
empire are all downplayed in a logic that turns Filipina/o migrants into subjects
in need of rescue from the space that corrupts them.

An impeccable figure of the "subject in need of rescue" is the hypersexual-
ized Asian "third world" woman, whose nativeness and motherly love signifies
a gateway to one's homeland. In *Cebu*, this figure is embodied in Ellen, an ex-
sex worker whom Ben's Aunt Clara has promoted from her own massage par-
lors in Quiapo to a life of administration and entrepreneurship (95). Ben quickly
identifies Ellen as a "vaunted pinay" who gives rise to "pleasant, pubescent fantasies" (92). He loses his virginity to Ellen, but becomes disgusted with his own
religious trespass only after she emphasizes that *he* was the main sexual aggres-
sor: "I'd be sleeping," she says, "or trying to, and then wake up with you on me,
pumping like a Nissan piston" (127). Ben's fetishization of Ellen as a hypersexual
figure of his homeland begins to dispel when he is faced with his own desires for
her. When they leave Ben's hotel, Ben attempts to grope Ellen in public, which
she reads as an act of possession. She compares him to her clients: "[W]hen I
worked, men always thought they bought me. But they were wrong. My services,
maybe, but never me" (129). Incapable of understanding his own privilege and
complicity with sex tourism, Ben conjures the voice of his mother, Remedios,
who once told him that "he wasn't like other men; he respected women" (129).

Bacho's *Cebu* offers the figure of the sex worker as a gateway toward intimacy
with an ethnic Other, allowing Ben to possess an ethnic solidarity that is reduced

to a patriarchal and imperial relationship. Ellen comes to represent the sin and temptation of the Philippines, and her imagined hypersexuality makes her an easy scapegoat for Ben's own religious trespass. Months after Ben's return to Seattle, he receives a letter from his Aunt Clara explaining that Ellen has died during an abortion for his child. Clara's declaration is a lie, an attempt to bring Ben back to the Philippines for Ellen's funeral. Yet even the devious Aunt Clara underestimates Ben's ability to justify his own actions. Rather than return to the Philippines to make amends, Ben pushes Ellen's death aside by falling back on the notion that "people have choices," and he "didn't force her" (194). As soon as Ben is faced with his own reproduction of imperial violence, the liberal tolerant injunction flattens Ellen into an individual who could not live up to the personal responsibility of her own choices. That this switch happens so quickly allows the reader to see the absurdity in this logic, and to question how the desire to rescue the "subject-in-need" reconstitutes Asian American identity as symbolically belonging to a space of liberal tolerance.

The sex workers in Lydia Kwa's 2003 novel, *This Place Called Absence*, also offer intimacy with an ethnic Other, though they differ from Bacho's Ellen by resembling the "bad subjects" who provide positions of passive resistance. Like the *manongs* and "fresh off the boat" migrants of Bacho's novel, Kwa's queer sex workers are distanced in space and time, imagined as historical figures in early twentieth-century Singapore. Where Bacho's Ellen is blamed for her perverse desire, Kwa's sex workers are depicted as innocent, oppressed figures who reflect the patriarchal essence of the distanced homeland. They emphasize queer tolerance in the Pacific Northwest, as they become meaningful ancestors for the novel's modern-day protagonist, Lim Wu Lan, a queer Singaporean migrant living in Vancouver, British Columbia.

After her father's suicide, Wu Lan is thrust into a psychological crisis, and she is forced to reflect on her distance from her family, her migration, and her queer desire. As a refuge from this crisis, Wu Lan becomes absorbed in history texts about turn-of-the-century Chinese sex workers in Singapore. The narratives of two sex workers, Lee Ah Choi and Chow Chat Mui, appear as first-person narratives interspersed throughout the novel. Lee Ah Choi's narrative begins with her escape from her father into the world of sex work and debt slavery. Though these first-person narratives are presumed to be Lee Ah Choi's intimate inner monologue, the narrative voice is constantly evaluating her lifestyle within the values of a middle-class, tolerant gaze, and with historical distance: "Here at 61 Upper Hokien Street. My cubicle, Number 2, next to the front room. Sum Tok told me when I first came, this brothel is special, used to be a mansion, I should be proud to belong. . . . And Sum Tok, our kwai po, wicked den-mother. Yes, this is a mansion, a temple of hell, where bodies must crush other bodies" (9). Ah Choi's narrative contains facts that locate her position in space, "61 Upper Hokien Street," and allude to the history of Chinese and Peranakan *babas* in Singapore, whose mansions were often sold and converted into brothels. Her naming of the exact address, rather than a mere description of the street or district (Chinatown), suggests a realm of historical fact, as if the writer is reiterating historical data rather than describing an urban landscape. The use of Christian figurative language—"temple of hell"—to describe the crushing of abstract, nameless "bodies" also belies the narrator's "authentic" voice. This historical gaze becomes even more prominent when Ah Choi first arrives in Singapore and the narrative splits into two decipherable voices: the first of a victim experiencing oppression, and the second of a distant voyeur gazing upon that victim: "[the auntie] told [my father] I would be able to return once I finished paying back the money for the passage. At twenty I would be a *kong chu*, with no rights over my own body" (22). The first use of "would" here describes a causal effect, that she would "return" only if she "finished paying back the money." The second "would," "I would be a *kong chu*," can be read as a historian might describe an event that "would lead to the First World War." This second voice of historical distance is also nearly identical to a passage in the history book that Wu Lan reads throughout the novel, James Francis Warren's *Ah ku and Karayuki-san: Prostitution in Singapore, 1870–1940*, where Warren describes the *kong chu* as "virtual slaves, 'outsiders' with no rights in themselves" (53). This voice of historical distance thus seeks to capture Lee Ah Choi's life-story as one of total "innocence," of a girl caught in a series of events that seem predetermined by her historical and geographic situation.

The two voices in the above passage parallel separate readings of the novel as an ethnic autobiography or as a satire. Taken as an autobiographical ethnic voice, we the reader access a figure who has been historically marginalized, and bear witness to the cruelty of the "third world" past, which constructs present-day Singapore as homophobic (though repressed by state legislation in the 1990s, queer identity has since the 2000s been catered to in nightlife advertisements and political speeches). Wu Lan's narrative of dealing with her father's death and her own queer identity thus appear as remnants of an intolerant Singapore. If we read the novel as satire, however, we must acknowledge that Lee Ah Choi's life-story is being imagined by the upper-middle-class Asian Canadian protagonist Wu Lan in order to help relieve Wu Lan of her own psychological crisis and social alienation from her family in Singapore as a queer Chinese daughter. In this reading, Wu Lan reimagines the trauma and violence of the past to reaffirm her own development from such origins, thereby establishing Vancouver as a utopic space of arrival. As Wu Lan continues reading about these sex workers through Warren's history book, her absorption into their lives turns into a desire to possess them as figures defined by their imagined subordination and resistance: "At the back of the book, there's a table with the names of *ah ku* who committed suicide. . . . I wish I could get under their skins, to know what it was like. . . . I already had begun to imagine details about the *ah ku* after reading that article, but now here were photographs, images that compel me, spur me on" (48). As a Singaporean migrant who suffers from her own "absence" from family life and gender normativity, Wu Lan seeks to "know what it was like" when migration meant occupying a space of illegal and oppressive sexual labor. Despite Wu Lan's position as a successful psychologist living in Vancouver, by the end of the novel she is convinced that "she is neither Ah Choi nor Chat Mui, although they are parts of her" (207).

The appearance of Wu Lan's gaze within the sex worker's own narrative allows the reader to see the construction of these figures, where their "ethnic authenticity" is invented to meet the needs of a liberal, tolerant audience, and to implicitly thank the host country for having rescued the migrant. Whereas traditional heteropatriarchy "produces the prostitute" as its Other, these transnational texts depict her as a queer migrant rather than a deviant one, setting her on a course of integration and progress within the infrastructure of global capital (Ferguson 10). These representations thus reimagine the prostitute as queer "third world" women, whose rescue comes in the form of market exchange, and is made possible through the neoliberal freedoms associated with development and globalization. As a satire, however, the novel points out how narratives of liberal tolerance become interiorized into even queer identity, as Wu Lan's coming out to her family—her "big shock," as she calls it—can only be achieved at a distance, after Wu Lan has felt at home in the safety of a tolerant North American space.

Like *Cebu*, *This Place Called Absence* has rarely been read in a satirical mode, despite the ambiguity of its multiple voices and reimagined histories. Critics such as Eleanor Ty have enforced a socio-historic reading, claiming that *This Place Called Absence* "preserves [prostitutes] from obscurity and rescues them from the seeming purposelessness of their lives.... [Kwa] renders nameless victims into heroes of a sort" (*Unfastened* 28). While this interpretation resists moralizing narratives of sex workers, such resistance seems reduced to a passive role that merely identifies with an abstract innocent subject, and does so from a position of moral and cultural superiority where only the liberal reader can give purpose to the "seeming purposelessness of their lives." When the novel is read as a satire, these sex workers are realized as mere representations invented by Wu Lan to offer herself and the reader a level of intimate access. The novel refuses this access simply in its form, as the two voices of the sex workers, as well as the voice of Wu Lan's mother (Mahmee), are Othered by having chapter headings with the name of the speaker, whereas Wu Lan's narration is never announced, but simply assumed as the normative voice. Like the Filipina/o migrants who seek Ben's spiritual guidance, the pluralist voices of the past are herein managed by a seemingly neutral subject, whose gaze occupies the position of the universal against pluralist particulars. By narrating the queer sex worker through Wu Lan's imagination, Kwa's novel reveals how the very act of representing the ethnic "subject in need" is bound within the needs and desires of the tolerant subject in order to provide a position of resistance within a context of undeniable capitalist complicity.

As in Bacho's *Cebu*, mobility in Kwa's novel intensifies the desire for the Other's intimate portrait. But whereas Ben Lucero needs this intimacy in order to distinguish himself from Ellen, Kwa's Wu Lan desires to know the Other so intimately that the Other is no longer Other, but rather part of herself. The sex worker thus offers a means for Wu Lan to heal herself in a context where her Asian success story shapes Vancouver as a space of liberal tolerance. Kwa's sex workers are abstracted into figures of innocence and oppression that embody difference in almost every way imaginable: by sexuality, race, class, space, and history. They are so distanced from the liberal tolerant consumer that any act of "rescue" can only be achieved through available forms of corporate or privatized charity rather than through political change. As Kwa's novel shows, it is the Other's life-story that both rescues us from psychological despair, and also allows us to forget our own complicity with forms of capitalist exploitation, military invasion, and institutionalized racism. What enables this logic is the assumption that the Other's story represents her in all her authenticity, conveniently ignoring any real features of that Other which may contradict one's emotive self-satisfaction. This presumption to innocence supplements a culture of liberal tolerance that, in order to see itself as free of racial violence, elicits sympathy for figures from whom we are radically distanced, rather than people who may not be totally innocent, sincere, or caring, and whose "need" exposes the systemic violence within a tolerant space. Kwa's novel forces us to ask whether or not we can empathize with subjects who are, abstractly, in need of support mechanisms, but in an intimate way, may themselves be cruel, abusive, or patriarchal. Satirical readings of Bacho's and Kwa's novels show how Asian North American narratives, which are often read as gateways to ethnicity or are ghettoized as novels "for Asian Americans/Canadians," can shed light on the deradicalization of our contemporary moment.

THE ROMANCE OF RECIPROCITY

The mobilities in both *Cebu* and *This Place Called Absence* reveal how the homeland's imagined intolerance, violence, and heteropatriarchy are integral to forming a narrative of rescue and multiculturalism that compel migrants to feel guilt, duty, and gratitude. For Marcuse, tolerance leads to a repressive state where the subject to be tolerated is turned from an active political figure into a passive recipient, one who must tolerate the contradictions of a liberal democracy in exchange for becoming "tolerable." Yet liberal tolerance takes different meanings when we consider the position of Asian North Americans, whose way of life must be tolerated, but whose very bodies reinforce a space's tolerant construction. In the Pacific Northwest especially, Asian North Americans play a crucial role, since without them, state institutions, universities, and corporations would appear racist, privileging whites over blacks, Latino/as, and indigenous peoples in almost every segment of society. In this context, Asian North Americans are brought into a contradictory position: on one hand, they are meant to idealize North America as a space where tolerance and multiculturalism are practiced, while at the same time, the price for participating in this utopic space is the constant performance of a tolerable cultural form, thus discounting the very ideals of cultural diversity and difference that liberal tolerance is built upon. As we see in Ben Lucero's Filipino American identity, the successful migrant body acts as a symbol of liberal tolerance only when performed in a particularly tolerable way.

As it appears in these novels, reciprocity supplements liberal tolerance through affective regimes of duty and gratitude.[12] Where emotion is constructed as individual, scholars like Brian Massumi have characterized affect as social, and affects such as "grief" or "trauma" can create what Jacqueline Rose has called "a monstrous family of reluctant belonging" (31). As a means of understanding the production of "ideological effects by non-ideological means" (Massumi 102), affects of social reciprocity reveal how minority subjects reinforce spaces of liberal tolerance through affects of guilt, sympathy and gratitude.[13] The desire for an empowered, recognizable identity can be framed as powerfully affective, where subjects adopt an identity as a crucial part of themselves, to engage and reinvest in seemingly apolitical identities. Affect in these novels points us in the direction of the Other, in this case, the "subject in need of rescue" who can free the Asian North American protagonists from the guilt of capitalist and imperial complicity. As the scholar Clare Hemmings has argued, affect can characterize marginal figures as "so over-associated with affect that they themselves are the object of affective transfer" (561). As Hemmings points out, the figure of the "third world" prostitute is a common example of this "over-association," since the prostitute is both objectified and overinvested with either shame or pity. To rescue her can legitimate the space of liberal tolerance as the utopic sphere it strives to become.

The affects of liberal tolerance allow us to trace a romance of reciprocity in *Cebu* and *This Place Called Absence,* as both Ben Lucero and Wu Lan strive to "pay back" both their homeland and their host countries through acts of rescue. Both texts explore and complicate notions of reciprocity as an ambivalent relation, where the gift functions to remind the subject of the generosity that likewise summons the obligation to give in return (Ricœur 232). As William Safran wrote in 1991, diasporic migrants are especially subject to regimes of reciprocity, as they are cast with the moral burden of "reconstituting a lost homeland or maintaining an endangered culture" (85). This "moral burden" can be exploited by both the host country and the homeland in order to mobilize pressure for purposes of war, remittances, investment, and political representation. The homeland myth, for Safran, reinforces feelings of guilt by emphasizing the homeland's historical violence, so that the subject feels both a sense of debt to their homeland and a sense of gratitude to their host country for providing a tolerant space. The myth distracts from the present-day ethnic and racial violence within the host country, and from the fact that homelands often "view the diaspora with a certain disdain for having been enticed by the fleshpots of capitalism and for retaining a vulgarized ethnic culture" (Safran 93). Though the myth itself maintains a level of social belonging and diasporic community, it also assumes particular nationalist identities that can inspire ethnic solidarity (91).

Expanding on Safran's conceptions of diaspora, Shirley Geok-lin Lim has focused on the way Asian migrants see social debt as a reciprocal debt toward the host country, not the homeland. For Lim, reciprocity signifies affects that mask the subjects' awareness that their "debt" continues to maintain the power of the "creditor," but instead they "perceive chiefly their [own] weakness and the others' power to assist them" (*Writing S.E./Asia in English* 33). Lim describes the debt that Asian migrants have upon arrival in the United States, which expects them to perform as dependent and grateful migrants, binding them into "almost involuntary" relationships of social debt—"involuntary" because they are not posited as incentivized, rational outcomes, but are invoked by guilt, gratitude, and shame. Lim sees reciprocity as a depoliticizing affective regime "in which the complicity of the oppressed, their silence, passivity, and yes, cooperation, support and contribute to the power of the oppressor" (ibid.). Coupled with Safran's homeland myth, Lim's conception of reciprocity as a debt toward the host country puts the migrant into an in-between position, where he or she is meant to choose between duty to the homeland and duty to the host country. However, as Bacho's and Kwa's novels show, both of these duties converge in liberal tolerance within the act of rescuing "subjects in need" from the intolerant homeland by turning them into tolerant (and tolerable) subjects. Acts of rescue thus function as the ideal, logical outcome to a romance of reciprocity. The duty to the host country is met through the repression of intolerable cultural practices, and the duty to the homeland is met by rescuing fellow migrants from those same practices, as Ben attempts to do with the FOBs in Seattle, and as Wu Lan attempts to do in turning marginalized sex workers "into heroes of a sort" (Ty, *Unfastened* 28).

If Bacho's *Cebu* exposes how reciprocity can be construed as the definitive subjective experience for Filipina/o migrants, it also works to expose how Asian Americans pathologize Asian migrants through their "entanglement" with social debt. *Cebu* foregrounds notions of reciprocity through the concept *utang na loob*, the Tagalog idiom for reciprocal indebtedness that "defines relationships through uneven gift-giving, where the subject cannot ever repay the debt in full" (Pisares 88).[14] Ben Lucero's ability to cast violence and inequality onto the Filipino/a migrant is made possible by viewing migrants as hopelessly entangled with their *utang na loob* (and thus their inability to overcome historical trauma). Ben's trip to the Philippines permits him to characterize Filipino/as through *utang na loob*, as he witnesses the afterlife of historical violence. His Aunt Clara's wealth, for example, is a direct result of the military Jeeps left behind by American troops. The jeepney business makes Clara "rich, very rich," and gives her the capital to "diversify" into "smuggling, assorted vices, and politics" (22). After the war, Clara's *utang* casts those around her into cycles of immense social debt for being "rescued." During the Japanese Occupation, Clara's mute driver, Sitoy, was "the sole survivor of a Japanese sweep" who devoted his life to his regiment, choosing combat because "in the Filipino way, Sitoy owed his life to his saviors [a guerilla patrol], and his *utang* to them would never end" (49). Carlito's place of crucifixion stems from Sitoy's *utang*, as Sitoy discovers the Korean soldier who Carlito, Clara, and Sitoy torture to death. Indeed, Sitoy feels relieved by the soldier's torture, since "in this war without rules . . . only as a soldier could [Sitoy's] *utang* be repaid" (58). Carlito's crucifixion convinces Ben of the violence within Filipino/a culture, as he associates *utang na loob* with the need for vengeance rather than its ethnographic associations with gifts or kindness. For Ben, *utang* reappears as a violent kernel of Filipino/a culture, first in Carlito's crucifixion, and again in the violence of Seattle's migrant Filipinos.

Though Ben uses *utang na loob* to define Filipino migrant subjectivity, *utang* also emerges in the narrative as a shared affect that has yet to be confined by liberal tolerance. For Filipino/a Americans, World War II was a seminal instance where the debt toward the homeland and the debt toward the host country became aligned for a single cause: the defeat of the fascist Japanese empire by the pluralist United States. The racism of the Japanese empire enabled the United States to present itself as a pluralist savior, allowing Filipino/a Americans to view the war as an opportunity to prove their allegiance to the United States (Baldoz 195). The sacrifices of Filipino bodies, however, took on a complex set of meanings, as Filipino/as "pledged their undivided loyalty to a nation that had long treated them as an unwanted and unwelcome presence" (ibid.). Indeed, this alignment against Japan lasted only as long as the war, and afterward Filipino veterans found that they had been paid far less than their white counterparts, and their participation was immediately forgotten as they continued to experience racist exclusions.

In *Cebu*, the historic alignment of social debt functions as an origin point for *utang*. While Ben's Aunt Clara stands out as one who has taken advantage of cycles of social debt to boost her own success, Ben's mother Remedios (whose very name is an attribute of the Virgin Mary) feels in debt to the godlike ideal of General Douglas McArthur. Remedios had "shot enemy soldiers, tortured prisoners, and executed Japanese wounded as eagerly as any male guerilla. Yet, despite the savagery of her existence, when she heard that MacArthur had landed, she knelt and prayed her thanks, crossing and crossing herself in Catholicism's universal sign" (30). World War II becomes a moment when the Catholic beliefs set in place by Spanish missionaries are transferred to conflate God with Douglas McArthur, and in turn to express gratitude to the American military. This vision of the United States as a pluralist savior was then integrated into the Filipino/a school system, which encouraged "the remembering of the war against Spain and the forgetting of the war against the United States" (Ileto,

"Philippine" 222).[15] For Remedios, McArthur's "rescue" produces its own social debts that compel her to move to the United States and place her son in the seminary. Her belief that "Douglas MacArthur was His indelible sign" demands the sacrifice of her first-born, making Ben's attempts to distance himself from *utang* a continually ironic realignment with American militarism (30).

Cebu's ending revisits the haunting of continued imperial violence to satirize (and thus expose) Ben's attempts to separate himself from social reciprocity. While the violence near Saint Mary's increases, Ben uses his own privileged position to rescue Filipino/as from their own cultural norms, distancing himself from the violence motivated by *utang na loob* (Pisares 91). Yet this distancing is not enough, not if he is to "pay back" the host country. Rather than an outright rejection of his *utang*, Ben's refusal to grant absolution to the "fresh off the boat" boy in his confessional can rather be read as "paying back" the Philippines from the point of view of the Filipino American who identifies with the American imperium. Ben tells the boy to leave his *barkada* by "giving up [his] friends [and] companions" (200). Once "Filipinoness" becomes associated with sin and violence, Ben's social reciprocity to the Philippines can only be returned through a narrative of rescue that presumes Asian American cultural superiority. The satirical effect of Bacho's novel, where the tolerable Filipino American is ridiculed as naïve and imperial, exposes a transnational history of historical violence that has been rendered invisible through gratitude and debt. *Cebu* represents the traumatic haunting of continued imperial violence when, in the end, Ben realizes that the same historical violence that was the catalyst for his Aunt Clara's atheism was the same catalyst for his deceased mother's devotion to the Catholic faith, which she then passed on to Ben, who became a priest. Ben's life in Seattle too is fused with a history of American empire, a history of violence that has made the "successful Asian American" possible.

MOBILITY AND THE GLOBAL IMAGINARY

As texts that can be read as both autobiographical and satirical, *Cebu* and *This Place Called Absence* play multiple roles for the North American audience, allowing readers to project their own notions of Asian North American identity, while also providing clues in the tone and the protagonist's naïveté that this authentic representation is also an effort to sustain one's psychological and physical survival in a context of pluralist governmentality. Whereas Ben's attempts to "rescue" Filipina/o migrants allows him to pay back his debts to the homeland and the host country, the novel's satirical style questions this ethical stance by illuminating the affective aftermath of these very desires. In its consistent comparisons between the Philippines and Seattle, *Cebu* sees liberal tolerance as specific to the Pacific Northwest. However, I hope to end this chapter by shifting from these national comparisons to consider the global (and thus imperial) imaginings of liberal tolerance that mobility affords. If liberal tolerance relies upon affective regimes of guilt, gratitude, and social debt, then to what extent do these affects broach nation-states? How has tolerance been imagined as a global standard to reinforce regimes of pluralist governmentality?

Lydia Kwa's *This Place Called Absence* provides a launching pad for this inquiry. The novel's implicit space of liberal tolerance is held up as a utopic endpoint for Vancouver as well as Singapore, as the Asian city gains greater access to a global imaginary. I first used the term "global imaginary" in a 2009 essay, conceiving it as a way to track "forms of racial and class hierarchization that are posited as global, and to track the contradictions within these forms" ("Global Imaginaries" 52).[16] I will expand upon this term in the next two chapters, but here I want to briefly define it as the utopic imaginings of pluralist governmentality as a globally equalizing force. Like thought-regimes based on religion, civilization, and the like, the global imaginary restructures the world upon a hierarchy of tolerance, where tolerance signifies global civility, and intolerance the provincial, violent, and uncivilized. Unlike "globalization" or "global multiculturalism," the global imaginary names an affective and collectivizing force where its members, as with Benedict Anderson's notion of an imagined community, "will never know most of their fellow-members, meet them, or even hear of them, yet in the minds of each lives the image of their communication" (*Imagined Communities* 6). The global imaginary is neoracist in the sense that any racialized body can belong, but each are measured by their "tolerable" or "intolerable" ethnic performances. It is "imaginary" because its affects create new desires for access to globality, and because it posits itself as the common destination for all people. It is "global" in the sense that it relies upon mobility as its most meaningful shared experience signifying belonging. Mobility of social class, of bodies, and of identity itself—such mobilities conjure subtle affective regimes of intimacy and belonging where the nation-state, the homeland, and one's own ethnic/diasporic group have become distanced. Finally, the global imaginary, while reliant upon North American modes of multiculturalism for ethnical recognition, need not necessarily be "liberal" or "Western" in practice, but is symbolically active within global cities like Singapore, Kuala Lumpur, and Manila, where the call to become "global" is often synonymous with policies and identities that appear tolerant.

The global imaginary appears in Lydia Kwa's novel as a shared affective construct between the narrator, Wu Lan, and the Singapore prostitutes. Affects such as guilt and thankfulness toward a global imaginary guide the characters' actions, and reappear throughout each life-story. Lee Ah Choi's narrative expresses frustration at the constant demand for her to feel gratitude for escaping the patriarchy of China into the globally relevant space of Singapore: "Yes, I'm supposed to be grateful for this new life, for the hungry ones who pass by, peering through windows on the ground floor, searching for merchandise they can run their coarse hands over. But it makes no sense to be grateful" (9). For both sex workers, the act of migration compels them to feel thankful for their escape into a "global" city, even as such thankfulness is enacted through a life of debt-slavery and prostitution. Even after Chow Chat Mui is raped on her way to Singapore, the men who commit the act expect her gratitude, as "thanks to them, [she] would be able to find wealth in the new country" (12). This "wealth" of course leads to only more debt even after her debt for migration is paid off, since Chow Chat Mui must keep her position in order to "pay for food and lodging and a new set of clothes each year" (36). More to the point, the gratefulness that these sex workers are expected to feel for Singapore reflects Wu Lan's experience as a queer Asian Canadian in Vancouver, where her acceptance within the globally imagined city demands acts of gratitude. Whereas Chow Chat Mui escapes the homeland to be free of her "father's cage," Wu Lan's migration to Vancouver escapes her family's traditional (heteronormative) values, allowing her to come out as a lesbian only after arriving in the more tolerant global imaginary. As with the two sex workers, the global imaginary here offers sanctuary for Wu Lan, even as class and racial inequality remain rampant. As she walks through Chinatown, Wu Lan wonders how she is "not like the bodies shuffling for space on the sidewalk," and asks "How many of these people are on the verge of utter despair? How many of them have tried to kill themselves, and which ones will eventually succeed?" (67). On Vancouver's Main Street, Wu Lan describes a shirtless white man with "a cookie tin for donations" and observes that "the people pass by, unsympathetic." Not long after she observes Vancouver's disadvantaged, she walks through Vancouver's streets hand-in-hand with another woman, Francis, and receives nothing but support from passersby: "Two gay men pass us by. Later on, three dykes together. They look at us with knowing smiles, openly showing their approval" (158). Later on, when they kiss in public, "no one seems to notice" and Wu Lan feels "like a kid again, not caring what's showing or who's looking" (159). Whereas the sex workers' story constructs Singapore as global by contrasting it to the patriarchal Chinese homeland, Wu Lan constructs Vancouver as global by contrasting it to the homophobic Singapore homeland. Vancouver thus appears as a utopic space that deserves Wu Lan's gratitude, despite the constant reappearance of inequality within the city's derelicts and ethnic enclaves.

Kwa's depiction of Vancouver helps us understand the function of the global imaginary as constructing a hierarchy of tolerance, where Vancouver sits comfortably above Singapore for celebrating both racial *and* queer diversity. In this sense, Wu Lan pays back her social debt merely through her visibility as Chinese, upper-class, and queer.[17] Here the similarities between old Singapore and new Vancouver seem hard to miss—the class inequality, the need to feel grateful for having been "rescued," the tacit indifference to the homeless. Wu Lan's focus on queer tolerance as the redeeming virtue to mark Vancouver as utopic seems to satirize rather than reinforce notions of Asian North American (queer) identity as, in itself, resistant.

Read satirically, Wu Lan's implied celebration of liberal tolerance can be seen as an ironic reiteration of the sex worker's celebration of Singapore as a space that provides access to a global imaginary. While *Cebu* offers satirical tones within the naïveté and self-hatred of its main character, in *This Place Called Absence*, the sentimental style can be reread as a performative act of impersonation, which Tina Chen defines as the act of fooling others into believing "a seamless performance" (7). Acts of impersonation pay homage to "notions of authenticity and originality" while at the same time challenge them toward "more resistant possibilities" (ibid.).[18] Wu Lan's identity as a Singapore lesbian holds value in Vancouver, as her very presence reinforces the space's utopic global imaginary. Yet despite her privilege and wealth, she continues to "impersonate" migrant victimhood, an impersonation that breaks down whenever she is confronted with non-Asian minorities and lower-class lesbians. The novel's very title *This Place Called Absence* refers to the year of absence that Wu Lan takes from her job as a psychologist, a privilege that very few can afford. This impersonation becomes seamless as Wu Lan spends this year-long absence at the gym and library. (Kwa never explains how Wu Lan can afford to take a year off without income.)

Wu Lan's finances only become an issue when she meets a casual sex partner, Stephanie, who is attractive, white, and queer, but of a lower class. Wu Lan assumes that Stephanie is bisexual, since she lives with a man named Dale in a one-bedroom apartment, but Stephanie explains that Dale is her brother, and that "one bedroom and one bed were the best [they] could do" (73). Angered by Wu Lan's assumptions, Stephanie bursts: "I don't know about you baby-boomer types . . . it's tough making it in the city. Lotusland indeed. Tight-assed hypocrisies of corporate culture. Just how narrow-minded can a person get, anyway?" (73). Frustrated by Wu Lan's upper-class privilege, Stephanie calls Vancouver "Lotusland," a nickname for British Columbia that alludes to Homer's Lotus-eaters, who were fed lotuses as a narcotic to keep them in sleepy apathy. "Lotusland" has also been used to reinforce Vancouver as a space for rich Asians, as the lotus is also considered a sacred symbol in China and Singapore, and is often present during festivals. Wu Lan's identity as a queer Singapore migrant enables her to ambivalently impersonate the "subject-in-need," making her imagined solidarity with queer Asian sex workers seem like the very "narcotic" that blinds (and binds) Wu Lan into affects of reciprocity. Indeed, Stephanie's lower-class position keeps her from being more than an "adventure" for Wu Lan (130). In contrast, Wu Lan's upper-class sex partner, Francis, provides more intimate company. While Stephanie lives in a small one-bedroom shared apartment, Francis lives in a large wood-floored apartment with "two large, red velvet cushions fringed with golden tassels" (168). This privileged space provides Wu Lan with a sense of safety, a "private temple of our own love making" (168).[19] This temple, like the utopic ends of the global imaginary, adopts narratives of queer tolerance to conveniently forget the marginalization of subjects like Stephanie. That the narrative never returns to Stephanie, but continues to bemoan the reimagined sex workers, speaks to the novel's ambiguity. The narrative reflects Wu Lan's psychological suffering as a queer Asian lesbian, but also satirizes this "resistant" identity by depicting her as a privileged Asian Canadian. Meanwhile, Stephanie's story never seems complete; her economic position is neither transformed nor even referred to again. She is simply featured and then indifferently forgotten.

If, as Tina Chen suggests, Asian American acts of impersonating oppressed peoples of the past can "resist the ways in which their identities as Asian Americans are legally and socially over-determined," then this "resistance" can also distance historical violence into an "intolerant" past (xxii). As Chen says, "impersonation becomes an imaginative act that helps to redress the wrongs of history . . . even as one keeps in mind the impossibility of becoming that subject" (xxiv). These novels point us to ways in which the "wrongs of history" can evade the structural violence that has been maintained in the long, continuous history of imperial violence. Such violence, when distanced, can live on through the very presumption that racial and anti-queer violence can be confined into the homeland, thus reinforcing a narrative of liberal tolerance that sees some as "tolerable" and others as "intolerable." Read as satires, Bacho's *Cebu* and Kwa's *This Place Called Absence* reveal how representations of the homeland as a discrete space of violence can sediment a global imaginary where spaces of tolerance remain at the top. *Cebu* reveals the danger in these histories when Ben discovers that the violence of World War II was the catalyst for his mother's devotion to the Catholic faith, and thus this Filipino American identity is itself branded as an extension of American imperialism. Similarly, in *This Place Called Absence*, the sex worker's very labor as an affective performance for rich clients parallels Wu Lan's occupation as a clinical psychologist. While Chow Chat Mui describes her labor as being "holed up in my box transporting men to some heavenly release," Wu Lan says of her labor that "if there's any religion in North America that supersedes Christianity, it's the business of secular confession" (186). In their association with religious symbols of "heaven" and "confession," both occupations are shown to fulfill a vital function within a successful capitalist society—the release from guilt, shame, and self-disgust. Wu Lan's resentment parallels the sex workers' positions as affective supporters of the colonial government in Singapore, and allow us to trace the subjugation of gendered migrant labor within the structure of pluralist governmentality.

The national comparisons in both *Cebu* and *This Place Called Absence* expose forms of pluralist governmentality that continue to the present day as a global form of belonging. Thus we can understand the characters' affects of debt and gratitude as related to depictions of North American space as antiracist, multiculturalist, and tolerant. In the following chapter, I consider how representations of the brown gay traveler reject the desire to belong within a global imaginary that neutralizes identities to reflect the exceptionalism of a particular nation-state. Instead, these texts reinterpret given identities by traveling to new spaces, where the complex positions that emerge from mobility offer new forms of transition and coalition. As depicted in *Cebu* and *This Place Called Absence*, mobility can reveal the imperial reach of pluralist governmentality, as divergent contexts expose the power and privilege invested in identities, and where Americanness/Canadianness symbolizes the cultural power of racial, queer, and gender tolerance. If mobility in Bacho's and Kwa's texts permits Asian North Americans to rescue or impersonate the "subject-in-need," mobility can also appear as a means of taking refuge from these North American political attitudes, where Asian spaces can play "host" (rather than "home") to alternative imaginings of global belonging. Detached from these North American politics, mobility can unsettle the seemingly sacred investments in minority identities by revealing them—even those coded as empowering, resistant, or antiracist—as adopting modes of recognition that rely on identifying, objectifying, and subjugating the intolerable.

4 · JUST AN AMERICAN DARKER THAN THE REST

On Queer Brown Exile

This chapter expands on the arguments in chapter 3 by considering how queer mobility and transition offer alternatives to a global imaginary characterized by tolerance, mobility, and multiculturalism. I treat novels of queer mobility from two Southeast Asian diasporic authors, R. Zamora Linmark, whose novels *Rolling the R's* and *Leche* explore queer Filipino/a migrants in Hawaii and Manila, and Lawrence Chua, whose novel *Gold by the Inch* (1998) follows a queer Thai/Malaysian/Chinese diasporic who returns to his multiple homelands. The brown and queer narrators of these stories begin by rejecting a global imaginary to instead transition toward new forms of identity in Southeast Asia, where their brown bodies transform from devalued working-class skins to ambiguous sites of meaning-making. While in Bacho's and Kwa's novels, mobility only made their protagonists more certain of the intolerance of the homeland, in these novels travel allows characters to collect tactics and local knowledges of identity and power, and to compare them across borders. These novels begin by refusing the desire to belong to a global imaginary that manifests as a disguised form of pluralist governmentality, which leaves their protagonists open to alternative forms of cultural belonging.

Here I expand on the global imaginary, loosely defined in the last chapter as the normative social imaginary for how race, gender, and sexual differences are lived within global spaces, that is, as an ideal, postracial social formation. As an imperial form, the global imaginary is always expanding to include others—new imperial subjects, new ways of performing gender, new sexualities—at the same time as it hierarchizes newly identified populations into regimes of global capital and state surveillance. While the narratives from chapter 3 reveal the desire to remain within the global imaginary and to insist on its tolerant superiority, the novels in this chapter explore the "colonial leftovers" and the "historical stains" that are left behind in the desire to become global. In both *Gold by the Inch* and *Leche*, belonging to a global imaginary is something that poor queer-of-color subjects particularly fail to achieve. They fail to become Thai, Malaysian, or Filipino/a, just as they fail to belong to a global imaginary built on diversity, multiculturalism, and homonormativity.

Lawrence Chua's 1998 novel *Gold by the Inch* follows a twenty-three-year-old gay Southeast Asian American unnamed narrator who travels to Southeast Asia after a failed love affair in New York City. This unnamed narrator is multiply queered: he is of Thai, Malay, and Chinese (Teochew/Peranakan) descent. He is sexually queer as well, as his omnivorous sexual desires tug him from space to space, from go-go bars to brothels and public toilets. He seeks out romance, love, sex, and belonging through monetary transactions, deluding himself that the pleasures he experiences exist outside a system of barter and exchange. The novel works episodically, and like a travel narrative it seems unsettled and wayward, tracking its mobile narrator to Paris, New York, Honolulu, Thailand, and Malaysia. Each new location reflects the narrator's unsettled identity and inspires a new erotic register, as the narrator transitions into bottom, top, sadist, masochist, fetishist, and lover. R. Zamora Linmark's 2011 novel, *Leche*, returns to the queer Filipino character from his previous novel *Rolling the R's*, Vicente de Los Reyes, now thirteen years older and returning to the Philippines for the first time since he left as a child. Instead of an awaiting homeland, Vicente finds a similar neocolonial state rich in guarded mansions and the need to fake a racial harmony for tourists. In a nation where Filipinoness is heterogeneous, hybrid, and predicated upon hierarchies structured by one's capabilities with English and American culture, Vicente is no longer able to identify simply as a Filipino, as he did in Hawaii. His attempts to understand his homeland through vexed notions of Filipino authenticity place him as a tourist, traveler, and American. Like Chua's narrator, Vicente transitions as both a "brown boy" and "rice queen," a trope that Eng-Beng Lim has identified as a central trope in colonial encounter. Indeed, both *Gold by the Inch* and *Leche* wrestle with the "white man" and "brown boy" dyad (also called the "white man/native dyad"), which Lim defines as "a pedophilic Western modernity bearing the homoerotics of orientalism" (4), wherein the brown or native boy can represent infantilized darker-skinned adults, and functions as an accepting love-child to "predatory capitalism, queer orientalism, and the white male artist-tourist on the casual prowl for inspiration and sex" (9). Hiram Pérez has similarly observed that for the white and Western "gay cosmopolitan," "brown" signifies "the fantasies about racial and sexual others who fascinate modern gay male identity with their instinctive, earthy, volatile, scatological, savage, and dirty allure" (14).

As with previous chapters, I focus on reading two novels together (*Leche* and *Gold by the Inch*) to focus on the slippages in identity across contexts, and to understand transition as more than an opportunistic tactic, but as a strategy developed through communal cultural crossover. Both novels feature traveling narrators who are challenged by mobile encounters that force them to broaden their ways of seeing their American-produced identities: Thainess, Filipino-ness, Malayness, queerness, Americanness. Both novels see transpacific travel as crucial to practices of transition, producing an intellectual cunning developed through mobile encounters. As both novels take place in the early 1990s, they capture a moment between the Cold War and the War on Terror, when brown bodies were, for a brief time, politically ambiguous and incorporated into the global imaginary as workers, consumers, and travelers. Indeed, the early 1990s could be seen as the "Rise of Asia," when Southeast Asia began to transform from a space of war and trauma into a space open to investment, consumerism, and political integration. While Southeast Asia itself was in a period of transition, Linmark's and Chua's texts shape their narrators too as figures of transition—people who can turn identity on or off as they choose, from closeted "Filipino" in Hawaii to "hooker" in New York, to "client" in Thailand, to "returned son" in Malaysia, to a "*balikbayan*" in the Philippines. Both novels expose the supposed authenticity of multicultural identities as forming the basis of biopolitical man-agement, where authenticity, in practice, means "being able to 'place' things and persons" in order to "assess the relative strangeness and/or acceptability of the thing or person in question" (Manalansan 290). These novels cause us to under-stand, as Vernadette Gonzalez has put it, "not the authenticity of these attach-ments, but their manufacture" (3).

Linmark's and Chua's texts provide a stage to explore the transitions that come with travel. They articulate feelings of loss and the desire for fulfillment for people of color travelers who seem deprived of the "soul-searching" narra-tives of white travelers, and who are instead expected to find their fulfillment by collapsing upon their ethnic orientation. These narratives of racial transition thus crossover into narratives of gender transition. That "he/she is transition-ing" suggests the incomplete maturation of a human being who is marked as undeveloped due to the viewer's own categories of identity. As Jack Halbers-tam has argued, to be "transitioning" need not reflect a deferred future, or a lack (spiritual or otherwise), but can simultaneously be "a symbol for postmodern flexibility and a legible form of embodied subjectivity" (*In a Queer Time* 17). An easy co-optation of transition thus emerges when flexibility itself becomes associated with a utopic, postracial, postgender future—a global imaginary built upon tolerance, flexibility, and mobility.[1] However, taken out of its associations with progressive futures, the temporal associations of transition can also allow both ambiguity and recognition by naming an ever-present condition, the begin-ning and end of which is irrelevant to their material presence of being in the now. Thus, these novels explore the intricacies of feeling unmoored from nationalist or even global futures. Being "unsettled" here complicates accounts of migration as a settling, or as an arrival. The brown, queer migrant remains unsettled in order to protect the self from the settled communities. Home and settlement are not only elusive, but undesirable. These narrators see the need to feel "safe" and "secure" as enacting the very authoritarian restrictions upon one's freedom to find oneself, a privilege given only to those in power who can occupy states of wanderlust and self-discovery. In these brown queer travel novels, transition emerges as a tactic that is recognized only by those who practice it. It characterizes a community that produces feelings of belonging, loyalty, and kinship—an alignment based less on racial identities and more on relationships with imperial power. These novels thus ask how transition can allow for growth, flexibility, and modes of self-discovery that do not simply lead back to presumed gender, sexual, or racial identities.

In spotlighting the transnational travel of brown queer bodies, these novels reclaim the privilege of feeling lost in oneself through a picaresque traveling form where encountering others both challenge and guide the traveler. Mobility not only offers new identities and selves, but through self-discovery, reveals the pains, structures, and violences that invoked the desire to travel in the first place. The travelers' education comes from a process of mobile encounters, as the American, poor, brown, queer travelers begin to imagine themselves in the optics of Southeast Asian contexts. Indeed, both novels share a sense of brownness as a form of racial ambiguity that aligns their narrators with Southeast Asian bodies, permitting them to enact transitional roles that would be unavailable to them in an American racial formation.

Throughout his career, José Muñoz formulated "brownness" as a conceptual framing that enables vaster considerations of how local and global forces degrade the value of brown people. "Brownness" comes without immediate value, and whatever value it achieves can be put down, attributed to "exotic" and "spicy" excesses. Yet "brown" only operates provisionally within identity categories, as "a waiting station of sorts between white and black, or white and Asian," and thus brownness can also reveal "how bodies are situated" within given binaries (white/black, white/Asian) (Pérez 175). In both novels, brownness becomes an everyday embodiment that shifts meaning in Southeast Asia, where brownness can signify a blended mixture of histories and races, and does not itself signify a particular class, race, or creed. This shift leaves transition open as a viable cultural practice, allowing these narrators to disidentify with the American sense of brown, toward a transnational brown commons. Muñoz describes his concept of "disidentification" as a process that "scrambles and reconstructs the encoded message of a cultural text" so that the "code of the majority" appears as "raw material for representing a disempowered politics or positionality that has been rendered unthinkable by the dominant culture" (*Disidentifications* 31). To queer Muñoz's own term, I ask if we can see the "cultural text" being "scrambled and reconstructed" not as a commodity, but as the brown subject and all the attached attributes deemed natural or given: Filipinoness, Hawaiianness, and an exotic gay "brown boy" identity that serves the homonormative.[2] In the global imaginary of the 1990s, to disidentify with the ascribed brownness of diversity and multiculturalism did not leave one marked as terrorist or communist radical, but left open a new, uncharted identity whose meaningful content was still in process.

ROLLING THE R'S AND "QUEER COMMUNAL SUBJECTIVITY"

In R. Zamora Linmark's 1995 novel, *Rolling the R's*, his adolescent characters of 1979 Honolulu contend with the unrelenting surveillance over masculine performance and Filipina/o American identity. Linmark's young Filipino migrant, Vicente de Los Reyes, wrestles with being closeted while he dreams of sex with celebrities like Scott Baio and Matt Dillon. He remains uncertain of his own queer performance and appears rather as a critical examiner, fascinated with gays, straights, haoles, Filipina/os, transsexuals, and others. From the first vignette of *Rolling the R's*, Vicente listens to his out-of-the-closet friend, Edgar Ramirez, who reveals to Vicente that he had a dream where "we saw you in the corridor givin' Parker Stevenson the Hardy Boys treatment. You actin' like you knew the ropes by trade, spreadin' your legs for spill out the one-and-only clue. You was so grown-up, you knew who you was, and was lovin' it too" (2). Edgar's dream that Vicente "knew who you was" hails Vicente into a recognizable gay identity, and the use of the second person "you" here stresses the conditioning of this hail as it becomes directed toward the reader. Vicente, like the reader, does not speak back in this vignette. Edgar's dreams of Vicente coming out of the closet are merely assumed to be Vicente's own. In Martin Joseph Ponce's reading of *Rolling the R's*, Edgar's call to perform queerness is meant to "disidentify" with heteronormative acts of expression. Edgar appropriates dominant images of male and female normativity, like posters of John Travolta and Scott Baio, and fetishizes them as objects of queer desire and consumption. Indeed, Vicente's refusal to come out of the closet could be read either as disempowering or as a means of resisting the homonormative identity wherein brown gay men are assigned into roles of "brown boys" who satisfy white "rice queens."

Vicente's desire not to be identified resists the image of Hawaii as a space of multiracial tolerance that has been promoted by both tourist and military regimes since the 1980s, and has continued in television shows like *Hawaii Life* where white settlers are invited to buy and auction off island land. This view of Hawaii as a multiracial utopia is met with scorn in *Rolling the R's*, which questions the relationship of ethnic identity with queer sexuality, transgender performance, and "islander" masculinity. Linmark's closeted Vicente is tormented for his queer sexuality by his family and friends through the language of self-affirmation and cultural identity, as he is never quite "Filipino" or "gay" enough, while Vicente himself seeks instead to withhold any gender, sexual, and ethnic affinities. This act of withholding marks him as a betrayer and fake in the eyes of Edgar, yet it also reflects a flexibility that allows Vicente to remain critical of pluralist discourses seeking to manage and incorporate him. In contrast, Edgar bears the brunt of his school's queer bashing. He learns to deal with the names he is called, "fag," "bakla," "homo," "sissy," "mahu," and "panty," and he "swallow[s] the names like the vitamins I gotta take before I go to school . . . cuz they supposed to make me grow big and strong" (5). The pain that Edgar learns to cope with makes him antagonistic toward the closeted Vicente, who expresses curiosity for other forms of queer identity. Vicente shares Edgar's desires but not the risk of social violence inherent to coming out. In the queer logic of the novel, the tension between Edgar's hypervisible gay identity and Vicente's closeted self takes the form of superficial surface markers, when the transgender woman, Exotica, names Edgar's pouting lips "ambitious, manipulative, and powerful," marking Edgar's affinity with gay identity as both courageous and as a means of controlling his own legibility through a recognizable queer discourse. Exotica then becomes "hypnotized" by Vicente's lips, with its "curves" that "mean eternity," and the fullness for "a kiss that means beauty and sadness" (15). Here the transgender figure of transition places Vicente's refusal to be hailed as gay in an "eternal" form like "the redness for birth," an opaqueness that decontextualizes his unspoken desires. The "secret" that Vicente is "trying to hide" is not merely his gay sexuality, but the unbound and unnamable sexual desires that operate in excess of it (15).

Vicente's refusal to align with a recognized identity makes him difficult to incorporate into multicultural narratives about overcoming racial and sexual barriers. His experiences give us pause, as his anxiety and frustration with maintaining his identity is set against the 1980s backdrop of a supposed Hawaiian "racial harmony" that is the afterlife of World War II and the Cold War, when attempts to depict America as multicultural gave unprecedented national attention to the territory of Hawaii, the first American state with a majority Asian population.[3] As the gateway to Asia, Hawaii's multiracial veneer covered over long histories of violence, servitude, and exploitation, beginning with the *Mahele* ("division") of 1848, when American missionaries and merchants bought up land from indigenous people to transform into industrial sugar plantations (Wu 211). With chattel slavery a thing of the past, and the Hawaiian natives decimated by Western diseases, growers looked to Asia to supply farm hands: Japanese seeking refuge from the unsettled society of the Meiji Restoration; Chinese as part of the coolie trade routed through ports in Hong Kong, Portugal, and Puerto Rico; and Filipino/as, who had been made colonial subjects. In *Rolling the R's*, the site of pluralist ideological reproduction remains the school, where Vicente's teacher, Miss Takata, teaches him the implicit racial hierarchies of multicultural Hawaii, threatening to take him and his friends out of class to teach them "a thing or two about integration" (49). As Dean Saranillo has pointed out, the production of multicultural space in Hawaii can be traced to American colonial education as part of a "deliberate, intentional, purposeful miseducation and disinformation by the government" to promote colonial pluralism (124). The public school system in Hawaii that valorized a particular brand of racial harmony coincided with the simultaneous establishment of other colonial schools in Puerto Rico, Cuba, and the Philippines. Saranillo's comments echo Renato Constantino's essay, "The Miseducation of the Filipino," where Constantino argues that Philippine schools inherited the miseducation of American colonial schools, which taught them "to regard centuries of colonial status as a grace from above rather than as a scourge" (49).

The valorization of a multicultural (and thus exceptional) American culture carries implicit superiority to Filipino/a culture, and does the work of reifying (rather than hybridizing) conceptions of both. As Meg Wesling wrote in her book *Empire's Proxy*, American literary education was made into a tool of American exceptionalism, as narratives about racial uplift were used to distance U.S. officials from the "openly exploitative" example of *British* colonial rule (8). As detailed in chapter 3, American exceptionalism helped constitute Filipino/a American identity as a separation from the *manong* generation. Saranillo reads this identity as thus an articulation of colonial miseducation (125),[4] and insists instead on the term "Filipino settler," as it stresses imperial subjectivity while "forcing non-Natives to question our participation in sustaining U.S. colonialism" (141). "Filipino settler," for Saranillo, inverts the nationalism inherent in "Filipino American," emphasizing instead the erasure of native Hawaiians and other indigenous tribes from American subjectivity, but also disrupts notions of "homeland" and "host country" by naming the overdetermined context of migration as neither totally "forced" (by U.S. colonization) nor totally "free" (in migrants moving for better opportunity).

Saranillo's call to replace "Filipino American" with "Filipino settler" troubles understandings of settlement and migrant arrival. To presently "settle" upon land assumes a prior "unsettling" of politics and/or land that prompted the migration—in this case, U.S. colonialism and sugar cane plantations. To be a settler reinscribes the individual within the political, economic, social, and environmental unsettlings that were the conditions of identity articulation. The problem with "Filipino settler," however, is inscribed within the term itself—the presumption that such groups have "settled," have claimed land that isn't their own, and thus the term takes for granted that the limited range of Filipino American identity in Hawaii reflects the transnational context wherein Filipino/as have become displaced, "unsettled" migrants even within the Philippines itself. "Filipino settler" can flatten the differences that Linmark's texts seek to draw out, where new forms of Filipinoness depend upon different histories of engagement with U.S. empire.

Indeed, Vicente's refusal to adequately "settle" into given identities speaks to the neocolonial context and distrust of mainland American discourses, where Asian American identity can operate within a contemporary form of pluralist governmentality. Its rehearsal of racial pasts also reveals a limited utopic horizon that continues to be reliant upon the institutional power of the state, on one hand, and the conditions of possibility enabled by empire (via settler colonialism) on the other. In refusing "settlement," Vicente also confronts the migrant's desires to feel settled—to have a recognizable and communal identity under the auspices of a stable (though imperial, unjust, and unequal) power structure.

For some Asian American scholars, Linmark's *Rolling the R's* demonstrates how queer and diasporic writing disrupts nationalist and racial identities through idealizing sexuality and its communities as a viable alternative, a community that victimizes Vicente for remaining in sexual obscurity. In David Eng's analysis, the novel exposes a notion of queer communal subjectivity that disrupts ethnic identities while also making available more politicized forms of affiliation. While ethnic identities are made tenuous, sexuality "binds them together as a social group with a common sense of purpose" so that "the coalitional possibilities of 'Asian American' as a viable or even workable group identity are engaged, renewed, and rendered efficacious by this detour through queerness" (225). Queerness in this case could reflect an identity indifferent to nationalist status, as Chandan Reddy has noted, where "identifying as a 'queer' immigrant rather than an American immigrant powerfully deflects identification with the U.S." (qtd. in Eng 225). Eng's focus on *Rolling the R's* pressures the text to formulate Asian American queer communities as "a name under which progressive politics can be strategized and rallied" (226).

Previous readings of *Rolling the R's* do not engage directly with Vicente as a closeted character who is bullied and harassed by Edgar, and who emerges as the main character of the book's 2011 sequel, *Leche*. Vicente's refusal to come out of the closet, in fact, sparks Edgar's ire and results in Vicente's sexual abuse at the end of the novel, when Edgar pimps him out to a teenager, Roberto, for twenty dollars, and abandons him with Roberto in a shed. Although Edgar acts as a gay hero through his revolt against straight white (haole) attitudes, his embrace of gay identity is laced with an excessive embrace of American consumer practices, spending "all his money on life-size John Travolta or Shaun Cassidy or Scott Baio posters" (3). The reading of *Rolling the R's* as rejuvenating Asian American political solidarity by "a detour through queerness" is belied by Edgar's consumer-obsessed performance of queer identity, and his desire to force Vicente out of the closet, even it if means subjecting him to a sexual assault. Edgar shames Vicente as "two-face closet-case," Miss In-Denial, and "major closet case," and attacks Vicente with the same queer bashing insults that he himself had learned to absorb: "missus" and "faggot" (135). Indeed, the familiar hatred that made words like "faggot" seem ugly to Edgar, motivates Edgar to use them toward

Vicente: "fuckin' fag," Edgar says, "he goin' get it. . . . No matter how many times you like run away from yourself, you cannot" (135). Enacting the gaze of colonial powers in reading the illegible, Vicente's friend Katrina diagnoses Vicente as an "unconscious two-face" and "schizophrenic" unable to choose sides (119).

THE BROWN BOY IN THE GLOBAL IMAGINARY

> Your skin is your uniform. A beacon and a membrane . . . Dark, but not dark
> enough to hide your insides.
>
> —Lawrence Chua, *Gold by the Inch*

In R. Zamora Linmark's *Rolling the R's*, Vicente's disidentification with queer consumption reflects an unease with settling into any prescribed identity. In Lawrence Chua's 1998 novel, *Gold by the Inch*, this unease comes from the narrator's repeatedly having to play the "brown boy" to his white gay boyfriend, Jim, in order to seek security and approval. In a French subway, the narrator is harassed by "ten men in black paramilitary uniforms" who throw him violently against a wall (56). Once the police realize he is American, they pat him on the back, just as Jim returns from the toilet. During the attack, the narrator realizes that his skin was "an act of resistance" (58): "Jim gave me the appearance of belonging," the narrator says, "to a place, to a time, to him. As decoration, I wasn't always able to articulate my value, but Jim knew it intrinsically" (57). The brown skin that Chua's narrator embodies necessitates Jim's presence as a constant symbol warranting the narrator's social value to belong. The belonging that the narrator feels as an American is only recognized by others insofar as he maintains the value given to him by a white interlocutor. "But," the narrator says, "it was the value I now knew was less than the worth of my skin. Skin the color of decay. Another layer crumbling in the rinse" (60).

Chua's unnamed narrator relies on Jim as a universal subject whose whiteness acts as a referral to give the narrator's brown skin value in a context where it is presumed to have none. In chapter 3, I introduced the binary between the "tolerable" and "intolerable" migrant, where the intolerable signified new migrants whose Americanness was still under question. The novels in this chapter extend these concepts by focusing on two categories of American brownness: one of rural poverty, whose presence in the city warrants surveillance, and one whose belonging is given value by the endorsement of a white (or more tolerable) American. Lisa Marie Cacho similarly divides brownness between the "respected" minority and the "deviant" minority (183), with the latter as being in excess of "ideological codes" that are "used for deciding which human lives are valuable and which ones are worthless" (186). In the United States, Jim does the work of ideological coding when he assesses the narrator's value, allowing him to be recognized and thus to belong, but always in spite of his race. As a brown queer man, the narrator's belonging is unstable, even as he finds himself in an apparently multicultural global imaginary. Thus he feels forced to emigrate from the United States where his skin only represents the fear of "Foreignness" and "Contagion" (121). His skin cannot be cast aside, but continually exposes the contradictions of the global imaginary. Jim refuses to see these contradictions: "When I had told Jim what had happened [in the subway] he didn't believe me," the narrator says, "He was certain I had made up the story just to amuse him" (57). The narrator's embodied brownness is his exclusionary mark, one that allows him to discover contradictions that Jim either cannot see or chooses to ignore.

While the narrator is tethered to a brown skin that marks him as either valued or devalued, Jim acts as a neutral universalist whose whiteness gives him access to a global imaginary without skin. Jim's addiction to cocaine allegorizes this feeling: "Jim always said that the cocaine made him feel as if he were unencumbered by his body. It left him free to indulge in mine" (88). The narrator decides to become a nomadic traveler when, in New York, Jim smashes a phone against the narrator's face. When the police arrive to settle their domestic dispute, Jim refuses to identify the narrator as his housemate or lover. The narrator's brown skin makes his innocence invisible: "He told them I was trespassing. That they should arrest me. I begged them to let me call our next door neighbor, who could vouch for my identity. One of them started to giggle when he put the handcuffs on me. I couldn't blame him" (59). Even as Jim denies the narrator's encounters with police harassment, he still is conscious enough of their racial difference to manipulate ideological codes, and to mark the narrator's race, gender, and queerness as "deviant." The narrator feels entrapped by the fixity of the American system, like vines that "always bring you back to the forest" (59). Southeast Asia provides a space of refuge from these ideological codes, as it is only after arriving in Malaysia that the narrator gets revenge on Jim by calling the American police from a pay phone and reporting Jim as a drug smuggler. Identified only by his American accent, the narrator is able to mark Jim with the same ideological coding tactics that Jim had used on him, naming whiteness within a set of criminal categories: "Six foot one. Blond. American passport" (89).

The narrator's disillusion with the global imaginary provokes his desire to travel to Southeast Asia, yet as he travels, so his skin, his queerness, his language, and his American notion of brownness travel with him. He thinks, "My own body is starting to return to itself in these weeks since I left [Jim]. . . . I think I can do things with it now that I never knew I could do" (88). Whereas in France and New York his brown skin marked him "as an illness," brownness in Southeast Asia permits him to transition to a wider array of identities, each of different value depending on the context. Mobility here unfixes categories and values that were once reliant on Jim's presence, as the narrator's skin no longer presumes the same cultural practices. But as values are relational, for the narrator to add value to himself often means devaluing others, particularly, his lover Thong, whom he fetishizes as a Thai national in the same way that the narrator was once fetishized as a brown boy. As he says, "At twenty-three, would you believe I've never been with anyone like him before. . . . What I mean by that, like him? Like me" (13).[5] *Gold by the Inch*'s narrative is held together by the narrator's overwhelming desire for Thong, a desire that reflects the colonial obsession for the native boy as "a sign of conquest . . . a savage domesticated as a child, and a racially alienating body in need of tutelage and discipline" (E.-B. Lim 9). Yet this desire manifests as an attempt to understand Jim's privilege in desiring the narrator. Whereas the narrator could never truly reveal himself to Jim for fear of losing Jim's referred value, neither can Thong do the same. The narrator articulates Thong's value whenever given the chance, describing even his sexual trespass within terms of value: "You used to like the fact that other men were having him. It made him more valuable to you" (165). Despite this casting of value, the narrator continues to grasp for an honest relationship. His own likeness to Thong, that they can "pass for brothers" (27), deludes him into buying into American racial hierarchies where brownness is a fixed mark of subjugation as well as solidarity.

As the narrator's mirror-image, Thong reveals the limits of the narrator's transitions: that despite his brownness the narrator cannot form himself into any identity he pleases; that to belong to some identities also means becoming structurally positioned at the bottom of a class hierarchy. When they first meet, Thong performs the "brown boy" to the narrator, complaining that "he doesn't know who his father is. . . . They all live in a shack with a dirt floor somewhere in the slums of klong toei" (31). Once they become more intimate, Thong invites the narrator to live with him in his father's house so that the narrator can save money. Thong's father, it turns out, is a sugar merchant, and the "shack" is in fact a mansion surrounded by an electric gate, a long driveway, and a garden (31). The narrator, unable to free himself from his skin in America, takes racial identity for granted as the only way in which groups are hierarchized. It is not the narrator's skin nor cultural behavior, but his American accent and passport that remain his most important signifiers. His previous desire for the global imaginary has framed culture as a commodity to be owned, stirring only anger when he is dispossessed of it: "I wish people here would stop trying to teach me the fine points of my own fucking culture, you know?" (170). Pushed into being Thai, Malaysian, and Chinese in the United States, his inability to understand the purposes behind Thong's transitions comes from the arrogance that he really is any one of those identities, that he "owns" these cultures. The more the narrator attempts to own Thong, the more estranged the two become, until the narrator catches Thong in bed with his "replacement," a woman (198). Even after Thong has slept with other men, and together he and the narrator had enjoyed threesomes together, Thong's bisexuality acts as the ultimate trespass for the narrator. It signifies a personhood as illegible to the narrator as his own brown queer personhood is in the United States. Even in a novel filled with upfront erotic imagery, the bisexual figure stands as the most unsettling sexual image. It reveals to the narrator that he cannot ever own or possess Thong (and therefore Thainess). In their last heated argument, Thong casts him as another foreign sex tourist, "just an American darker than the rest, doing things in Thailand you could never do at home" (201). Despite having so little privilege in America, the narrator finds that his own desire to conquer and own other cultures—even those that were "given" to him in America—has left him disconnected, consigned only to see the smiling surface of the locals.

QUEER EXILE AND THE TOURIST GAZE

These novels about queer exile contrast with the mobilities of Bacho's *Cebu* and Kwa's *This Placed Called Absence*. Rather than harden imposed identities, here mobility allows these travelers to deny given identities—queer, minoritarian, or otherwise—and to instead permit the affective growth and self-discovery so often restricted to white travelers. While in *Cebu*, Ben's return to his homeland ends with a reaffirmation of his Filipino American identity, in these novels, mobility destabilizes the identities of these queer brown travelers, and every transition enables new relationships with others. Once becoming travelers and nomads, these characters cannot be confined within an identity that fits easily into the structure of the global imaginary. Their unstable identities reveal transpacific structures of stratified ethnicities, as their brown ambiguity keeps them from belonging within any particular space. Rather than rediscover their racial identities by returning to their homeland, these travelers instead appropriate the pleasure-seeking wanderlust of white travel by queering travel literature itself.

More often than not, travel narratives are figured as optic extensions of what Mary Louise Pratt famously called "imperial eyes," wherein an empire "becomes dependent on its others to know itself," and creates "an obsessive need to present and re-present its peripheries and its others continually to itself" (4). Travel literature, from Herodotus to Lord Byron, has helped imperial powers get a sense of what lies in the prospective colonies, from "discovering" the types of rituals and food to identifying (and thus casting) racial, gender, and sexual characteristics upon local populations. As Edward W. Said argued in *Orientalism*, this literature shapes people and cultures from "the Orient" as undeveloped, unchanging, exotic, backward, uncivilized, and at times dangerous, thus producing the West as advanced, developed, civilized, progressive, and safe. Countering this imperial form of travel, Pratt insists on reading and producing autoethnographies, referring to the accounts of creoles, indigenous peoples, and natives who countertravel and write of the imperial center in order to evade imperial eyes.[6] Extending these arguments, John Urry has argued that travel writing can help understand the orientalisms of a "tourist gaze," which Urry describes as the tourists' expectations of the foreign in relation to the mundane and the everyday of their lives. Travel texts for Urry are unique in that they invest certain objects with pleasures that "involve different senses or on a different scale from those typically encountered in everyday life," and such pleasures are often reflected back by locals for financial benefit (*Tourist Gaze* 12). Indeed, travel literature can be integral to understanding how imperial powers produce socio-cultural sensescapes wherein the performance of the traveling body and its perceptions are contrasted with the everyday.[7] For example, postcards of Hawai'i routinely contain romanticized and idyllic visions of the islands' beaches, though one may spend five days in Hawai'i and in only 5 percent of that time lie out on the beach (if there is no storm). Yet the memories, photographs, and travel writings will be almost solely focused on scenes that re-create the postcard. The sensescapes of a place, the very feelings and physical sensations one has within a travel experience, are limited to the already established tourist gaze.

Both *Gold by the Inch* and *Leche* appropriate travel literary forms to express the experience of queer brown exile. First, both texts explore how postcards and other touristic objects articulate the limits and potentialities of travel. Chua's narrator carries a "sheaf of postcards" with him across Penang, which he calls "windows onto a river of lust" (61). He uses a postcard of the Chao Phraya River to reflect on his own relationship to imperial history by calling the river by its colonial name, "the menam," and writing of himself as a colonial mimic: "I'm twenty-three," he writes, and wearing a counterfeit "black suit" that's "not real. . . . But I wanted to wear it. It makes me look different" (7). Similarly, Linmark's *Leche* includes a pastiche of touristic writings, beginning with a "Tourist Tips" section that Vicente (now going as "Vince") uses as a survival guide to Filipino/a culture (12). These sections, which contain tips like "'Filipinos' to Westerners; 'Pilipinos' to nationalists," not only maintain a distance between Vince and the locals by reinforcing his position as a tourist, but also allow him to distance himself from imperial power. Even as the tips enact an orientalist geography that separates (and thus produces) Filipinoness, Vince's self-reflexivity chops away at these binaries, as the tourist tips are slowly outnumbered by Vince's own postcards, which offer his thoughts of Manila inspired by his annoyance at the city's heat and loud music. As Manila assaults both his senses and his categories of meaning, he writes on a postcard, "All that crap about Western metaphors, signs, and symbols is useless here" (180).

Both *Leche* and *Gold by the Inch* depart drastically from typical travel forms by parodying tourist commodities like postcards, and in providing a historian's knowledge of the cities they encounter. Both narrators display an archive of historical knowledge about the places they visit, and their analytical voices counteract their initial travel encounters. In *Leche*, Vince at first makes naïve and often racist judgments about Filipina/os: "Filipinos talking loudly behind your back is their indirect way of showing you that you are important enough to kill time with" (9). This intimate narrative of Vince's frustration, after a woman gossips about Vince being gay, is entirely absent at other times in the narrative, when we are faced with a disengaged voice, as in this description of Malate (downtown Manila): "MALATE Pulse of Manila. Crammed with bars, restaurants, hostels, motels, cafés, and potholes. A small fishing village during the Spanish colonial period, the name was derived from the Tagalog 'maalat'—salty—because of the seawater from the nearby Manila Bay that seeped into the drinking wells" (82). This historical voice operates like an exterior shot in a film before cutting to an interior scene, where Vince's naïve reactions occur. The narrative functions as an expert informant, historically informed, semi-academic, and compared to the pleasures of Vince's intimate narrative, pessimistic. It offers a hyperawareness of the space, and gives historical information that doesn't complement Vince's simple impressions so much as highlight his naïve mode of tourism.

Gold by the Inch's unnamed narrator similarly has an academic knowledge of history, one that is often conjured in moments of gay sex. Chua juxtaposes a statement from the American Department of Defense on the importance of "security" with a dreamlike scene of a white angel who chains the narrator to a public toilet and cums in "your mouth," leaving "you" with "a wish to die a hundred times this way, the object of someone else's history" (81). Rather than oppose the pleasures of the intimate travel narrative, the historical voice here reinforces the pleasures of sub-dom erotic practices by adding the historical weight of colonial violence to the encounter. Earlier, a quotation from the *Hikayat Abdullah* focuses only on the book's representation of sex slaves (41), and later, a historical meditation on the colonial extraction of rubber from Malaysia intersects with a scene where the narrator enacts sexual vengeance on a white tourist in a rubber suit. Transitioning into a native brown boy by "fumbling for the English word" (115), the narrator tries "to make [his] body disappear" by urinating inside the man's rubber suit: "He is surprised, but it only takes a moment before it fades into indignation. You put your hand over his mouth and continue urinating ... you push him down, still peeing. Cover him with your body. The rubber takes on a new sheen" (116). A scene that invokes the colonial violence of rubber plantations is here made into pleasurable sex, and the narrator's transition into the "brown boy" takes on an attitude of fetish and fun. Where the narrator could only be seen as the "brown boy" in America, his ability to become this figure as a choice rather than a devalued stigma opens the encounter to new forms of eroticism (and erotic vengeance).

The historical reflections in these novels displace the excitement and thrill of travel with a historian's knowledge of colonial violence that seems to "kill the party," so to speak. But historical knowledge does not leave a pessimistic view of travel so much as bear the burden of historical accountability, where travel provides a platform for historical violence to be made more intimate. As queer travelers, these narrators cannot speak for local communities, but instead rely on historical facts to inform their encounters, erotic or otherwise. Their historical diatribes reject the sensescapes of the global imaginary to instead broaden spatial understanding. Both authors are familiar with the academy: after publishing *Gold by the Inch*, in 2012 Chua earned a Ph.D. from Cornell where he studied under Benedict Anderson; Linmark was a Fulbright scholar in the Philippines and a professor at the University of Hawai'i during the years he wrote *Leche*. Their novels can be read as the expression of intellectuals in exile, as Said has called it, those thinkers imbued with a metaphysical sense of "restlessness, movement, constantly being unsettled, and unsettling others" (*Representations* 53). Their styles reflect a condition of exile where unhappiness becomes a mode of being and thinking that resists the trappings of the national, the local, and the global. The exilic intellectual thus "tends to be happy with the idea of unhappiness," and dissatisfaction with every new space brings upon a new "curmudgeonly disagreeableness," that operates as both a style of thought and as "a new, if temporary, habituation" (ibid.). Indeed, the narrators of both novels derive pleasure from the spaces they inhabit even as they remain highly critical of their own positions within them. Such historicized encounters contain the pleasure of being surprised, as Said writes, "of learning to make do in circumstances of shaky instability that would confound or terrify most people" (ibid., 59).

Leche and *Gold by the Inch* queer travel literature through appropriating travel objects like postcards, through rehearsing imperial history, and lastly, by applying the second-person plural narrative typical of travel guides, which employ the second person to focus readers on sensations of food, landscape, and sex. "You can't really say you've been to George Town unless you've stepped inside China House," says the Lonely Planet guide to Malaysia. A tourism brochure for Angeles City, the most well known prostitution site in the Philippines and the previous location of the U.S. Clark Air Force Base, advertises go-go bars with "young women eager to show you a good time" who can help *you* get "loaded and laid" (Ralston and Sutherland). And so on. As travel narratives often use the plural "you," to make the reader feel included in the experience, the traveler then is made to appear "neutral" or "universal" in respect to the target audience—in nearly all cases, the traveler is presumed white. In response, *Leche* and *Gold by the Inch* use the second person to impose historical responsibility upon the pleasure that readers absorb from travel writing.[8]

Leche appropriates the second person to queer travel as a mode of seeing, where travelers often inhabit "lumpy, fragile, aged, gendered, racialized bodies," yet they perceive new places by inhabiting a white imperial gaze that is enhanced by the use of the second person (Urry, *Mobilities* 48). *Leche* recognizes this in its "tourist tips" sections, which separate "you" (white) and "them" (Filipino): "Don't use Spanish on them because their Spanish is not your Spanish" (120). The second-person narrative expresses the dissociation of travel, where the traveler is always presumed to be a white tourist, who knows little to nothing of the space. Vince, as the reader of these tourist tips, seems to adjust them as he spends more time in Manila, replacing their frequency with his own postcards, and revising them to expose the colonial violence that tourist sensescapes only occlude. A tourist tip on Filipino stares says: "Staring can't kill you; Philippine colonial history would have lasted in a blink rather than four hundred years" (85). The last tourist tip section becomes critical of its own genre: "Your Manila is only one of the hundreds of millions of versions. . . . Keep tourist tips where they belong: at the International Dateline" (316).

In Chua's text, the second person is used liberally to double the narrator into different selves, and to implicate the American reader into the narrator's own imperial complicity. At first, the second person seems to name the American version of the narrator himself, who he seeks to leave behind. "I died when I was ten," the narrator says, "and that's when you were born ... you came into the world when the plane took off, circled Subang International Airport, and then tore off into the clouds" (52). The second person allows the author to make sense of his transitions among multiple identities, as the "you" figure shifts back and forth from his American self, to his ideal Thai self in Thong, to the reader, and to the "brown boys" who pop up in his dreams, where "you" names Graham Greene's local lover (126). In the end, when the narrator allows himself to reconnect with his American side, his self is imagined as the Western world reinhabiting his body with New York, Paris, and Los Angeles (207). But on the next page, the second person breaks into a direct call to the reader, the implied "second person": "You thought this was something in which you wouldn't have to participate. Thought this was a story you could just watch unravel" (208). The novel's intimacy, direct calls, erotic imagery, and invocations of historical violence continually implicate the reader into the pleasures of travel.

BROWN ILLEGIBILITY

> Illegibility, then, has been and remains, a reliable source for political autonomy.
>
> —James C. Scott, *Seeing Like a State*

Gold by the Inch's second-person narration envisions the self as made up of multiple identities, where "you" acts as a center tethering them together. "You were not born pretty or a bitch," the narrator thinks, "you are a piece of work" (19). The second person is "you" the voyeur, the central self, and the reader who watches the narrator as he transitions and moves about Thailand and Malaysia. Indeed, in both *Gold by the Inch* and *Leche*, the travelers' brown bodies permit access to new identities within Southeast Asia across a spectrum of race, class, gender, and sexuality. *Gold by the Inch* typifies transition in Southeast Asia on its first page, where it opens with a story of gender transition from Singapore's newspaper the *Straits Times*. The story details how Thai migrant factory workers in Singapore paint their fingernails red to "dupe murderous 'widow ghosts' who are hunting for husbands into thinking the men are really women" (3). These opening lines introduce a radically different form of gender transition than the individual (or liberal) transitions in the West, one that spotlights group-oriented transitions based on religion and superstition. These migrant workers are depicted not as enlightened, traveling subjects, but as foreign bodies who bring the transsexual with them as smuggled ghosts. The brown queer traveler thus discovers new gender and sexual norms that would be illegible if not impossible to imagine in the United States. At times these norms confuse the narrator: "I can see men touching other men here all the time. I see woman walking together hand-in-hand, but I don't know what union of our particular limbs mean" (21–22). At other times the norms seem imbricated within global capital. The narrator's cousin, Martina, works in a Penang microprocessor factory, where she informs him of *latah*, an affliction "in which subjects were unable to realize their own identity" and instead "could only imitate the actions of others, accompanied by cursing and swearing" (92). *Latah* becomes easily appropriated by the factory's management as a disciplinary instrument, to "make [the workers] do anything by simply feigning it." At the same time, the factory permits women to transition in ways previously unavailable. Martina points out that the women "try to copy men" by wearing "baggy jeans and basketball jerseys," and that "they forget their sex" (92).

If Thailand, Malaysia, and Singapore offer new modes of transition, they are modes unavailable to white tourists, who will only be identified as just that. Indeed, the narrator's brown skin acts as the everyday embodiment of these transitions, a "suit" whose color can be either dirt, shit, or gold. On a beach in Penang, Malaysia, the narrator lies "under the sun, hoping it will bake the answer into my skin. Bake my belonging. But it's not me that's lying back this afternoon, just my skin" (121). In the West, his skin and mixed heritage are enigmatic, and mark him as an ambiguous Other.

In describing the brownness of Latino/as in the United States, José Muñoz formulated brownness as "the ways in which minoritarian affect is always, no matter what its register, partially illegible" ("Feeling Brown, Feeling Down" 679). Brownness for Muñoz could not be white or black, but was always seen in relationship to them, complemented by a "self-knowing" that is "cognizant of the way in which it is not and can never be whiteness" (ibid., 680). Brownness thus begins like Chua's unnamed narrator—it rejects the promises of whiteness as the impossible ideal. For Muñoz, brownness becomes well defined only as it exists "in relation to an official 'national affect,'" where feelings and erotics are normatively white ("Feeling Brown" 68). Of course, this national affect is only the racial identities of the United States reimagined as a global imaginary. But in one of his lectures before his early death, Muñoz sought to expand brownness into a transnational context that described not just brown subjects in the

United States, but "the multitude," a "Brown Commons" of underprivileged and undervalued ("Brown Commons"). These novels of queer brown travel allow us to develop Muñoz's conceptions of brownness into the transpacific, where the "national affect" and white norm are displaced, scattered, and uncertain, and where brownness operates as a "commons" sensitive to other modes of affective belonging (feeling lower class, feeling female, feeling queer). These characters escape white normative modes of affect and erotics in America only to find themselves confronted with radically different sorts.

In *Gold by the Inch*, the unnamed narrator's desire to transition comes in part by his fixation on his grandmother, who in his mind was a figure of transition in dress and illegibility. He spends a month in Penang seeking his grandmother's story, a story that been hidden from him (70–71), knowing only that she was "the daughter of a Siamese father and a Nyonya mother" (134). He sees her as "the illegible Nonya," a matrix of various ethnicities: "Siamese, Teochew, Hokkien, Hakka, Acehnese, Tamil, Sinhalese, Portuguese" (134). She died during the Japanese Occupation amid rumors that she starved to death because members of the family withheld food from her, perhaps, as punishment for her sexual disobedience, "because she was having an affair with another man" (110). Seeking to rescue her from illegibility, the narrator discovers a picture of a woman who might be her at the Batu Ferringhi beachfront: "You could be any grandmother," he thinks. "There is a shape to your face ... that reminds me of my own face in the mirror" (109). He gravitates to the image because of its artful fakeness: the sparse jewelry, the difficult smile, and the replicated background. The image, however, is merely a postcard dressed in a wooden frame, mark(et)ing his grandmother as "a sales pitch, a hot tropical fantasy" (109). When the narrator visits his grandmother's grave, he again finds that "[t]here is no prepackage of identity or ethnic heritage left to possess. No folk tales passed on from Grandmother's knee" (135). Finally, at the end of his journey, he asks a medium to conjure his grandmother's spirit. The spirit manifests and recalls sitting for the photograph he found, only to chastise the narrator for finding it. She says that she burned all the photographs but kept one for herself, thinking that "if my children didn't know what I looked like, then I could be everywhere for them" (141). In adopting the same desire for categorization as the colonial powers before him, the narrator realizes that making her legible has only betrayed her own attempts to obscure her life story. Her decision not to be remembered in a photograph was her own effort to control how her identity was envisioned throughout the years, to remain unexposed, "torn in pieces that never form a whole reflection" (142). The narrator here finds not identity in his grandmother, but the power of illegibility, that without image, without identity, she can continue on through others, so that "I would never know where her body ended and mine began" (142).

As in *Gold by the Inch*, in *Leche* transnational travel offers a range of brown identities that Vicente was previously unfamiliar with, all of which are different types of being Filipino. In *Leche* it is 1991, and Vicente, now twenty-three and calling himself "Vince," has come to define himself as Filipino, that is, until he wins runner-up in the "Mr. Pogi" (cutie-pie) pageant and is given a free trip to the Philippines. In Hawai'i, Vince's identity as a Filipino came as a casual checkmark in the "Filipino" box, but in the Philippines he is seen as a *balik-bayan*, a returned Filipino from overseas. In *Out of This Struggle* (1981), one of the first books on Filipino/a history in Hawai'i, the authors mark the Hawaiian Filipino as having "no discontinuity between the history of the Philippines and the history of overseas Filipinos" (Teodoro x). While Hawaiians like Vince may imagine the Filipina/o as diasporic, he is met with frustration at every attempt to authenticate himself as Filipino. Because his family fled during the Marcos years, Vince is associated with a legacy of neocolonial brain drain and self-exile. In contrast, by 1991 the Filipina/o heroes had become the overseas Filipina/o workers, or OFWs, who work in foreign countries as maids and entertainers, and who send money back through the overseas remittance program. Indeed, Vince's slippery grasp of his Filipino identity overlaps with the white tourist's dream to identify with the locals in order to escape the guilt of first-world citizenship, even as he pursues sexual escapades with them. But Vince's desire for this identity also maps his own critical political alignment, which is antagonistic to American imperialism. The constant hailing from Filipino/a children around him as "Joe" and the compliments he receives as a beautiful film-ready mestizo only reaffirm the alienation he experiences from both his Americanness and his Filipinoness.[9] Vince's devalued Filipino body in Hawai'i suddenly holds value that reproduces the unearned capital of colonial subjectivity, and contradicts his queer desires. Though the locals see him as a rich mestizo or a "Joe," Vince could only afford to come to the Philippines by exploiting his body in a beauty competition, or as he calls it, his "great humiliation," which, like his sexual abuse as a child, was orchestrated by Edgar. Vince's frustration stresses the desperation of asserting a political identity that does not travel easily. What seems resistant in a context of neocolonial Hawai'i becomes, in the Philippines, a mark of colonialism itself.

    Leche is told in a postmodern pastiche style reminiscent of Jessica Hagedorn's *Dogeaters* and Linmark's previous novel, *Rolling the R's*. *Leche*'s variety of narrative voices—from tourist tips to academic treatises of Filipino/a culture—reflects different understandings of Filipino/a identity. In the main narrative the extended metaphor of the *balikbayan* box complicates notions of Filipinoness. The *balikbayan* box, a strengthened cardboard box that Filipino/a migrants have used for decades to send goods to the Philippines, becomes a symbol for the shifting Filipino/a identity as carrying colonial leftovers: "cans of Hormel corned beef, Libby's Vienna sausage, [and] Folgers" (2). Such foods, as Martin Manalansan has pointed out, are remnants of American colonization, like the overseas Filipina worker herself. The *balikbayan* box reappears throughout the novel in italicized vignettes that portray Vince's dreams, where "a procession of canned goods, led by a can of Libby's Vienna sausage, floats past him" (14). In a later dream, a *balikbayan* box falls from the sky, killing one of Vince's white ex-boyfriends. The migrancy of the *balikbayan* box into Vince's dreams foreshadows the associations of the box with death and haunting, when Esther, a domestic worker from Hawai'i who Vince meets on the airplane, is murdered along with her two children for the goods inside her *balikbayan* box. The *balikbayan* box, seen as an object that can "invite crime" (124), here upends the privilege associated with migrants to mark them as precarious workers vulnerable to the violence of migrancy.

The *balikbayan* box unsettles Vince's understanding of Filipinoness, which, like his education in *Rolling the R's*, reflects American colonial education. In *Rolling the R's*, Vince's understanding of American diversity came from the Japanese American teacher Miss Takata, and in *Leche*, Vince's notion of Filipinoness comes from a Filipino American Ethnic Studies professor at the University of Hawai'i, Bonifacio Dumpit. Professor Dumpit's academically certified definitions from *Decolonization for Beginners: A Filipino Glossary* appear strewn throughout the narrative in grayed text boxes. These snippets ascribe Filipinoness to cultural objects, as Dumpit lectures, "a Filipino is not a Filipino until he has climbed into a jeepney and paid his share of the ride" (152). Vince derisively renarrates Dumpit's authority as sacrosanct because Dumpit himself identifies as a true Filipino, and his authority goes unquestioned by the students who remain astonished "at how much truth was in Dumpit's definition of a Filipino" (152). In light of Dumpit's authority, they accept the jeepney as "One hundred percent certified Pinoy" (152). Against this discourse, Vince remembers jeepneys only as producing feelings of claustrophobia, of being "trapped inside a box reeking of perspiration," a feeling of confinement akin to Filipino identity itself as narrated by an authority like Dumpit (153). The tourist tips and historical narratives, in other words, call into question the rarely questioned authenticity of the source, and slowly these authorial sources give way to Vince's own "low culture" modes of representation: the postcards he collects and writes upon, the creative Taglish signs he notes down, and the stories he collects of fellow migrants. While the tourist tips sections are written in a form that homogenizes locals, the concluding tourist tip accounts for the multiple forms of Filipinoness: "Remember: in Manila, contradictions are always welcome, including—and especially—yours" (316).

In their rejection of American forms of brownness, the queer brown travelers of *Leche* and *Gold by the Inch* confront the limits of brownness as a common identity. Chua's narrator, seemingly free to transition within brownness, finds himself marked by his American accent and loss of the local languages. In Malaysia, he lacks Hokkien, a language of Chinese diasporics and Peranakans. His family in Georgetown "smile at my awkwardness, my stumbling through the language. As if they are looking at something inhabited by more than one self" (52). The narrator blames this lack on his father, "Ba," who forbade him "to speak anything but English" because "it was the key to everything in the world" (136).[10] The brown skin that gave him access is limited by his linguistic codes, which the narrator resents: "Every time I misunderstand a word I curse Ba. Curse him in the only Hokkien I have managed to retain" (137). Similarly, in *Leche*, language plays a crucial role in revealing the limits of transition. In Honolulu, Vince works for over a decade to gain recognition as something other than a Filipino worker or effeminate Asian American, losing his Tagalog and choosing to converse "in standard English with a minimal Filipino accent, so he could talk his way out of the plantation of stereotypes and discrimination" (104). Yet in the Philippines he must start from scratch, or be judged as a "brain drain" *balikbayan*. When, at the airport, an immigration officer tells Vince that his line "is for returning Filipinos only," Vince replies, "But I am a Filipino. I was born here.... It says so right there on my passport" (45). Vince attempts to conjure other symbols of recognition—his birthplace, his cultural identity ("In Hawaii, Filipinos don't see themselves as Americans"), and that the sign indicating the line does not say "nationals" (45). In response, the immigration officer corrects his Tagalog ("It's ba-LIK-bayan") and points out that the sampaguita flower, which decorates the sign, is the national flower, adding, "If you're a true Filipino, Mr. Vicente ... you'd know that" (45). From the airport on, Vince's odyssey becomes a series of misrecognitions, as his inability to explain himself in Tagalog or pidgin English marks his brownness as a reflection of whatever identity others cast upon him. Just outside of the airport, Vince is confused for a woman's dead son because "you have his face" (48), and later a woman in mourning confuses him for her deceased niece's pen pal (198). As in *Gold by the Inch*, the traveler's inability to linguistically and knowledgably perform as a local limits his transitions only to the transpacific identities that signify mobility (38).

QUEER VERSATILITY

For both Vince and Chua's nameless narrator, their failure to obtain the identity they want also enables them to become more versatile, and to change the very meaning of success (or "inner fulfillment") in a system fueled by pluralist categories. In *The Queer Art of Failure*, Judith Halberstam argues that success is too often seen through a heteronormative and capitalist lens that equates success to "reproductive maturity combined with wealth accumulation" (2). Within such a context, "failing, losing, forgetting ... [and] not knowing may in fact offer more creative, more cooperative, more surprising ways of being in the world" (ibid., 2–3). Failure, in other words, offers queer subjects the means to change the meaning of success. In the global imaginary that these characters resist, success depends upon being assimilated into a state multicultural order, but one rampant with nationalist, racist, heteronormative, and moralistic presumptions. Thus the travelers of *Leche* and *Gold by the Inch* do not merely fail at normative notions of success, but also fail at being normatively gay.

Vince's failure begins in *Rolling the R's* as a "closet case," where he appears unsatisfied and ashamed. In *Leche*, Vince's failures too take the form of sexual failures: he has been "dry" for six months; he attains sexual pleasure from zero potential partners in the narrative; and when he is offered sex from a Filipino actor for a mere $12, Vince refuses, admittedly more out of pride than principle (179). In *Gold by the Inch*, the unnamed narrator fails by falling in love with the prostitute, Thong, and sees their relationship as a transgression: "I think I'm breaking rules, taking a prostitute on a date during the day . . . I'm transgressing roles, crossing borders, that kind of thing" (21). His biggest fear is feeling like "just another client" (29), and he tries (and fails) to invent a relationship "outside laws, rules, and habits" (106). In both novels, failure comes from the refusal to "give in" to another's terms, rather than becoming receptive to another's will. Both characters lack sexual versatility, where, as Vince states in a conversation with Edgar, "'Versatile' is the euphemism for a big bottom" (31). As both characters refuse to take part in sex work as a client, they both dismiss the sexual versatility of "big bottoming" that stresses gay sex as an indicator of personal (and political) pride. Vince's anxieties around gay sex, particularly in not having enough of it, emerge in his unwillingness to be versatile himself, or as Tan Hoang Nguyen puts it in his book *A View from the Bottom*, in refusing to adopt the effeminate and "passive" positioning of the bottom, which would work to reveal "an inescapable exposure, vulnerability, and receptiveness in our reaching out to other people" (2). For Nguyen, positioning oneself as a receptive bottom opens affective and social bonds that are otherwise closed in the power-positioning of the top. As both characters in these novels project masculinity, their greatest anxiety is emasculation, a fear doubled by both their brownness and their queerness.

Vince's failure to be recognized as Filipino brings forth a cataclysmic self-shattering (rather than a self-fashioning) of his identity, forcing him to eventually let go of his identity and to take on a more receptive, versatile, and vulnerable position. His failure to gain recognition in the way he wants is complemented by the failure of his body to diarrhea (171), the failure to have a sustainable relationship (160), and the failure to have sex. It's not that Manila is hostile to him, but that he cannot help resisting Manila on its own terms, a "capital city of Vince's frustrations, daydreams, nightmares, reflections, and wonderment" (185). The act of travel produces failures, but also pleads with these characters to act receptivity, to own versatility, and to shatter identities that once seemed natural. Vince's "last straw" with Manila comes while buying batteries, as he writes, "I lost it. I started shouting. Two guards with guns had to escort me out" (187). Resigning himself to failure, Vince surrenders: he "doesn't qualify to be a Filipino," an identity that in Hawai'i was "never questioned" (249). For Vince being Filipino was a given, an easily checked-off box on "surveys, college grants, job applications, and affirmative action scholarship forms," but in the Philippines, "the ethnic ID Vince has been carrying around is no longer valid" (249). In his vulnerability he begins to consider alternative ways of being and performing, of claiming a more versatile attitude toward his own "ethnic ID": "He has to be cautious with what he says," he thinks, and to "choose his adjectives carefully" (262). Similarly, in *Gold by the Inch*, the narrator reflects on his own desire for Thong as a desire for a new "building" that is "not described by the word *home*," but that can "find[] expression in other forms" (106, italics in original). Unable to be part of romantic relationships dependent upon monetary transactions, the narrator plunges into the vast, illimitable world of travel, armed with a new versatility, as a subject who, as Viet Thanh Nguyen says, "refuses to be hailed by dominant ideology [but] can also refuse to be hailed by resistant ideology" (*Race and Resistance*, 157).

The versatility of bottoming reclaims individual agency, but also limits it to the categories and expectations of the "viewer"—in this case, the top. Similarly, transitive culture does not eliminate, disrupt, or transcend identity categories so much as act upon them. For Paulo Freire, too, transitive consciousness was not yet about full agency, but about the ability to detect categories and conduct movement from one recognizable sphere into another, an "agency" insofar as the individual assumes a versatile position. One then does not identify with being the bottom so much as understand the point of view of the bottom, a view that "allows for the switching and assumption of multiple positions, but not the transcendence of them," so that the "feminine" abdication of power provides a kind of agency that is "already socially structured by existing relations of power" (12). In *Leche* and *Gold by the Inch*, brown queer transition rests on recognizing (and at times surrendering) privileges: Americanness, and straight male performativity. Indeed, Vince's masculinity emerged as a Filipino migrant in Hawai'i, where his "brown boy" body had been dominated by orientalist representations of the Asian male body as effeminate, soft, or childlike. But in the Philippines, the "Filipino Nation" has rarely ever been imagined as queer or anti-imperial, but instead as "Tagalog, colonial, bourgeois, Catholic, lowland, macho" and "heterosexist" (Garcia 12). Indeed, as Bobby Benedicto has argued, the queer Filipino or the *bakla* is seen from many in the Philippines as a derisive, Western caricature of the brown boy that "conflates homosexuality, transvestism or effeminacy, and lower-class status," and belongs to a colonial American global imaginary (318). Indeed, as J. Neil C. Garcia has observed, queer literature in the Philippines does not follow the U.S. model of pursuing national inclusion, but rather rejects attempts to see "Filipino" as anything but militant and masculine.[11]

One could say the same for the presumed "bottom" position of Thai and Malaysian men, whose "hand holding" most Americans (including Chua's narrator) would presume as homoerotic. But it is only through recognizing his failures to understand "his own culture" that Chua's narrator too can recognize his privilege. In the end, after Thong identifies him as "an American darker than the rest" (201), the narrator admits the artificiality of the belonging he sought: "You will build your love on a lie. A lie so beautiful that you will forget it's pure fiction" (205). Here the second person shifts from the fantasy of the "beautiful lie" of identity to the "view" of versatility, pushing the reader to recognize the narrator's own privilege as crucial to understanding the region, and to recognize the self as one who can always leave: "You call the airline. There are still seats on the plane back to New York the next day. Flights to Hong Kong every few hours. Tokyo. Taipei. Dubai. Beirut. Berlin. Los Angeles. Flights to anywhere. The world is yours" (205). In accepting versatility, Chua's narrator accepts the performances of fetish and role-playing that Thong was able to provide on his own terms. In turn, the narrator no longer desires the reality behind the charade, and relinquishes the search for an ideal brown and queer belonging that cannot easily travel. What he has, instead, is the same quality that his missing grand-mother cherished—transition.

UNSETTLED ARRIVALS

> "But how have I managed to arrive, when I have not yet left?"
>
> —Italo Calvino[12]

Rather than live within Thong's "beautiful lie," Chua's narrator chooses to find solace in the arbitrariness of his own identity, now armed with a better under-standing of the limits and privileges of his own transitions. The narrator returns to global itinerancy, imagining globality not through a global imaginary built on tolerance, but through the transitions afforded by brown queer failure. The narrator begins to imagine himself within a state of nonarrival when he watches a white man with a U.S. military gym bag who could be "businessman, tour-ist, torturer, Mr. America" and "Miss Military Adviser" (191). The narrator witnesses the man punch a local Thai man on a motorbike for driving in his path. The narrator feels his "fury melt[] into a low-grade sorrow. I'm overcome with something. Some need. Maybe it's the need to feel pity for Miss Military Adviser. Or the need to fuck him senseless" (192). The white man sees the vari-ous encounters of travel as mere obstacles in his "straight" path. Rather than something "to be shared or transformed through presence," the new spaces offer only "a place to own," a place "ripe for development" (192). The narra-tor realizes, in seeing his own desires mirrored in the white American, that the global imaginary has disconnected him from his own body as a mere obstacle: "my body," he thinks, "the obstacle to its linear progression." Where arrival is often imagined as the continuous evolution of the self, a form of renewal or reinvention, it also always anticipates an ending, an ownership of a space or an identity that one can settle into.

I hope to end this chapter on queer brown travelers by exploring their intentions to never arrive. As in *Gold by the Inch*, in *Leche*, Vince's failure to meet the standards of recognition in Manila causes him to seek out a queer refuge elsewhere, what José Muñoz might call a queer utopic space where queerness operates as a collectivity aimed at imagining "futurity and hope" (*Cruising Utopia* 11). Much of this alternative futurity emerges only after recognizing the limits of heteronormative (and homonormative) attitudes toward success and freedom, an awareness that can be attained by failing to find success. Muñoz conceives of queer utopia not within a queer identity (like transgender, gay, lesbian, or the like), but as a "formation based on an economy of desire and desiring" that is "not yet here," but can be made present through "objects and moments that burn with anticipation and promise" (ibid., 26).[13]

Vince finds such a utopic queer space in Leche, a daytime museum and nighttime sex club often dismissed for having "too much mixed history" (282). The club contains a wide variety of patrons: Arabs, Filipina/o youth, Chinese Filipina/o matriarchs, transvestites, white expatriates, overseas workers from Tokyo (Japayukis), mestizo gay men, and prostitutes. As with Alfred Yuson's afterlife jungle café, Club Leche invokes a community characterized not by the hierarchy of identities outside of it, but by the interactions among its members, in this case, the fetish, role-play, and pleasures that coexist within the very real and complex colonial history. It is only within the walls of Leche, where Vince focuses on meeting his sexual desires, that he forgets himself (and his identity), and lets go of his own name, as he writes "Vicente" rather than "Vince" on the guest list: "Let it go, Vince," he thinks. "Just this once, let it go" (271). Queer utopia here is more than just a refusal to adapt to social norms, but entails a self-reflective virtuosity that discredits the standards for success expected outside of Leche's walls. It is a space where to fail to be recognized is to succeed in fulfilling sexual desires, and failure as a moral category means success in sex (what we might call "succsex"). Even the club's sexual identity is also in perpetual deferral, as Vince's Intramuros tour guide, Jonas, frequents the club with his ex-girlfriend because she was "turned on by watching guys make out" (264). Vicente asks, "Which makes you gay? Not gay? Semi-gay?" (264). Leche does not advertise a recognizable sexual identity, but is, as its transgender manager, Tita G, says, "the gatekeeper of secrets" (273).

Club Leche contains a "queer utopic memory" that narrates the Filipina/o past as producing well-fostered skills of adaptability and transition. Its history begins as a milk distribution center "started by wives of Spanish generals"; then in 1899 Americans transformed the building into an "orphanage for children whose parents were killed in the Philippine-American War," and then during the Japanese Occupation it was converted into a military headquarters until, finally, it was made into a brothel for Marcos's mistresses, before becoming a sex-club/film center/museum owned by a secret proprietor (probably Bino Boca, the novel's stand-in for the openly gay filmmaker Lino Brocka) (260). The shifting purposes of the building reflect the varied strategies of dealing with transforming power structures. Tita G's focus on the history of Leche as a route to "de-tour" the facility marks its history of mixture and transition, as it has adjusted to new regimes of power by collecting the leftovers from every regime change: the orphans, the prostitutes, the censored films and books. It performs not a nostalgic recollection of the past but a queer utopian memory that seeks to form "a utopia in the present" (Muñoz, *Cruising Utopia* 37). Leche thus functions as an everyday semblance where queer utopia is imagined as an alternative to the utopic global imaginary. Like Chua's focus on global brown queer failures, this utopic imagining is not built upon state recognition, but "better relations within the social that include better sex and more pleasure" (30). In rejecting the global imaginary of postracial success, both novels push us to imagine a brown queer global utopia of transitional "succsex," an ongoing and unfinished project that resigns itself to the failure of heteronormative and homonormative success. Their succsex is formed in the unexpected and illegible forms of desire, pleasure, and receptivity to others.

The de-tours of *Leche* and *Gold by the Inch* can be read as formative sojourns from an understanding of rigid brown identities to an understanding of the transitions that can occur by making oneself vulnerable. In their journeys, these travelers shift from masculinity to femininity, from power-top to receptive bottom, from prostitute to client, to seeing themselves within a rigid, essentialist identity to deploying recognizable signs of brownness, queerness, and language to "let go" of their former trappings. Both narrators realize that their desires to identify as Filipino, Malaysian, or Thai were not misplaced, but were effective means of controlling their identities only within an *American* context. Their failures were in presuming that the global imaginary of America was really global, rather than merely a form of pluralist governmentality masked as global. Thus their sense of their own brownness could not fit within Southeast Asian contexts, and they remained oblivious of the situation and expectations around them. Their mistake was in claiming an identity without foreknowledge or concern of the appropriate strategy and context.

Chua's narrator's journey ends with finding solace in the arbitrariness of his own identity. "Home," for the narrator, cannot exist in a place, but is the condition of exile, of traveling through different cultural forms and identities, where it is always "almost time to go" (208). Like *Leche*'s own Club Leche, these travelers are too products of imperial conflict, who have survived through methods of identity transition. Vince recognizes this when he reflects on the mixed "halo halo" nature of Leche, and realizes that Leche too resembles Filipinos, for "it is in their nature and dreams to roam, to seek a better life, to adapt and adopt another country" (306). As a communal space, Leche acts as a metaphor for transition as a cultural practice, as Vince says, "Maybe the ways of the West is just a switch that they can turn on and off whenever they like" (318). Rather than "Them, Filipinos, against me, American," Vicente understands that he, too, was engrained with this practice, "That I, too, can switch it on and off if I like" (319). This acceptance of "switching" as a mode that remakes the queer, the brown, and the traveler reinterprets cultural belonging as a property (a belonging) that says little about the material essence of an individual, but rather, is seen as a Nietzschean pure concept—a "conventional fiction for purposes of designation, mutual understanding, not explanation" (33).

CONCLUSION: GENRE

This chapter has focused on expressions of brown illegibility, queer versatility, and transpacific travel. Like those in chapter 3, the novels read here explore how such concepts have been conditioned by colonial views of violence and sexuality, where binaries like tolerant/intolerant, respected/deviant, and brown boy/white colonial have been informed largely by the presumption that Southeast Asia offers radically different form of sexualities than those found in the West (whether they are termed queer, perverse, sinful, or patriarchal). Similarly, both chapters have considered how transpacific Anglophone literature can dismantle these binaries through metafictional forms of satire and queer travel. In part III, I focus on how such aesthetic forms offer ways of imagining transitive cultures by operating within the confines of genre expectations and identities. If, for James C. Scott, legibility itself "is a condition of manipulation" (*Seeing Like a State* 183), then how does transpacific Anglophone literature represent the illegible, without quite conforming to the standards of legibility of pluralist governmentality? Responding to Scott's insight, Jack Halberstam calls on scholars to imagine how we can see "*unlike* a state," with "different aesthetic standards for ordering or disordering space, other modes of political engagement than those conjured by the liberal imagination" (*Queer Art of Failure* 10, italics in original). With this call in mind, I ask how genre forms of distance and speculation permit us to imagine an aesthetics of transition.

PART III GENRES

People of color have always theorized—but in forms quite different from the Western form of abstract logic. And I am inclined to say that our theorizing (and I intentionally use the verb and not the noun) is often in narrative forms, in the stories we create, in riddles and proverbs, in the play with language, because dynamic rather than fixed ideas seem more to our liking.
—Barbara Christian, "The Race for Theory"

I am trying to insist that "race" is really a code-word for "genre." Our issue is not the issue of "race." Our issue is the issue of the genre of "Man." It is this issue of the "genre" of "Man" that causes all the "–*isms*."
—Sylvia Wynter, "PROUD FLESH Inter/Views"

"It's illegal to yell 'Fire!' in a crowded theater, right?"
"It is."
"Well, I've whispered 'Racism' in a post-racial world."
—Paul Beatty, *The Sellout*

5 · MUTANT HYBRIDS SEEK THE GLOBAL UNCONSCIOUS
Cynicism, Chick-Lit, Ecstasy

In Hwee Hwee Tan's 2001 novel, *Mammon Inc.*, the young Oxford English graduate student Chiah Deng Gan leaves her literary career for the world's most successful multinational company, Mammon Inc., to become an adapter: a consultant who teaches up-and-coming business elites how to employ their racial and cultural signifiers to raise their social capital. Chiah Deng's training takes her through London, New York, and Singapore, as she learns techniques to turn symbols of "Chineseness," "Britishness," and "Americanness" into corporate emblems that symbolize belonging to the global elite. At the New York club Utopia, her trainer—a fellow employee of Mammon—suggests that to fit in, Chiah Deng should start "ranting about lower-income ethnic groups, like cab-drivers" (145). Chiah Deng invents an anecdote:

> So I step outside and see this mega protest against Police Brutality. All sorts of groups—African-Americans against Police Brutality, Arabs against Police Brutality, Mothers of Victims against Police Brutality. . . . And the people look at me like I'm *so* shallow, because they're out doing their bit to wrestle justice for humanity, while I'm out here shopping for beauty products. But I was like, *whatever*, just get out of my way. (148)

The story succeeds, and Chiah Deng discovers that among the "Generation Vexers" (Gen. Vexers), she finally "found where [she] belonged" (274). Her acceptance within the global elite is conditioned by her ability to distinguish herself from "lower-income ethnic groups," those "African-American" and "Arab" Others who are "doing their bit." Despite her discomfort with telling this story, the tale's performative effects bring her the feelings of belonging, identity, and comfort that she has been seeking all her life—feelings that her study of literature could never quite fulfill.

Tan's novel cynically exposes how the global imaginary, like many imagined communities, defines itself by contrasting global belonging with "ethnicized" Others. Chiah Deng's desire to transcend her ethnic position leads her to take a managerial role in "adapting" ethnic subjects, and her expertise in cultural mores only adds to her global self-depictions as a global subject. While her ability to adapt seems to reject pluralist categories by offering an identity beyond her ethnicity, the novel's cynical tone questions how her desire to distinguish herself from "real ethnics" actually reinforces reified conceptions of culture, as she and the Gen. Vexers must continually identify ethnic Others as foils to their own transcultural identities.

Like Chiah Deng, the queer Filipino protagonist of Han Ong's *Fixer Chao* (2001), William Paulinha, also transitions to new identities within the terms of the global imaginary. Yet as a migrant who has worked in the service sector all his life, Paulinha knows well that his desire for the global imaginary can act as an incentive to play the part of the ethnicized object of ridicule. Paulinha's desire is thus not to become part of the global imaginary, but to destroy those at the top of its hierarchy. Paulinha transitions from his queer Filipino identity to the more valued identity of a Chinese feng shui artist, "Master Chao," who claims to "fix" the condos of rich elites, while actually arranging their furniture to bring them bad luck. *Mammon Inc.* focuses on the global subject's desire to distinguish herself from ethnic Others; *Fixer Chao* considers the ethnic subject's ability to placate this desire by transitioning among ethnic identities in order to gain vengeance.

As the characters of *Mammon Inc.* and *Fixer Chao* unsettle identity categories, the texts themselves flip the typical themes of their own genre forms: *Fixer Chao* speaks like an ethnic autobiography, but follows a man who fakes Chinese ethnicity; *Mammon Inc.* uses the chick lit genre form to follow a Singaporean woman's market-driven identity transitions. Indeed, both texts disrupt the global imaginary by upending the traditional genre forms that their texts claim to inhabit. Unlike analyzing aesthetics, form, and technique, to speak of genre for a literary audience often invokes the ugly world of market-based distinctions, wherein sameness is reproduced for a capitalist culture industry (Adorno and Horkheimer), and literary merit is measured by how a text transcends identifications (or identity politics). Genre, however, provides a unique lens for discerning how a literary text participates within (rather than "above") established ideological categories to mediate between artistry and audience. Genres are politically and culturally active forms of categorization, which embody "values and ideological assumptions" depending on the audience and historical period (Chandler 4). They are a set of stylistic conventions that change over time, and are produced by the relationship between the audience and the producers. In turn, genres articulate cultural values, and are active in attempts to change those values through a "constant process of negotiation and change" (Buckingham 137). While some texts can be called "prototypical" in that they establish the conventions of a genre, most genre texts are instances of both repetition and difference.[1] Genres are always in process, and represent shifting categories that result from negotiation within new contexts.

The pressure for artists to work within genres shares similarities with the pressure to speak from within an established identity. Like identities, some genres are seen as empowering (ethnic literatures), transcendent (global literatures), or overpowering and privileged (British and American literature). Like identity politics, thinking in terms of genre can "ideologically close" a text or an individual, but can also increase communicative efficiency between the individual and their audience. Indeed, the desire to name a text's genre echoes the desire to name an individual's identity, as it marks the subject/text within a mode of recognition and legibility.[2] Genre overlaps with identity in revealing and disturbing ways—its reliance on market incorporation, its expression of certain conventions (read: ethnic traditions) that the audience then expects the genre-text to perform, and its power to dictate how we imagine the real world, especially in moments of confrontation with the unfamiliar, the uncertain, the unexpected. The uncertain future defines the genre of science fiction; the unexpected car chase characterizes Hollywood action films;[3] difficult encounters with racialized Otherness manifests in ethnic autobiographies. If genre is what we collectively name and create, and its forms are invoked in the way we perform the everyday, then it matters who "we" are. And if Asian American literature is thought to provide a gateway to an intimate Other, then what does this mean for readers who claim this very identity in how they imagine their own identity-genre? Put another way, what does it mean for those on the periphery of this imagined identity of Asian American (Southeast Asian, diasporic, queer), whose difference might radically disrupt the social realities that genres create?

I begin part III by asking how a focus on genre reveals the ways in which transpacific Anglophone literature disrupts the desire to belong within the global imaginary by revealing this global community's dependence upon consuming the products, knowledges, and intimate life-world of ethnicized Others. In using a cynical tone that distances the reader from notions of ethnic authenticity, both *Mammon Inc.* and *Fixer Chao* refocus on the ethnic service worker, who, like the authors themselves, employs performative modes of cultural expertise in order to satisfy, insult, and punish their audience. Both texts confront the global imaginary with a visceral sarcasm and cynicism that exposes the capitalist violence underlying its spiritualized global center. Tan's Chiah Deng employs the idealization of the global imaginary to further her career, while Ong's William Paulinha makes a small fortune by passing as a Chinese mystic. Their texts allow us to envision a twenty-first century where transitive cultural practices—the practice of managing and reinterpreting one's cultural identity—are common among a global migrant underclass, especially among service workers who are cast as ethnic subjects in order to bolster "global" communities. Both novels, written in 2001, depict the dyad of the global subject and the ethnic subject in a way that shifts our understanding of power from postcolonial models of East versus West and white versus Other to neocolonial models of "the global client" versus "the ethnic service worker."

Mammon Inc. and *Fixer Chao* both explore how the global imaginary functions within its centers of symbolic power, that is, within the "global cities" of New York, Singapore, and London. In chapter 3, I defined the global imaginary as a contemporary form of pluralist governmentality built upon the desire for belonging to a global community characterized by tolerance and multiculturalism. This imaginary is perceived as an autonomous culture of the globe that can be tracked in terms of one's mobility and participation within global cities. Unlike "globalization," which binds the effects of global capitalism to production, finance, and trade, the "global imaginary" spotlights desires, affect, and the longing to belong, which arise alongside and are constitutive of global capitalism. Since the rise of hybridity theory in the late 1990s and the new cosmopolitanism in the early 2000s, understandings of race that resist multiculturalist categories have increasingly valued a global imaginary built upon mobile, transcultural, and transnational subjects, who often have economic privilege. In contrast, the "transcultural" characters of these novels unsettle notions of authenticity by transitioning among ethnic types and rearranging their positions within the global city. The global imaginary thus seems less like an alternative to multiculturalist categories, and more like a way of sustaining pluralist governmentality by producing "neutral" global subjects as natural managers of ethnicized peoples. Here knowledge of ethnic history and cultural traditions, even one's own, can support one's position as a global subject.

Through their cynical styles, both novels depict the desire to belong to a global imaginary as containing a deep, spiritual function: in becoming a citizen of the world, the global subject reaches a level of enlightened understanding concerning how race and ethnicity function. This "enlightened" sense of the global imaginary raises questions about literature itself as a commodified object that produces ethnic understanding and expertise. As these novels show, the global subject relies heavily upon artistic representations of Others to keep their expertise intact. The cultural knowledges found in art, literature, and the performance of ethnic service workers all offer forms of global belonging, which together signal that the subject has surpassed ethnicized Others. In turn, the ethnicized subject fosters tactics and strategies for gaining recognition and pursuing his or her own interests (even if that interest is revenge). As genre texts, these novels refuse to meet the expectations cast upon them and deny the global reader's desire to affirm his or her superiority. Both texts thus speak to the ways in which literature itself has played an integral role in constituting the global imaginary, where racialized bodies are categorized along a spectrum of tolerance and financial success. It is in the ambiguity within this scale of ethnic categories that transition reemerges as a political tactic for disruption and revenge.

MAMMON INC. AND GENERATION VEXED

In *Mammon Inc.*, Chiah Deng's narrative voice characterizes her as a sarcastic young woman caught up in the joys of celebrity culture, fashion magazines, corporate hierarchies, cultural exchange, hairstyles, and *Star Wars*. Her vast expertise in consumer culture marks her as a subject laden with cultural power, a symbolic identity of "chic" and "in-the-know" that gives her value within global cities. Her knowledge of cultural mores and "coolness" makes her especially valued in the global imaginary, where knowledge of cultural practices can be used to produce niche market strategies. All the while her journey follows a plot sequence reminiscent of that of Doctor Faustus, of a genius caught between her cherished Jedi-like Oxford professors and the lure of "selling her soul" to belong with the global elite, which she compares to the devil, Chinese dragons, and the Dark Side. In the novel's cynical take on the global imaginary, cultural knowledge has become deprived of everything but symbolic value, and ethnicized subjects must be "adapted" into depoliticized commodities to be valued on the world stage.

Like her protagonist, Chiah Deng, the author Hwee Hwee Tan also grew up in a highly mobile environment. Tan first moved from Singapore to the Netherlands as an international student, and then to Oxford where she received her master's degree in English. With the publication of *Mammon Inc.*, Tan grew to become, as the scholar Robbie Goh has written, "the poster girl for the 'global' generation of Singapore writers," exemplifying "the split between the local and the global, traditionalism and progressivism, ethnographic and 'international' writing" (240). Like Suchen Christine Lim, Tan has also been highly critical of Singapore's economic obsessions that produced a "quantitative prism" for viewing arts and development (ibid.). Tan's critique is grounded in her life as a migrant for whom "identification with national narratives [become] increasingly difficult," and her migrations seem less like the economic migrations of Singaporean and Malaysian history than a series of departures and returns (Holden, "Interrogating Multiculturalism" 285). Her second novel, *Mammon Inc.*, was one of the first Singaporean novels to be published by Penguin and distributed internationally, and shows greater influence from global popular culture than from earlier generations of Singaporean writers.

Mammon Inc.'s narrator, Chiah Deng, similarly feels displaced between the Singapore city-state, which she sees as cultureless and materialistic, and England, which she fetishizes as a bastion of high culture. In the novel's beginning, Chiah Deng showcases her knowledge of Chinese and British identity, yet the British students at Oxford exclude her "not with a slur but with a compliment" (9). Frustrated by how her racial signifiers continue to mark her as a foreigner, she is presented with a way out of this dilemma when she receives a letter from Mammon Inc. inviting her to train to become an adapter, a professional with masterful knowledge of cultural performance who adapts the "professional elite: those executives who grew up in one country, were educated in another, and are now working in a third" (2). As an adapter, she would train elites how to transform their cultural signifiers—which might be marginal, intolerable, or associated with a particular type of labor class—into profitable symbols of global belonging.

The novel follows Chiah Deng as she passes three tests to become an adapter, beginning with her British flatmate, Steve, who must successfully navigate a Singaporean dinner; then her Singaporean sister, Chiah Chen, who must be accepted at an Oxford gathering; and finally, she must adapt herself into a "Generation Vexer," a member of the global elite who has "no fixed cultural identity" (143). The novel's language of "adaptation" conjures connotations of evolutionary adaptation, where a biological organ is modified in order to make it fitter for its changing environment. Chiah Deng's task to adapt "Global Nomads" ("bankers, diplomats, lawyers, and consultants") means that she must shift their behavior so that they are tolerated and respected in global cities (2). They must not only perform a tolerable cultural identity, but a consumable one. The corporatized language of adaptation sees identity as a strategic shift for new global environments, where only the wealthy can afford to adapt, while others remain stuck in their immobile cultural attitudes. To "adapt" is thus to "evolve" into members of a proper global elite who belong to a higher mode of civilization than their ethnicized counterparts. To become an adapter, for Chiah Deng, means her own inclusion in this elite, as she is promised "a lifetime of free global travel" (2).

Chiah Deng's place as an adapter-in-training catapults her from being a poor English graduate student to being a globe-trotting high-salaried global elite. As the only Asian in her college at Oxford, she is convinced that the university has only accepted her in order to legitimate itself as a diverse institution, marking her as "the token foreigner from a poor underdeveloped country" (168). Yet she continues to fetishize Oxford as "an ancient and immortal Atlantis," and her gaze seems typical of the colonized subject raised on literature praising the landscape of rural Britain rather than urban Singapore (108). But her gaze also seems updated for the globalized world, where the halls of Oxford represent the esoteric knowledge and traditional cultures that have been extinguished by capitalist industry. She feels "envious of the professors who sipped wine from the college's private vineyard in Tuscany" because they "seemed like sentinels who guarded secrets from an enchanted age" (108–109). Her desire for Oxford is a desire for an occidentalized Englishness, a desire to "become one of the wise guardians in this mysterious, magical wonderland" (109). Englishness here embodies a culturally rich past, which offers an alternative to Singapore's rapid development and materialism. Yet the racism Chiah Deng encounters forces her to admit that her love for Oxford was contributing to the structural role that the university played in cultivating "the feeling that they were the possessors of some sort of esoteric knowledge available only to the elite" (20).

Once she joins Mammon Inc., Chiah Deng views Oxford as an over-ethnicized space, and sees its elitist xenophobia as provincial rather than superior, as "out of date" and irrelevant in the new age of global cities. The adapters of Mammon contrast with the Oxford students, as they too are wealthy and highly educated, but are also mobile and racially diverse. Like Chiah Deng, the young "Gen. Vexers" "had no fixed identity," and felt "equally at home in a 212 or 0207 area code, equally well versed in the work of George Lucas and Joseph Campbell to be able to analyse the mythological archetypes in *Star Wars*" (143). As Chiah Deng meets more Gen. Vexers, she notes that "for the first time in my life it was normal not to be a native" (138). Unlike her acquaintances in Oxford and Singapore, the Gen. Vexers seem to have transcended national roots, and take pride in lacking a single racial or national history. Despite their differences in race, they all share in the ideals of the global imaginary: that they, unlike the vast majority of the world, have transcended monolithic ethnic types, so that even the whiteness of Oxford seems provincial.

Although the Gen. Vexers presume to have transcended the provincial racism of their homelands, they do not ignore race—rather they make it hypervisible, turn it into a farce so they can cynically distance themselves from it. To meet with these Gen. Vexers, Chiah Deng must get into New York's hottest club, Utopia, by using the "Glam-o-meter," a guide that helps determine whether or not an individual is high enough on "glam" to be considered a global elite. On the scale, being Asian can earn someone ten points, being "Black AND look[ing] hip-hop AND [being] in a group of < four" earns one thirty-five points (112), while being white *costs* ten points, and being "Black and look[ing] hip-hop and [being] in a group of > four" is minus fifty points, suggesting that groups of more than four black people might be construed as a gang (113). Though the Gen. Vexers consider race as an indicator of social value, they are more concerned with how that race is performed. The "Glam-o-meter"'s implicit concern is to weed out those "ethnicized" peoples who may breach decorum by revealing an "authentic" or "fixed" identity. To break these implicit conventions shows that one is subjected to one's cultural background rather than cynically distanced from it. Chiah Deng calls this convention "the Look," an ambiguous set of expectations that depends upon the culture one is performing, so that any racial construct is determined by one's clothing, hairstyle, friends, education, and knowledge of cultural coolness. Having "the Look," as Chiah Deng discovers, indicates that the wearer shares a common lack of culture but has also memorized a vast array of cultural knowledge. After weeks of shopping for the right clothes, toning her body at the gym, and waiting for the best hairstylist in New York, Chiah Deng finally has enough "glam" to enter the club, but once inside, she discovers her "Glam-o-meter" rating is actually higher than she thought, since "being Asian will be the new It thing during the summer" (141).

Chiah Deng's second task in adapter training is to enable her Singaporean sister, Chiah Chen, to blend in at Oxford, a task that requires creating a cynical distance between Chiah Chen and her given ethnic culture. When Chiah Chen praises Oxford, Chiah Deng writes in her notebook: *"Explain to sis that people come to Oxford not because it is a great academic institution . . . but because they want some of the elitist mystique to rub off on them"* (177, italics in original). She puts these notes into short guides for her sister that separate valued cultural signifiers from those that are lower class and crude. Her "Swank Up Your Speech" guide suggests that "anything you say in Latin [or French] will make you sound *cheem*" (Singaporean slang for "cosmopolitan obscure"). Her guides use cultural signifiers while ignoring their historical meanings, often giving no definition for terms, but simply stating "You don't have to understand . . . you just need to know how to insert it in your conversation" (184). In her final test, Chiah Deng attempts to adapt her Oxford flatmate Steve to fit in with Singaporean Chinese, which similarly requires a cynical assessment of Singapore culture. She makes a note to *"replace Steve's enthusiasm for walking around museums of fine art with a passion for strolling through the air-conditioned corridors of food courts and shopping malls"* (242, italics in original). Despite Chiah Deng's guidance, both her sister and Steve fail their tests, as both of them seem too at home in their given communities. Unlike the mobile and transcultural Chiah Deng, both characters are unable to find value in "overcoming" their respective national identities.

When the novel ends, Draco Sidious, the head of Mammon Inc., reveals that Chiah Deng's trials to adapt Steve and her sister were never meant to succeed, but were designed to expose her own lack of belonging in either national culture: "You could never be totally Singaporean, since you were so ashamed of their lack of culture and sophistication. . . . And you knew that you could never belong to England, because they would never accept someone as Chinese as you" (274). Chiah Deng's desire for the global imaginary here reveals itself as a response to the racism of the English and the lack of culture that she perceives in materialist Singapore. She thus chooses to become a Gen. Vexer and to pursue a career deploying her knowledge of cultural performance for the world's largest company. Because she understands racial categories as socially constructed, Chiah Deng is able to spend her life managing and teaching wealthy clients how to take advantage of these racial assumptions. Her choice is both cynical and pragmatic, as she assumes the commodification of cultural forms, and employs her knowledge of them to game the global elite.

COSMOPOLITAN/MULTICULTURALIST/GLOBAL

As a meditation on the overlapping of consumerism and cultural knowledge in Singapore, London, and New York, Tan's *Mammon Inc.* explores the global imaginary as a historical reiteration of colonial pluralism, which contained, for J. S. Furnivall, "a lack of a common social will," since every group had different values and gods. This social "lack" monetized cultural exchanges and fragmented social demand so that economic production became the only unifying focus (450). The only common values, for Furnivall, were in generating more wealth: "In a plural society," Furnivall wrote, "the only common deity is Mammon," the biblical deity of greed (308). As Sumit K. Mandal points out, since Singapore has turned from an industrialized economy toward a service and intellectual economy, the pluralist social structure has operated like a global, cultural supermarket, with the nation-state, "Singapore Inc.," as the "modern holding company" ("Boundaries and Beyond" 179). Singapore Inc. was tasked only with generating wealth, and to "incessantly reinvent itself ... to retain its competitive edge" (ibid.). The pluralist discourse that emerged saw Singapore's diverse cultural groups as signifiers of commodified difference, making them easier to conscript into structural hierarchies, and allowing the state to maintain ideological dominance so long as the nation's economic success continued. Through its cynical outlook, Tan's *Mammon Inc.* casts attention on how such commodified difference garners overseas investment and intellectual capital through forms of global inclusivity.[4] Rather than have identities dominated by a national narrative, which places some as diasporic and others as local, cultural meanings are provided through a neo-racist global imaginary that attracts ethnicized subjects through the unreachable desire to fully belong within a global community. Chiah Deng's sister and flatmate Steve are partial products of this reified culture, who take seriously their identities as Chinese Singaporean and British, while Chiah Deng's transcultural attitude sees them as monocultured. Her desire to be global thus does not deny or upset the reified cultures of pluralist governmentality, despite her awareness of their construction.

Imbricated with transnational capitalism and the cosmopolitan city, the global imaginary produces normative members who fully belong by being "ethnic free," and others who are members but are not "proper subjects," or who are "too ethnic," and have yet to be adapted (or "evolve"). Here the global imaginary overlaps with theories of cosmopolitanism, which often divorce the cosmopolitan attitude from its structural role as identifying "ethnic" subjects, who seem stuck in a provincial behavior that borders on intolerance. In Taylor Astra's 2009 film *Examined Life*, Kwame Anthony Appiah discusses cosmopolitanism while walking serenely through airport gates, standing on escalators, and gazing at planes landing. He reflects that "within a few minutes you'll have passed more people than our remote ancestors will have passed in their entire lives." The airport invokes the gaze of a busy nomad within a discourse of mutual under-standing and tolerance through globalized infrastructure. Yet Appiah's invocation of cosmopolitanism as a cohesive group ethics smuggles in a hierarchy that val-ues cosmopolitan subjects over what Appiah, in his book *Cosmopolitanism*, calls "counter-cosmopolitans," those hopelessly ethnic subjects for whom "universal-ism issues in uniformity" rather than diversity (144). If the cosmopolitan accepts that there must be many different ways of living, the counter-cosmopolitan prac-tices a "universalism without toleration." This counter-cosmopolitan is mono-cultural, unable to overcome his or her presumably "authentic" culture, and is marked as "intolerant" in a world where tolerance characterizes the elite.[5]

Appiah's take on cosmopolitanism insists on "Othering" the ethnic subject. Bruce Robbins's early work on cosmopolitanism attempts to downplay the ide-alization of a cosmopolitan class. He admits that cosmopolitanism can invoke a globe-trotting prestige, but insists that it can also stress "the more general sense of 'belonging' to more parts of the world than one's nation" (173). Here the trans-cultural subject is extended to anyone who can be educated out of provincial atti-tudes. Meanwhile, marginalized Others remain absent from Robbins's theory, as many "transcultural" subjects may have never "belonged" in their own nation-state in the first place. Indeed, this "positive" sense of cosmopolitanism pre-sumes a cosmopolitan subject who can choose to belong to "one's own nation," which discounts those who seem exiled or nationless, such as refugees, migrant workers, diasporic subjects, and minorities, who seek to belong within nations that refuse them. Robbins goes on to note that cosmopolitanism can provide a "normative edge" that adds to "the inclusiveness and diversity of multicultural-ism" (183).[6] Robbins's attempts to salvage cosmopolitanism means placing it as an ideal outcome of multiculturalist dominance. Yet the multicultural education he defends, especially when pursued in the Global South, dangerously reiterates the history of imperial education onto subordinate countries, where the figure of the tolerant and diplomatic cosmopolitan stands in for the civilized and religious colonial. If cosmopolitanism, in this construct, figures as the result or the "unre-alizable ideal" of multiculturalist education, then those who consume symbols of cosmopolitan belonging—Tan's "Global Nomads"—represent the *realized* ideal. They are products of an intense multicultural education who find that their transcultural attitudes can be repackaged and commodified to place themselves at the top of a hierarchy construed as the only form of global belonging.

In his book *Inhuman Conditions*, Pheng Cheah questions the implicit desires and exclusions of such cosmopolitan ideas, tracing the cosmopolitan tendency to become "entwined with a normative concept of culture as the human power of transcendence" (5). For Cheah, cosmopolitanism can never be separated from the desire that buttresses its structural role: the desire to transcend or escape from one's "given culture," as Cheah calls it, to a cosmopolitan identity that views its community as "the world," but can only see that world through particular consumerist optics and capitalist networks. As an imagined community, cosmopolitanism results not from grand theories of diversity so much as "the development of forces of production on a global scale" (28). Through this materialist understanding, Cheah invokes two distinct layers: the *high cosmopolitanism* of middle- to upper-class migrants (what Aihwa Ong calls those with "flexible citizenship"), and the *low cosmopolitanism* of lower-class migrants often employed in service work, who must adopt a cosmopolitan ethics as a strategy to better serve clients (199). Cheah illustrates these two types through the figures of the traveling "liberal middle-class professional woman" and the "docile foreign domestic worker" (202), who is thought to possess "a form of culture that the local population generally regards as annoying babble" (199). For the liberal middle-class professional, cosmopolitan networks provide a sense of transcendence, an "emotional reward of striving toward a higher goal that transcends mere economic self-interest" (203). Even as cosmopolitanism is produced by the infrastructure of global capital, it appears to grant transcendence from one's given culture, making it an ideal that exists as its own raison d'être. In contrast, "low cosmopolitan" foreign domestic workers see "global culture" as the means to financial remuneration, and do not seek to transcend their "given culture" so much as their "given conditions."

Cheah's analysis of "high" and "low" cosmopolitanism allows us to develop the global imaginary as similarly structured with "high" and "low" subjects, depending on their tolerance, cultural knowledge, and economic success, but also to understand how those "high" global subjects are produced through the affects provided by ethnicized Others, particularly their affective labor.[7] Affective labor finds value in an immaterial and immeasurable substance (affect), meshing racial identities with an affective economy that marks some populations as valuable and others as without value, or as "superexploitable or exhaustible unto death" (Clough 25). The trend of migrant affective labor coming out of the Global South, especially from Southeast Asia, marks the service worker as the ethnicized subject par excellence, whose labor remains a necessary condition for migrancy, and therefore compels her to reiterate ethnicity as a trained attribute. The global imaginary extends Cheah's materialist view of cosmopolitanism by accounting for the particularly "nonethnic" spaces carved out within the global, which follow from histories of colonial powers disguising themselves as "umpires" managing the divisive interests of ethnic communities. Hiding within the global imaginary are migrants who transition among recognizable multiculturalist identities, but who are presumed to be ethnic or monocultural. If the global imaginary values attributes such as "multicultural, reasonable, feminist, and law-abiding" and stigmatizes attributes such as "monocultural, irrational, regressive, patriarchal, or criminal," then those who transition are marked as the latter (Melamed, "Spirit of Neoliberalism" 87). Indeed, the claim that cosmopolitanism enables an appreciation for other cultures can be dangerously close to treating "each local culture the way the colonizer treats colonized people—as "natives" whose mores are to be carefully studied and "respected" (Žižek, "Multiculturalism" 44). For Chiah Deng, the global imaginary resembles a colonial structure wherein she can occupy its most privileged managerial position.

CHICK LIT AND THE CYNICAL GLOBE TROTTER

> "in a plural society... the only common deity is Mammon"
> —J. S. Furnivall, *Colonial Policy and Practice*

Hwee Hwee Tan's *Mammon Inc.* disrupts the desire for the global imaginary both through Chiah Deng's narrative on becoming a Gen. Vexer, and through its genre as an Asian chick lit novel, which gives the novel a first-person cynical tone that expresses "self-distancing irony, satiric orientation, and sharp self-parody" (Wee 200). The novel is one of the first from Singapore to use the chick lit style, which has risen to popularity with the publication of Kevin Kwan's *Crazy Rich Asians* (2013) and its sequel, *China Rich Girlfriend* (2015), which both similarly aggrandize and satirize the excess wealth and corporate attitudes of Singapore's elite.[8] In taking a cynical distance from ethnic identities, such satirical forms allow us to consider the multiple positions and transitions that such "distance" can allow. Chick lit emerged in the late 1990s as a genre that examined the nature of commodity culture in which young women were primary targets for the marketing of consumer goods (Mazza and DeShell). The name "chick lit" came from two anthologies whose postfeminist authors invoked "chick lit" as an ironic title aimed at those who would devalue its authors because of their gender and readership (ibid.). The genre's prototypical text, Helen Fielding's 1996 book *Bridget Jones's Diary*, was taken from a column Fielding wrote criticizing the way women obsessed over consumer culture and women's magazines. Her book defined chick lit in spotlighting a humorous, single, urban, confessional narrator who is well versed in pop culture, obsessed with fashion and shopping, and constantly searching for romantic encounters.

Though chick lit authors of the 1990s often saw their work as a parody of female consumerism, their books have continued to be read as encouraging a consumerist and apolitical female identity. Some scholars have pointed to the limits of chick lit as consumer-oriented rather than politically oriented, finding that the brazen attitude and sexual freedom of chick lit narrators expresses "a freedom predicated on desire rather than politics" that conflates "feminism and consumption" (Ommundsen 108). Despite the obvious counterargument that desire and sex are often political acts, we can also understand chick lit outside the United States as parodying the consumerist female voice within a global imaginary that has commodified race and ethnicity. In countries like Singapore, China, and India, chick lit has risen to challenge portrayals of passive and exotic third world women, to instead portray "young women from non-Western countries as denizens of a global, cosmopolitan modernity" (ibid., 110). In a 2002 book review, Hwee Hwee Tan revealed that *Mammon Inc.* was written in the chick lit genre to contrast with Chinese novels that portrayed Chinese women as people who were "regularly beaten with belt buckles and ha[d] to wrestle with big issues like the struggle for political liberty and the freedom to love" ("Ginger Tale" 66). For Tan, the major issues of the globe-trotting Singaporean "chick" was "how to lose weight," and how to wrestle with livelihoods that were "more like Bridget Jones than Madame Mao" (66). As Western audiences have been infatuated with Asian heroines who suffer under patriarchies and intolerant attitudes, chick lit has offered a useful genre for replacing these stereotypes. As Eddie Tay has observed, Tan's genre appropriation is strategic in distinguishing "the new Asian" from "Asians [who] had a reputation from the smell and mess of Chinatown" (*Colony, Nation, and Globalisation* 125).

Mammon Inc.'s own chick lit style comes through in the presentation of global cities as "late capitalist urban jungle[s]" with "temptations and dangers ... in store for young single women worldwide" (110). Chiah Deng navigates this urban jungle armed with the knowledge of coolness and expected cultural norms. Symbols from *Star Wars*, Lara Croft, and "the opening scenes from *Hawaii Five-O*" make frequent appearances, borrowing from the lore of each cultural reference, while other references seem to ridicule political figures, as names like "Hoover" become synonymous with great loss or failure. The style reflects a woman able to navigate through pop culture and consumer products, while at the same time, it seems reliant upon them to express ethical dilemmas. Her decision to join the global elite then can be seen as a logical result of her cynical and materialist outlook. For Slavoj Žižek, such cynicism, while critical and distancing, can work to maintain existing power structures, as it refuses to take the ruling ideology seriously, but continues "following an illusion" (*Sublime Object* 28). While the global imaginary may be founded upon false assumptions, the cynical global subject still has too much invested in this hierarchy, and thus adapts to it while also distancing herself from the system of power that provides her privilege. Cynical reason becomes a "paradox of an enlightened false consciousness" (ibid. 29), as it seeks to negate the authenticity of pluralist governmentality while still deriving material success from it. Chiah Deng's global identity depends on the meanings of an ideology that she knows to be false, yet she takes advantage of others' beliefs in it. Rather than resist the global imaginary, knowledge of its falseness is in fact the very condition that enables her to maintain her belonging within it. Tan's appropriation thus explores chick lit as a genre wherein consumption defines membership in a transnational elite, yet the objects being consumed are not mere commodities, but ethnicized Others themselves, made tolerable and thus consumable (Melamed, "Reading Tehran" 98).

Tan's novel appropriates chick lit's cynical tone ultimately to critique the desire for global belonging, which can be seen in its Faustian plot, where the novel provides an Asia-centered update of Marlowe's and Goethe's takes on the legend of Doctor Faustus. *Mammon Inc.*, however, replaces the devil with the multinational corporation, Mammon, and sees Chiah Deng's own desire to belong to a global imaginary as her fall from grace. Mammon's reputation, from the novel's beginning, is of an all-consuming deity, a company that "owns everything," so that "[w]hether you were in London, Singapore or New York, you would find people in mcJeans drinking mcLite beer while talking about the latest mcMovie" (4). The comparison of Mammon with the devil appears in jokes, as an allegory for "corporate hell," and in biblical illusions, as Mammon Inc.'s logo depicts "the red dragon," which could be the "sign of Satan" from the Book of Revelations (31). The company's absolute dominance, coupled with its connection with Satan, adds a mythical element to the realist style of chick lit that unsettles the reader's attempts to identify with Chiah Deng's cynicism. Indeed, rather than consolidate the identity of the individual consumer woman of color, her journey into Mammon's "corporate hell" can be read as a Faustian fall, a damnation to the hollow world of the global imaginary. In this condemnation of its main character, Tan's appropriation of chick lit can be seen as a break from its "postfeminist" investments toward a transnational feminist (and anti-imperial) critique of global capital. When we interpret Chiah Deng less as a "material girl" and more as a version of Doctor Faustus, we see her desire for the global imaginary as committing the sin of pride, which, in biblical terms, comes before the fall.[9]

GLOBAL ECSTASY

Mammon Inc.'s Faustian plot of sin and damnation is enhanced with moral and religious dimension when the chick lit form is disrupted stylistically by sections where Chiah Deng is pulled from her cynicism and into experiences of religious ecstasy. These ruptures seem to reflect Hwee Hwee Tan's own lifestyle as both a mobile cosmopolitan and an evangelical Christian, two identities that have become a common coupling in countries like South Korea, China, and Singapore, where evangelical Christians make up a significant portion of the English-speaking professional class.[10] Tan herself has been a figure in the evangelical movement, and after the publication of *Mammon Inc.*, she devoted herself to writing nonfiction Christian works, where religion functions as an ideal alternative to the materialism of the Singapore lifestyle. Her Christian blog, as she states, is "full of divinely-inspired insights that will help readers on their spiritual walk with God" ("Launch"). She describes her religious experience through prayer, feeling "a palpable energy" ("Peace"), and explains how her faith has been strengthened by her dire circumstances, comparing herself to friends who drive "big, expensive cars and live[ ] in big houses and costly condominiums" ("Comparing"). For Tan, these friends have the "Singapore dream" of the "Five Cs": Cash, Car, Credit Card, Condominium, and Country Club membership, while she has obtained little, but has been "called by God." Opposed to the materialism of the "Singaporean dream," Tan's material poverty means that she "get[s] greater spiritual attention in the body of Christ."

Tan's religious beliefs are visible in *Mammon Inc.*, and add a spiritual dimension to the longing for global subjectivity that discourses of globalization and cosmopolitanism can only hint at. Chiah Deng's cynical narration is interrupted by forms of ecstasy, as she experiences the global through ecstatic experiences that, at first, conflict with her desire for global belonging. Yet these experiences are later reinterpreted by Mammon Inc. as experiential proof of the global imaginary's freedom from ethnicity. Ecstasy brought about through encounters with the "global" or "universal" depicts the global subject as not merely superior, but as transcendental, in that ecstatic experiences imply a position of enlightened superiority over those who have not yet experienced it. Chiah Deng's multiple ecstatic experiences trace instances of globality and world travel by encountering the "the global" within multiple global imaginaries, each offering incentives of ethnic escape and global belonging.[11]

Chiah Deng first encounters ecstasy with her ex-boyfriend, Tock Seng, who has never felt at home in Singapore due to his whiteness. She describes Seng as an angelic figure, calling him "the most beautiful creature I had ever seen," with "curly hair" that made him "look like the cherubs in paintings stored in museums far away in the West" (43). The racist overtones seem inescapable in her religious analogy, as she calls "[a]ll the other Singaporean boys ... brown, skinny monkeys ... screeching racial abuse at him while his pearl-grey eyes welled with tears" (43). Like her depiction of Oxford, her description of a white male as angelic seems driven by a fetish for Britishness, and her attempt to cast racial prejudice as barbaric employs simian racist diction to divide the "civilized" tolerance of the global imaginary from the "barbaric" prejudices of ethnicized Others. After traveling the globe, Seng persuades her to join him at the top of the Statue of Liberty, which only disappoints and frustrates her, until, on the ferry back, the sunset gives her an ecstatic experience: "Everything suddenly flared into an incandescent glory. Never had I ever seen such a sight, the perfect fusion between artifice and nature.... Tongues of fire, Pentecostal, like the spirit descending on the apostles.... it was a perfect marriage between the man-made and God-created" (95). The ecstatic experience seems to have no origin, but forms in the perfect balance of the rocking waves, the descending sun, and Chiah Deng's own heartbeat, which has been stressed by the long climb up the Statue of Liberty. The experience comes from a space of pure transit, the emotional, ecstatic pay-off to the trials of never fitting in. This ecstatic moment contrasts her cynical narration, as her ecstasy is represented through direct and intimate religious imagery, providing an insight into her "hybrid soul" that gives the reader "a kind of poetics of the global unconscious" (R. Goh 254–255). As Chiah Deng puts it, she and Seng "are freaks, mutant hybrids of East and West like transcultural X-men" (53). Lost without a recognizable cultural community, these "mutant hybrids" seek out the elusive global unconscious, and like the "X-men," the thing that makes them strange (their "powers" or "talents") is the very thing that gives them domain over others.

Chiah Deng's second ecstatic experience encounters a different global imaginary, one found in spiritual fetish rather than in pure transit. It comes from her graduate school advisor, Professor Ad-oy ("Yoda" spelled backward), who blends the elitism of the university with the transcendent Christian faith. She meets Ad-oy in Dagobah Hall (20), where he lives in Coruscant Tower (21), two place-names taken directly out of *Star Wars* iconography of the Light Side of the Force. In blending geek culture with chick lit, the novel's Faustian narrative posits Ad-oy as the universal, spiritual power. Indeed, Chiah Deng finds Ad-oy sitting beneath "an African crucifix," serving his own special blend of tea made from "Polynesian Kava Kava, Roobios, Dong Quai, and Black Cohosh from the Native Americans" (22). Where Seng's experiences seem fleeting and reliant on the power of transit, Ad-oy's is a mystic, spiritual conglomeration of world religions and cultures that can "bind the galaxy together" ("Star Wars"). Ad-oy persuades Chiah Deng to become his research assistant by teaching her to pray "as the mystics did" (201), which gives her another ecstatic experience. First she sees a vision of Christ crying on the cross (206), and then: "My soul blazed with the fiery seraphim, singing and rejoicing, consumed by the love of Christ, bursting like a sweet red flame" (207). Chiah Deng's experience in Dagobah Hall, like Luke Skywalker's on the planet of the same name, throws her in "a wave of ecstasy ... like I had finally attained Jedi Knight mastery of the Force" (208). Like the ecstatic experience on the New York ferry, Tan's language ruptures the novel's chick lit genre to pull ecstatic feelings from a grab-bag of references, using allusions that are biblical and natural as well as consumerist and pop cultural. Appearing as narrative ruptures, these ecstatic moments expose the narrator's sincere interest in discovering a universalizing and transcendent "Force."

In popular chick lit like *Bridget Jones* and *Sex and the City*, the cynical distance obtained by an empowered professional woman is ultimately shattered by the desire for a family. The "chick" identity thus continues to operate as a temporary space until reaching a domestic lifestyle. Yet Chiah Deng's desire for global belonging resurrects a different sort of domesticity, where material wealth must overlap with experiences of religious ecstasy and global community. While Tock Seng's travel and Ad-oy's Christianity are individualizing and financially ruinous, Mammon's Gen. Vexers represent a wealthy community for the transcultural subject, "a tribe to belong to" (274). When she meets Draco Sidious, head of Mammon, he appears draped "in Chinese Imperial robes" with a voice that sounds like "the mechanical voice you hear on PA systems in airports and shopping malls" (59). The voice is ethnically "neutral," "hint-free with regards to locale," and "exudes professionalism." He introduces her to six adapters, each representative of global cultural identity: an African, a Western European, a Scandinavian, an Asian, a Hispanic, and Draco Sidious himself, the empty universal subject, chief over them all.

To convince Chiah Deng to join Mammon, the adapters show her images of global spaces: the "Piazza della Signoria," the "Beijing opera house," and others, all of which recall an Eden where she could become "a cosmopolitan jet-setter" (71). Finally, Chiah Deng has her last ecstatic experience when Sidious reveals a New York skyline where "everything in the world was on this island, all its glory and grim wrapped in a cloud of fiery pale chemicals" (277). Standing in for "the world," New York City makes the workers below seem "like subway rats," (278). In its reiteration of Doctor Faustus, Chiah Deng inevitably chooses the demonic Mammon, a choice that reproduces the inequalities of pluralist governmentality, but offers her belonging within the elite global imaginary, with people who look like her "if I'd received a million-dollar salary upgrade" (62).

FIXER CHAO AND THE FILIPINA/O OVERSEAS WORKER

In *Mammon Inc.*, years of transitioning among multiculturalist identities leads the protagonist to desire a stable identity and community, which she finds in the global elite. In the end, Chiah Deng's chick lit narrative style seems cynical toward everything but her own transcendence, as she continues to contrast herself with ethnicized others like her flatmate Steve and her sister Chiah Chen. In Han Ong's 2001 novel *Fixer Chao*, the division between the global subject and ethnicized Others manifests in the relationship between the global client and the ethnic service worker. Lower-class Filipino/a migrants offer upper-class global subjects—like Chiah Deng—cultural access to an authentic, ethnic subjectivity, one that seems paradoxically opposed to the very global capitalist forces that produced the service relationship. Migrant service workers are incentivized by the global imaginary, which hails them not with an Althusserian interpellation, but with a spiritual sort of hail—the hail of ecstasy, of communion with a global unconscious. Unlike *Mammon Inc.*, *Fixer Chao* depicts the global imaginary from the point of view of the service labor class whose survival in the global city relies heavily upon their performances of accent, education, and religion. Ong's novel, written in a cynical first-person narrative, explores global belonging beyond a hierarchical, developmental structure from "monocultural" to "multicultural" or from "low" to "high," but rather as a relationship generated through affective labor.

Born in the Philippines to a Chinese Philippine family, Han Ong migrated with his family to Los Angeles's Koreatown as a teenager where he gained recognition as a young playwright and earned a grant from the National Endowment of the Arts. After writing dozens of plays, some as collaborations with writers such as Jessica Hagedorn, Ong became one of the youngest people to receive the MacArthur "genius" grant in 1997. Since then Ong has devoted himself to writing novels that tend to be about outsiders, like Ong himself, who are "Othered" by being queer, migrant, lower class, or of mixed racial origins. His novels cast alienation at the center of migrancy, as his characters seek cohesive new identities against a white citizen-subjectivity. As with Tan's use of chick lit, Ong's cynical style can be seen as speaking back to the text's genre, in this case, the ethnic autobiography.[12] As scholars such as Betsy Huang, Viet Thanh Nguyen, Jodi Melamed, Tina Chen, and Jeffrey Partridge have pointed out, Asian American literature is often read within an "autobiographic imperative" that sees marginalized voices as always within a form of lifewriting (Huang, *Contesting Genres* 7). In turn, such texts are marketed as authentic gateways to a homogenized ethnic subject.[13] Ethnic autobiography is often read as autoethnography, which is invested in telling white audiences "something about another culture in a truthful manner" (P. Lai 56). This slide from autobiography and memoir to autoethnographic expectations makes minority subjects legible to a normative mainstream.

Though memoirs like Maxine Hong Kingston's *The Woman Warrior* were first received as experimental mixed-genre publications, today novels that blend autobiography, memoir, and autoethnography have become easily incorporated into postracial notions of immigrant progress. In response, scholars like Stephen Hong Sohn have pushed for "reading practices that move away from an autobiographical or autoethnographic impulse attuned to authorial ancestry" (*Racial Asymmetries* 3), as such reading practices can reinforce the ghettoization of ethnic literature and restrict race narratives to particular times, histories, and spaces that seem to "illuminate only Asian American social contexts" (ibid., 209). As Jodi Melamed has argued, ethnic novels have a history of being deployed to defend state multiculturalisms, to depoliticize radical antiracisms, and to mark the United States as an exceptional imperial power. As the U.S. state attempted to depict itself as the pluralist power during the Cold War, "positive" minority representations remade U.S. culture so that successfully integrated minorities "would be seen as culturally embodying the U.S. nation," and attest to "the racially inclusive nature of U.S. citizenship" (*Represent and Destroy* 22). But ethnic literatures were tricky in this respect, as many challenged narratives of the United States as the antiracist savior of the free world, especially in the late 1960s and early 1970s, during the emergence of multiple ethnic nationalisms (Chicano/as, Asian Americans, Native Americans). And with the appearance of new migrant groups after both the 1965 Immigration Act and the Vietnam War, multiculturalism in the 1980s shifted to providing new terms of social solidarity that attempted to depoliticize radical antiracist critiques through literary texts, especially those by African Americans and Asian Americans (ibid. 27). By presuming ethnic literature to be "authentic, intimate, and representative," literary texts helped inculcate young people to "appropriate sensibilities for a multiracial, multicultural professional-managerial class" (ibid. 32).

Poised against the dominant way of reading Asian American narratives, Ong's writing style has been described as an "unrelenting aria of high bitchiness and scathing satire" (Benfer). Like Tan's chick lit voice, Ong's humorous style keeps the reader viewing ethnic identities from a distance. The novel follows the Filipino migrant William Paulinha as he seeks revenge against the upper-class elites in New York City who have gentrified Paulinha's queer, lower-class havens. Paulinha introduces himself through his past identities, which are defined not by his race, nationality, or sexuality, but by his history of service work positions: mail delivery, answering phones, data entry, typing, street hustling and sex work (3–4). This range of labor identities exemplifies what the literary scholar Hsuan L. Hsu calls Paulinha's "chameleon-like qualities" ("Mimicry" 680). His capacity to adapt to new types of service labor gives him a cultural capital that is strengthened by his ability to racially transition into other lower-class forms of Chinese, Puerto Rican, Dominican, or Brazilian ethnicities. With the help of an upper-class stranger, Shem C., who shares Paulinha's rage against the elites, Paulinha becomes a con man, and weaponizes his chameleonic abilities to fashion himself into a Chinese feng shui artist, "Master Chao," so that he can exploit the elite's desire for exotic ethnic culture. After Shem publishes an article in a made-up European lifestyle magazine, the New York elites are more than willing to believe in Paulinha's fake identity, and they ask Paulinha to help placate their modern anxieties through the spiritual release of Chinese culture. As Master Chao, Paulinha's clients discover a counterpoint to their own privileged, globe-trotting lifestyle, as they each take Paulinha "into their homes and reveal[ ] the thing that they would never dare speak of in public. . . . They had sons and daughters who were drug addicts. . . . They were the children of country bumpkin parents" (85). For the clients, Master Chao represents an authentic Other who functions as a perfect counterpoint to their psychological anxieties.

As Paulinha's fake persona becomes popular among the city's elite, he begins to see Master Chao as a new identity that can rescue him from his own alienation after the queer bars of the village have been gentrified out of existence. As he says, "I too wanted to be changed just like these people wanted to be changed. I wanted to put on a new shirt and discard the old, sweat-soaked one I had" (84). His attempts to transcend his social position rely entirely upon his performance of an ahistorical, apolitical Chinese identity: "I had no core," he thinks, "I merely went from one identity to another guided by nothing more than mimicry" (168). Transitioning into "Master Chao" gives him access to wealth and social standing that contrast with the seediness of the Savoy bar. When a second article about Master Chao appears in the trend-setting magazine *H*, Paulinha's clients shift from "women who had tragedies they wanted operated on" to "creatures who 'lived and breathed' fashion and wanted to be 'up' on trends" (195). Paulinha's position in this fashion magazine–based society increases when one of his clients, Rowley, leaves him his Manhattan apartment as an inheritance (188). By transforming into Master Chao, Paulinha as ethnic trickster is thrust from being a queer prostitute in a seedy bar to an accepted worker for the global elite, but only insofar as he molds himself "according to a pattern that seemed—by its very age and durability—authentic [and] original" (168).

But as a worker hired to "fix" people's homes and anxieties, Paulinha himself never seems convinced that his material position can offer him spiritual transcendence, and unlike Chiah Deng, he continues to maintain a critical gaze on the global elite. His experience as a service worker makes him suspicious of such transcendence, a form of spirituality he sells to clients by masking himself as "a soul directly linked to the ancestral past, shot through with the very thing which the white man had given up in exchange for technological advancement—spiritual enlightenment—and the lack of which now made him inferior, in need of guidance" (66). Paulinha's sarcastic voice here allows the reader to see his service role as providing an idealized ethnic Other whose magical powers follow modern imperial histories of technological advancement. These histories manifest in the obsession with Asian culture that many of Paulinha's clients project onto Master Chao: "The [client] had it bad. His huge crush on Asian culture was much bigger than Shem had led me to believe" (70). These "crushes" far surpass the curiosity of the tourist, and are represented as genuine efforts to belong within an imagined culture of the globe. As a service laborer, Paulinha confirms the global elite's desire to transcend their materialism through his performed identity of Master Chao: "Marvelous, I told him. You have done my culture proud. My instincts told me to put my arms around him, and I did, welcoming him to a club" (72). Like Tan's Chiah Deng, Paulinha's clients seek a spiritual globalness reliant on ancient wisdoms that are inaccessible through the mere consumption of global products, but rely on the affective labor of ethnicized Others. Paulinha's ability to perform Master Chao is not an authentic gift he was born into, but a skill that he developed through a lifetime of service work: he becomes the "fussy housekeeper" when arranging furniture, and portrays himself as a psychologist when clients reveal "the thing that they would never dare speak of in public" (85). For Paulinha's clients, the desire to transcend mere ethnicity is followed by a spiritual desire to escape an automatized, profit-driven culture.

Paulinha's migrant journey as a Filipino service worker contrasts with Chiah Deng's, whose frustration with racial prejudice emerges in the "passive politeness" of the Oxford academy. In an era when Filipina/os have continued to be branded as overseas maids and seaman, Paulinha's Filipino racial markers limit his ability to escape his position as a service worker, making global transcendence seem an impossible (and thus less desirable) option. Paulinha's desperation as a migrant stuck in service work is common today when Filipino/as are often figured as the "servants of globalization" (Parreñas).[14] While Filipina/o identity has been bound up with service work, Chinese (especially Chinese Singaporean) identity has been bound up with consumption and business, as Chiah

Deng calls it, *"the air-conditioned corridors of food courts and shopping malls"* (242, italics in original). William Paulinha's lack of material wealth too marks him as an ethnic service worker, whose homeland dictates his identity. To transition to Master Chao is not merely to perform an ancient spiritual guide, but to be marked as Chinese, part of a recognizable and trusted business class, free of the racial markers of the migrant Filipina/o. His choice to become Master Chao takes advantage of the demand for the performance of a wise Eastern mystic, a figure associated with Chinese philosophers such as Confucius and Lao Tzu, who represent a culture mark(et)ed as "over five-thousand years old."

A POLITICS OF REVENGE

In *Fixer Chao*, William Paulinha's experience as a Philippine overseas migrant has made him bitter and resentful of the upper-class elites who preach multi-culturalism and tolerance while relying upon the affective labor of ethnicized service workers. Unlike Ben Lucero of Peter Bacho's *Cebu*, Paulinha makes no attempt to fulfill his duty to the host country for having "rescued" him; rather, Paulinha's response is to enact a politics of revenge, a refusal to be grateful or to pay back his supposed debt. His antagonism against the global elite seems unbreakable. Even after he inherits a Manhattan apartment, the upper-class life-style only stokes his fury as he continues to fix his clients' houses to invite evil spirits. Revenge here refuses the historical narrative of multiculturalism and the promised utopia of the global imaginary, and rather stays steadfast to marginal-ized histories of imperialisms that have afterlives in the present day, particularly within service work and the gentrification of queer-of-color spaces. As a queer Filipino migrant, Paulinha indulges in a politics of revenge similar to Roderick Ferguson's "queer of color analysis," which aims to oppose liberal ideologies that see the nation-state and capitalism as "sites of resolution, perfection, progress, and confirmation" (4).

In contrast to Paulinha's politics of revenge, his friend Preciosa believes in the ideals of the global imaginary. Preciosa is cast as the widely recognized persona of the Filipina affectual migrant, and while Paulinha transitions to Master Chao for revenge, Preciosa transitions to the affectual Filipina in order to fulfill her own desire to become global, seeing the U.S. nation-state as a site of universal progress. At first, Preciosa's story is told in a typical ethnic autobiography form, where the victimized Asian woman sees the West as her savior. After working as a maid to a Chinese family in the Philippines, and then being "waylaid into pros-titution" and escaping her brothel, Preciosa advertises herself in a mail-order bride magazine "intended to unite old white Americans with potential brides from the Third World" (309). She chooses a dozen American suitors to come to the Philippines, and hires a group of strangers to act as her family, transition-ing herself into the identity of a "traditional girl, a girl close to her impoverished family, for whom marriage to an American—regardless of how fat and ugly most of them were—represented an upswing in life" (309). Preciosa adds to her market appeal as a foreign bride by increasing her ethical value, presenting herself as a poor and disadvantaged brown woman, offering clients the chance to rescue her. In portraying her potential marriage as a virtuous act, as a means of taking up the "white man's burden," her strategy has great effect on Vietnam veterans haunted by the guilt of the war, and she ends up picking the oldest of her suitors. Since she can barely imagine marrying him, she invents a mantra for the occasion: "This man doesn't have long to live. And besides, an American passport would be hers forever" (310). The image of the passport recurs through Preciosa's journey as an ideal object worthy of servitude and the risk of domestic abuse: "Preciosa all the while thought of the dark blue cover of her new passport, thought of the Philippines as of a dilapidated building on the wrong side of town passed by without a second glance from a dark-windowed, air-conditioned car. She had transcended something, and it was now at her back. Even if the sex was disgusting, it was still in Texas, USA" (311). The attachment to the United States, even the "dry and boring" state of Texas, is not merely a reflection of Preciosa's need for remittances, as Pheng Cheah's "low cosmopolitan" might be understood. Rather, the United States comes to resemble a transcendence within the global imaginary, where the "air-conditioned" United States can provide a space of rescue from the "dilapidated" Philippines. The passport offers Preciosa global mobility, as a "regulatory instrument of residence, travel and belonging" (Ong 120). Yet the narrative's sarcastic tone, apparent in phrases like "even if the sex was disgusting," exposes the passport as a fetishized object. Even after her American husband dies, Preciosa surprises his family by refusing the inheritance, choosing to keep "only a small sum—enough to start a new life elsewhere" (311). Preciosa leaves the money as she left the Philippines, "at her back," as she embarks on the next step to the global imaginary: the global city of New York.

Preciosa's journey invites her into a realm of global belonging only to resign her to the role of an ethnicized affective laborer. Her movement reflects Filipina migration patterns since the 1970s, as Filipina migrant identity has become bound to service and domestic labor, no matter the migrant's previous training.[15] As Anna Guevarra has written, Filipina migrants have been made "emplowered" (employed and empowered) by state rhetoric and brokerage companies to have pride in an ahistorical Filipina identity based on matronly affection and care, an identity that migrants are then expected to perform as condition of their employment. This vision of femininity is also that of a responsible neoliberal subject, whose "emplowerment" "fulfills the goal of producing 'responsible' (that is, economically competitive, entrepreneurial, and self-accountable) and therefore, ideal workers and global commodities" (Guevarra 8). Indeed, the Filipina's education, English-language fluency, and "tender loving care" attitude, as Guevarra calls it, become a "comparative advantage" (2) formed through the

national and global media. In this contribution to global multiculturalist networks, the Filipina migrant has become one of the most successfully embedded national identities that make up pluralist governmentality today. It speaks
to a transnational investment in this identity, as the Philippine state encouraged
workers who were "mothers [and] wives ... [and] who must uphold a particular
image of femininity" (Guevarra 5). In Neferti Tadiar's terms, the religious (both
colonial and Protestant) upbringing combined with Filipina/o notions of curing
and healing have helped constitute Filipinas through images of sacred women
who have "sampalataya" (faith), and whose libidinal energies are proof of their
life-producing activity that can "be recognized as domestic labor" ("(Miracle)"
724). Indeed, like the ethnicized laborers of these novels, the Filipina's affective life-force becomes objectified for its "capacities for suffering, for relieving
suffering for others, [and] for using their selves as the instruments of others'
relief" (ibid.). This commodification of healing power shifts from an example
of religious femininity in the Philippines to a national identity, and the cultural
background of the Filipina—Cebuano, Tagalog, Ilocano, mestizo—becomes
homogenized to produce the affective Filipina servant as a national type recognized across the globe. Han Ong's novel thus speaks from within our current
global division of labor that relies on a pluralist logic, where national difference
is deployed to revise racialized (and gendered) work hierarchies within a global
division of labor (Guevarra 64).

   If Preciosa's story follows that of a victimized Asian through her intimate rec-
ollections of her homeland, the story later ruptures these conventions of ethnic
autobiography through a politics of revenge upon the very values of tolerance
and diversity that ethnic autobiographies are thought to produce. Despite Preciosa's attempt to transition herself into a traditional Filipina, and to give back
the money entitled to her, she discovers in New York City that she can still only
participate in a global imaginary by continuing the performance. After refusing
to look for service work, Preciosa finds herself performing the barbarian Filipina when she is typecast as a Central American "primitive" in a Broadway play,
wearing only a loincloth and poised to attack white missionaries. At first Preciosa is proud of fulfilling her dream to act on Broadway, but "after a few Filipino
friends came to see the performance and she saw their faces ... she realize[d]
that what she'd perceived as a triumph was the farthest thing from it" (313). In
every instance of upward mobility, Preciosa must fulfill her role as an authentic Filipina in order to belong among a higher, "transcendent" culture, thrusting
her back into the ethnicity she thought herself free from in everything but territory. She feels her new role "turning back the hands of time so that she could be
returned to the pages of a history book, all her English unlearned, her beautiful
blue-black American passport handed back. In her mind, she was being returned
to the Philippines" (313). Similar to the sections of ecstasy in *Mammon Inc.*, these
sections of epiphany rupture the novel's cynical tone to take on a more poetic

style, with phrases that give agency to metaphors ("hands of time," "history book"). In stark contrast to Tan's novel, these moments of structural epiphany lead the characterizers away from the global imaginary rather than toward it. In this moment Preciosa realizes she has compromised to the expectations of a global elite, and the once cherished status symbol of the American passport transforms into an object of resentment. Her shame comes from performing the primitive ethnic for a global imaginary to which she can only belong to as an affective laborer. Incensed by this betrayal, Preciosa joins Paulinha in his quest for revenge, performing as a feng shui priestess who grunts unintelligibly, shakes multicolored beads, and steals expensive decorations.

WRITER/PERFORMER, READER/CLIENT

Fixer Chao has been described as a "satirical narrative of passing" (Hsu 2006), though it fits well within the ethnic autobiography form, as the main character, William Paulinha, is a mirror reflection of Han Ong himself—mixed Chinese Filipino, queer, living in New York City, and a master of performance (Ong as a playwright, Paulinha in masquerade). Indeed, the novel's autobiographical form seems to seduce an audience of Asian American readers with the same intent as "Master Chao" in luring the global elite: to disturb, shock, and curse them. Throughout the novel's "authentic" form, it foregrounds a critique of an Asian American politics that views authentic representation, cultural tolerance, and inclusion as its main goals. This critique is made explicit when Paulinha witnesses an Asian American intellectual, Paul Lin, ranting about "hegemony, proletariat, diaspora, dichotomy, hagiography, [and] calligraphy" at a dinner party. Paulinha identifies Lin's remarks as "a complaint" that seems to ignore the speaker's own mobility and class dominance, while Paulinha's strategy of "revenge" takes all of this immediately into account (109). Paulinha's performance seems just as solicited by the socially unaware global elites as it is by Asian American intellectuals, as Paulinha's greatest act of revenge is directed at the Japanese American socialite, Suzy Yamada. Paulinha fixes Yamada's apartment to give her bad luck by repositioning mirrors so that she and her son Kendo would "run into mirror versions of themselves" that would "serve as pincushions for their ire" (181). Rather than rescue them from their own anxiety and anger, Paulinha uses the mirrors to reflect back their hypocrisy as Asian Americans who seek Master Chao as an authentic gateway to their "Asian" roots. This mirroring is reflected in the novel's genre form toward its very audience. The audience who reads *Fixer Chao* expecting an authentic gateway to Filipinoness or Filipino/a American identity will read the satirical, cynical narrative, with themselves as the butt of the joke.

Whereas ethnic autobiographies often help constitute the Asian American identity (even through its heterogeneity), *Fixer Chao* offers a radical politics of revenge for the nationalism that such an identity implicitly supports. After her disillusion with the belonging promised by the American passport, Preciosa feels an immense responsibility toward her own given culture, reflecting upon "the places of her childhood turned foreign by development, by neglect, by the symbol-heavy defacings of various political movements" (160). Preciosa realizes that her desire to become Western reflects the desire for a tolerant and multicultural global community, a desire that in turn brought decimation to marginalized nations subjected to American capital. Her newfound rage sees the desire for global belonging as merely a means of escaping "the most rigorous sense of responsibility to the given" (Cheah 119). Her desire for such belonging rationalizes the dispossession of third-world spaces like her hometown, a city demolished to make way for development projects. For Preciosa, the homeland is not a symbol of spirituality, but a territory appropriated by the "tolerant" peoples who reside in global cities. Her loss left the United States and global New York City as alternative communities that could only be pursued through her subjection within the global service industry. Whereas Tan's Chiah Deng continues to desire the global imaginary despite its relationship to global capital and racial hierarchies, Preciosa chooses to remain antagonistic to the global elite, seeing reappropriation of space and material resources as a shared struggle for the global underclass.

Paulinha's desire for the global imaginary also comes through the loss of cultural space, in his case, through the gentrified displacement of New York City's "seedy" bars (259). Paulinha's queer positionality restricts him from adopting the masculine identity of the Filipino overseas worker, who, according to Steven McKay, must act as both "subordinate" and "masculine" to follow orders from white managers, and to return to the Philippines as a "seasoned adventurer, as sexually experienced, as provider and patron, as father and husband" (628). Rejecting the characteristics of this ethnic labor niche, Paulinha gives up the Philippines as a place of return, and instead takes refuge in the queer of color space, the Savoy bar, the last "seedy" place left (150). The Savoy, named after a Manila vaudeville house where General Douglas MacArthur's mistress once performed, is marked as a space for lower-class queers to convene and share experiences of subordination. The Savoy also alludes to the 1969 Stonewall riots, which occurred after a police raid on the Stonewall Inn, a drag queen bar that existed when cross-dressing was illegal (Stein 156). The desire to masquerade as a different gender in the Savoy contrasts with the demand for service workers to masquerade as ethnic guides for the elite. The impending loss of "seedy" bars deprives William of his community, leaving global "transcendence" as an attractive alternative.

Paulinha's Master Chao brand enacts "revenge politics" by reflecting the gaze of the reader of ethnic autobiography. It recalls a type of spiritual fetish akin to Professor Ad-oy's global mysticism, as it offers spiritual tranquility through symbols like feng shui and Roobios tea. Paulinha's client Lindsay similarly fetishizes

"Oriental art" through a collection of Chinese "teapots and teacups, Japanese swords, calligraphic ink sets," along with "hundreds of Buddhas of dazzling variety" (71). At the end of *Fixer Chao*, Paulinha is caught as a fake, and is maligned as a scammer, not because he seeks wealth through ethnic performance, but because that performance is Chinese, when he is "authentically" Filipino. Like the novel's Chinese Filipino author himself, Paulinha's adopted identity is exposed as mere performance once the individual's "real" racial history is revealed. Master Chao's "fakeness" is invoked not because he is consciously performing an identity, but because he is preforming *someone else's* assigned identity-type. Ironically, he is excluded from the global elites for daring to possess the same distance from ethnic authenticity that they have used to define themselves. Once Paulinha's Master Chao persona is revealed as a performance, the clients (and in turn, the novel's readers) are faced with their own desire for an authenticated narrative capable of releasing their anxieties as global subjects. The cultural capital that had once freed clients like Lindsay from their own complicity was, as Shu-mei Shih has said of cosmopolitanism, a politics of "selective recognition," where the ethnicized Other is only recognized through modes of orientalism ("Toward an Ethics of Transnational Encounters," 78). In this framework, the ethnic service worker (and in turn, the ethnic autobiography writer) acts as an "authenticator," whose race, accent, and lower-class position transfers affective value to cultural symbols, allowing the clients/readers to cloak their lack of sincere political investments.

ABSURD ENGAGEMENT

In both *Mammon Inc.* and *Fixer Chao*, the transpacific migrants' desire to transcend their "given culture"—and therefore their "given labor"—is captured through forms of cynicism and distance. Yet in the novels' genre disruptions, they also express how being distanced from racial identities in order to manage, reinterpret, and transition among them is quite different from a retreat from political and social public life. Indeed, the mistake with valuing distance from ethnic identity is that such distance is too often seen as a unique perspective. To see such distance as a white, mixed race, or an Asian American experience presumes that other racial minorities are trapped within their cultural performance, while one type of people better understand their own self-conscious performativity. The notion of a minority Other who is unaware of his or her own performativity is itself a ruse, one that makes self-reflexivity appear as more transcendent than ethical, as if a "critical dimension" toward identity was available only to certain subjects. In their attempts to "game" pluralist governmentality, the characters of these novels expose inauthenticity and transition not as cultural attributes, but as shared affective strategies conceived in contexts where ethnic authenticity and performance are given the greatest value.

The genre appropriation of these novels can enable disruptions in our very way of reading ethnicized (rather than ethnic) literary fiction. These texts lay bare the political stakes of representational labor, and amplify politicized identities against the consistent remobilization of white supremacy. They point to the ironies and absurdities of literary culture, and the effects of ethnic literary forms upon how we imagine ourselves. Through their cynical distance they enable an absurd engagement for the reader, an attitude that takes on multiple identities despite the absurdity of their presumed authenticity. As Chiah Deng transitions among identities to manipulate the multiculturalist game, her desires for global belonging are rendered absurd. She strives to transcend ethnicized Others through a company that resembles Satan as much as it does the Dark Side of the Force. Similarly, Paulinha's decision to manipulate the upper class by performing a Chinese stereotype becomes immensely successful, and makes his own desire for the global seem absurd. In a moment of self-reflection, Paulinha tells Preciosa that he too came to America for a "better life" constructed from images of luxury: "wall-to-wall carpeting" and brand names like "General Electric, Sunbeam, Hoover, Proctor-Silex, Pfizer, Zenith" (262–263). For Paulinha, these commodities once possessed a magical quality, and functioned as "a short-hand for beauty, for quality, [for] things that wouldn't break—as our appliances often did" (263).[16] By the time Paulinha adopts the persona of Master Chao, his dream has faded with the racism he experienced as a service worker, and he begins to see global transcendence as a consumerist desire that he can profit from.

Though Paulinha is disillusioned with the global imaginary, he is still unable to escape how others imagine it. Like Chiah Deng, he tries to make the most with what he has (which is considerably less). Indeed, his options at the novel's end seem dire, as even returning to the Philippines "seemed like an admission of defeat" (308). His position as an ethnicized service worker has visualized the structures of pluralist governmentality, but his vengeful reaction is not community-oriented so much as an effort to exploit the system for his own gain. Paulinha's politics of revenge against the global elite see him going undercover by catering to its desires for escape, and in pretending to believe in the "fabled U.S." as a global imaginary.

If there is a definitive difference between the migrant service worker and the global elite in *Fixer Chao*, it is that the trickster, William Paulinha, seems critical of global transcendence, and his cynical voice can both distance himself from ethnic struggles and mediate absurd engagements with the global imaginary, as his fake persona amasses absurd amounts of wealth and prestige. Whereas Chiah Deng's sarcasm creates a cynical distance from her own ethnicity in order to bolster her global belonging, Paulinha's defies these temptations to instead engage fiercely in a politics of revenge. Likewise, Preciosa, after realizing that her inclusion in New York's elite is only possible through performing "the primitive," is also able to see the global imaginary—and the ecstatic experiences that go along with it—as necessitating affective service labor. Indeed, their cynical distance does just that—distances the reader from the "empowerment," the "pride," and the sacrosanct histories of ethnic identities. It provides a darker image of the global imaginary, not as cosmopolitan communities of tolerance, but as imperial elites formed by the labor of ethnicized migrants who are meant to desire the global imaginary, but can only belong as servants.

6 · SPECULATIVE FICTION AND AUTHORIAL TRANSITION

"Identity would seem to be the garment with which one covers the nakedness of the self: in which case, it is best that the garment be loose, a little like
the robes of the desert, through which one's nakedness can always be felt,
and, sometimes, discerned. This trust in one's nakedness is all that gives one
the power to change one's robes."

—James Baldwin, "The Art of Fiction"

In this book's previous chapters, I briefly outlined how each text
contained nonrealist elements that resisted nationalist literary traditions and
deviated from pluralist forms of expression. Part I focused on how texts from
Malaya and the Philippines disrupted social realist histories with magic, myth,
and intimate genealogies. Their nonrealist takes on history, I argued, were fundamental to understanding how they revealed a genealogy of pluralist governmentality that extended from colonial pluralism. In Part II, I foregrounded novels
that featured satirical engagements with migrancy, travel writing, and rescue.
Similarly, in the previous chapter, I spotlighted the importance of genre theory
and audience awareness to consider how novels employed chick lit and ethnic
autobiography to access transnational audiences and to disrupt their own genre
expectations. Thus far, the discussion of genre has been limited to tracing how
fixed genres are disrupted by unexpected (and unsettling) literary forms of
metahistory, satire, and cynicism. In this chapter I seek to expand this notion of
genre by asking how genres themselves (rather than their disruption) can mediate diverse historical and social processes to produce formations that respond to
various forms of pluralist governmentality.

Recently, scholars have employed genre theory to assess how literary texts
stage debates among multiple audiences from various historical contexts. Jane

Elliot and Gillian Harkins have helped revive the "literary-historical terminology of genre" to illuminate the relations among aesthetic form, capitalism, and "institutionally sedimented forms of reading" (11). Genre reveals how literary forms transect historical periods to "conjure an imagined community across regions and periods" (ibid. 1). Elliot and Harkins take this understanding of genre from Raymond Williams's foundational work, *Marxism and Literature*, where Williams begins his section on aesthetics with "conventions" and "genre," two concepts that speak to bourgeois literary practices.[1] Williams's theory of genre observes attempts to reduce literary forms into fixed recognizable types and reveals the "impossibility or inefficacy" of doing so (180).[2] He spotlights "form" within genre, because form displays ambiguity. It is "a visible outward shape, and an inherent shaping impulse," that does not merely define or categorize the literary text (186). Form need not be identified immediately, but exists as a literary practice, a common property between writers and readers that must exist "before any communicative composition can occur" (188). Williams sees genre then not merely as a set of traditions or rules, but as "constitutive evidence" that combines and fuses abstract levels of the social material process (185). Genre can help understand the practical and social processes that the (socially embedded) author is able to express, as well as the traditions, conventions, and forms made available to that author within a given historical context.

This final chapter reflects upon these genre inquiries to ask how we might envision transitive culture as a nonrealist, responsive aesthetics that transitions among genres and genre conventions in the way an individual might transition among various forms of identity. The "nonrealist" forms of the novels in this study render the obscurity of pluralist governmentality into recognizable forms of imperial, state, and capitalist violence, precisely because these novels do not fit into the national ethnic norm, nor into Anglo-Saxon genre expectations. As Viet Thanh Nguyen argues, ethnic texts implicitly cement ethnic identities when read as "social realist," as authors are driven to satisfy an "urge for self-representation and self-determination" that is "deeply embedded in ethnic literature in general," where the genre tag of "ethnic" becomes appropriated as a sign "of the ethnic speaking of and for the ethnic population" (*Nothing Ever Dies* 209). In the project of consciously managing and reinterpreting multiculturalist identities, transitive cultures are expressed as non- or antirealist because of their refusal to reiterate "the real" of recognized ethnic identities. To see beyond these logics of the real, the authentic, or the autobiographical, transpacific Anglophone literature conjures the unreal, the doubtful, the *speculative*. Thus it makes sense to speak of this literary archive within the framework of speculative fiction, a genre that has allowed audiences to meditate on the very presumptions that make an ethnic text an ethnic text.

Speculative fiction represents nonrealist texts without a particular genre or subgenre, and operates as a metagenre that comments on the assumptions of ethnic socio-historical narratives. Indeed, every text in this book has in some way been read as "nonrealist," "antirealist," or "imaginative," which all operate within the speculative. They all imagine alternative ways of representing the complexity of our globalized moment, where regimes of capitalist, state, and imperial violence overlap in systems that seem unreal and remain indecipherable by multiculturalist narratives of liberal (and inclusive) progress. In its critiques of "the real," speculative fiction focuses not so much on "what it was" but "how it remains so," and the feelings and procedures that emanate from one's positionality in relation to the whole. As I showed in readings throughout this book, the potential of nonrealist forms is not to describe "what happened" historically but "how it continues to happen," and how literary representations participate in continued reiterations of state and capitalist power. As Madhu Dubey points out in her readings of neo-slave narratives, speculative fictions "overtly situate themselves against history" (784) and "suggest that the truth of this past is more fully grasped by way of an antirealist literary imagination that can fluidly cross temporal boundaries and affectively immerse readers" (785). Speculative fiction has the capability of continuing projects of antiracism, as their mode of analogizing (rather than historicizing) racial, class, and gender identity can better imagine new forms of cross-ethnic and transnational coalition.

Speculative fiction has become a genre of increasing popularity within Southeast Asian Anglophone cultures, and its availability has expanded through speculative fiction journals and anthologies (many free online or sold as e-books). Online availability has brought these literatures to digitally literate audiences, who would not be surprised at portrayals of race and identity as virtual roles to be played. Online cultures make it possible to reinterpret depoliticized ethnic identities by exposing their versatility and practicality given our pluralist social structures. By meditating upon the performative aspects of identity, these texts focus on the audience who is to be affected (the spectator), the one who gazes and desires monolithic conceptions of race.

This final chapter breaks from the comparative mode of previous chapters by discussing multiple texts that express transition within a speculative mode. I begin with the work of performance artist Anida Yoeu Ali as a gateway to discuss the transformative nature of the speculative within Southeast Asia. I then turn to Anglophone speculative short stories by Alfred Yuson, F. H. Batacan, Mia Tijam, and M.R.R. Arcega, and trace the arguments of the artists-turned-anthology editors Dean Francis Alfar and Charles Tan, who have sought to use speculative fiction as a means of writing outside of their given ethnicity and nationality. Finally, I will reflect on my own speculative fiction, the use of my pen name Kawika Guillermo, and my own artistic challenges in expressing nonrealist forms.

SPECULATIVE READING

If speculative fiction can reveal how violent structures of the past continue to recur, then reading within the genre of the speculative can open new possibilities for treating artwork as both critical and transformative. Anida Yoeu Ali's 2012 performance work *Enter the Field* was created while Ali served as the Java Arts' Inaugural Artist in Residence in Phnom Penh, Cambodia. Ali is a refugee born in Cambodia, whose family fled the Khmer Rouge to raised Ali in Chicago. If Ali's poetry, as Cathy Schlund-Vials describes it, concerns melancholy, loss, and a journey from "grief to grievance," her performance art takes from history to speculate upon a not-so-distant future (189).

At first, Ali's image of a dancer dressed in black and white stripes conjures histories of genocide and imprisonment. We read Ali's own refugee autobiography within a genre of diasporic writing, where loss and grief reappear within the fields (read: killing fields), while the captured dancer offers a stage for resilience and overcoming of the homeland's violent history. Schund-Vials has written of Ali's other performance piece, *Palimpsest for Generation 1.5*, as "Cambodian American memory work" that "enunciate[s] (by way of performance) Cambodian American selfhood" (192), and "attempts to remember a history of U.S. imperialism, Khmer Rouge authoritarianism, and involuntary refugee dispersal" (193). This is one way of reading the image critically, as it captures the struggle to remember the complex set of events that preceded displacement within a context of amnesia propagated by multiple state powers.

Another way to read the image is within a speculative mode that bridges the historical violence of the "memory work" to the displacements of the present and the future. The dancer's black and white stripes are more reminiscent of American prisons than, for example, Prison S21 in Phnom Penh, where prisoners

Anida Yoeu Ali's 2012 performance work, *Enter the Field #1 / Arch Pose*. Performance and concept by Anida Yoeu Ali. Photo documentation by Vinh Dao. Archival inkjet print, 2012. Photo courtesy of Studio Revolt.

wore black. The symbolic prison then invokes the present-day associations of Cambodian Americans and incarceration within the "hyperghetto."[3] The dancer performs at the nexus of the rice plantation where lines crisscross to segment seed groups, a highly structured pattern of agricultural control that resurfaces on the black and white stripes of the dancer. These symbolic comparisons yoke the dancer to the various subjects of pluralist governmentality, whose identity categorizations segment and control an otherwise organic body. Even so, the dancer moves in unpredictable and improvised motion. The order of the stripes mimicking a prisoner are put into a dress that seems to flutter in the wind and a veil that, in the context of the War on Terror, signifies a radical and monstrous Other. This aesthetic shift does not enunciate an identity so much as render visually what Eric Tang calls "refugee temporality," which names "the refugee's knowledge that, with each crossing, resettlement, and displacement, an old and familiar form of power is being reinscribed" (21). The atrocities committed during the reign of Pol Pot and the Khmer Rouge are broadened to include all these contexts—the prison, the hyperghetto, the War on Terror.

From the purview of the speculative, "Cambodian American" resembles one possible identity among many along a route of displacements within the past as well as the unforeseeable future. The stripes are imprisoning because they speak to a need for categorization attached to the body. Stripes in a sense give the body skin, and thus they move, bend, buckle, and curve with the body's movements. The piece's most speculative dimension is in the futuristic appearance of the dancer's garb, which levitates around the dancer's body in a way that defies physics (two assistants hold up the artist's dress). The surrealism here suggests a return, not (merely) of the diasporic kind, but of the ghostly kind that combats the historical amnesia of the present. The white-and-black order that signifies futurity gives the ghost some recognizable form, just as the organic rice fields are structured into segments for food production. Identity is expressed here, as Baldwin wrote, "like the robes of the desert," which can be worn "loose" by learning to trust "in one's nakedness"—one's real histories, vulnerabilities, and hopes for the future. Here is not a rejection of the labels cast upon oneself, but a way of giving organicism to the labels. The setting becomes futuristic, a peek into a time when we have come to terms with the construction of identity while retaining its importance, when we can dance with it, play with it, and bend it as easily as arching our back. The speculative mode of reading radically revises the text by allowing it to speak across multiple genres—the genre of loss, of diaspora, as well as the genres of science fiction, fantasy, and the surreal. What makes this reading speculative is not merely accounting for various genres within an "umbrella" term, but seeing the text's abilities to transition among genres as a political and social act, what Williams called seeing genre as the "constitutive evidence" of real social processes, in this case the prison, the movements of refuge, the organicism within identity labels themselves, the process of imagining new futures.

Ali's work pushes us to consider how the speculative has functioned as a politicized genre resistant to the presumptions of genre categorization. In 1959, Robert Heinlein coined the term "speculative fiction" as an alternative to genre categories, a term that also marks a text's political investments (Gomez). Heinlein saw the speculative genre as a critique of realism that critically examined social norms hidden by notions of "the real," and in its truthful speculations, could actually be "much more realistic" (24). Similarly, in 1979, Darko Suvin defined "fantastic genres" as genres that pushed the limits of shared cognitive norms and defied dominant logics (Suvin).[4] To assign the label "speculative" to a text thus recognizes not merely its speculative elements, but how those elements refuse conventions that orientalize or exoticize the "alien" Other, and avoid "the space age settings and scientific jargon that had previously dominated the field (and that appealed essentially to adolescent boys)" (Gomez 949). Speculative fiction operates more as an Other to genre fiction, establishing alternative imaginings that, once they become conventional, are no longer labeled speculative fiction, but become a genre to themselves (slipstream, steampunk, biopunk). In this sense, speculative fiction does not merely "umbrella" nonrealist genres, but excludes many texts based on their implicit (Anglo-Saxon, heteronormative, pluralist) politics.

Speculative modes of reading are political in the way that many ethnic literary texts are presumed political by representing and commenting upon a social realist universe, and speculative fiction's political investments speak to its popularity in the United States, where positive minority representations in much film and literature confine minority histories into the past by making them seem solved (and thus forgotten). In turn, the speculative broaches constructed histories by allowing writers to depict (and thus compare) the various experiences of marginalization from the past to the present and prospective future.[5] Such texts are not only critical of confining genre labels, but also of similarly confining identity-based labels (African American, Chicano/a, Asian American). By "identity-based labels" I don't mean to dismiss the material form of the racialized and gendered body. Indeed, a speculative reading cannot ignore the prominence of the brown female body in Ali's image. Yet this body is transitional, covered by the bars of identity and masked from the audience's gaze. He or she is not an identity that can be sorted into categories of victim / victimizer, or whose subjectivity can be reduced to a shared figure ("migrant subjectivity," "diasporic subjectivity"). Instead, the body remains body, one that carries a haunting poetic potential for collective reconciliation by creating compassion for those locked into the distancing identities cast upon them. Ali's image envisions the embodiment of freedom and pleasure, ecstasy and dance, within the confines of the black-and-white imprisonment of our real-world conditions. Instead of the melancholic poetry of the written word, here the body itself becomes poem within a skin both futuristic and strangely familiar. The skin is also a veil, symbolizing the

Muslim woman in an age of Islamophobia, and inescapably brown, conjuring the ambiguous brownness of refugees stamped with the iconography of "crises." In this context, dance can only be rendered through an imagined body, a speculative mode of art.

"WHAT CAN WE DRAW FROM YOUR CULTURE?"

Since the early 2000s, speculative fiction has become more common among Anglophone cultures in Canada (Hiromi Goto, Derwin Mak, Larissa Lai), the Philippines (Charles Tan, Dean Alfar, Charleston Ong, Kristine Ong Muslim, Kenneth Yu), and other parts of Southeast Asia (Verena Tay and Hwee Hwee Tan in Singapore, Zen Cho in Singapore, Tiffany Tsao in Indonesia, Eliza Chan in Vietnam). Though these writers are often grouped under national rubrics, their works tend to refuse recognizable narratives of national progress or narratives that congeal national identities. Under state regimes that censor Anglophone writings, or under capitalist regimes that demand marketable ethnic stories, Anglophone fictions have become known for using speculative elements to couch contemporary criticisms of local states and their Western allies. As the critic Andrew Ng has written concerning speculative fiction in Singapore, the speculative mode has become "a strategically useful literary vehicle to air criticisms against the current state of affairs ... a textual strategy attempted, perhaps, to deflect away from the writer any accusation of sedition" ("Nation and Religion" 117). Though novels since Lloyd Fernando's *Scorpion Orchid* have contained speculative elements, Singapore speculative fiction has mostly been accessible online, assembled through networks of blogs like "Speculative Writers of Singapore" the 2012 print anthology *Fish Eats Lion: New Singaporean Speculative Fiction*, and the journal *LONTAR: The Journal of Southeast Asian Speculative Fiction*. Much speculative fiction is published in small presses or in online literary journals, where the goal of marketing a science fiction or fantasy subgenre is less of a concern than the production of innovative and politically invested texts. Journals like *Expanded Horizons, Strange Horizons, Scissors and Spackle,* and *Mobius: Journal of Social Change* have sought to use the speculative fiction label to consciously refocus antiracist art toward re-presenting the transnational experiences of marginalized groups. One of the most popular of these journals, *Strange Horizons*, details a "Stories We've Seen Too Often" list that aims at ridding submissions of racist, sexist, or otherwise prejudiced clichés.[6] In the Philippines, Anglophone literary culture has fostered the growth of speculative fiction through granting National Awards (Palanca Awards) to authors and through publishing speculative fiction in English-language web and print journals, finding audiences far exceeding that of previous Anglophone writing.[7]

If speculative fiction can be seen as a response to various genre fictions, speculative fiction from Southeast Asia also responds partially to its own contexts of censorship and pluralism and partially to Anglo-American science fiction and fantasy, which has reproduced much of the orientalist gaze by employing Asian mythos to idealize "premodern" Asian societies or to depict "techno-orientalist" futures.[8] As David S. Roh, Betsy Huang, and Greta A. Niu have argued, many Anglo-American genre fictions contain a "futurist spirit of contemporary existential, racial, and technological anxieties," yet they continue to be bound by a "disciplinary narrowness" when dealing with Asian cultures (4). Anglo-American speculative fiction writers are known to use the mythos of Eastern or African cultures as their inspiration, presenting alternatives to the Anglo-Saxon-based worlds of writers like J.R.R. Tolkien. This use of Asian cultures and histories call attention to unknown spaces and myths, but such texts also reduce "the East" to an alternative to capitalist alienation. Anglo-American speculative fiction in this case can be understood as "looking at" the Other as a spectacle in order to construct imaginative worlds, while conveying Asian practices and beliefs deprived of imperial histories. Ursula Le Guin's *Earthsea* chronicles offer a Daoist fantasy setting, yet also overemphasize this world's difference from Anglo-Saxon cultures, making the mythic past seem irrelevant to an era of capitalist modernity. As the literary scholar Betsy Huang has argued, even science fiction novels by writers like Le Guin, who seek to reverse racist trends by "appreciating" Daoist culture, consider Daoist thought as "sufficiently alien from Western psychorationalist models," and reinforces the notion that Western power can only be suffused by employing Eastern ways of being "passive, restrained, and nonthreatening" ("Premodern" 28). The passive Daoism in such novels also helps resolve anxieties concerning the rise of Asia within any imagined future.

Speculative fiction authors in Southeast Asia are marginalized by science fiction novelists who have already taken modern Asian cities as their inspiration, representing the East as a foil for the lack of spiritual development in the West, as places "where Westerners go for identity modifications, cultural experimentations, and even existential revaluations" (Huang, "Premodern" 38). The American writer Paolo Bacigalupi gained major success with his speculative fiction novel that takes place in twenty-third-century Thailand, *The Wind Up Girl*, which won both the Hugo and Nebula awards in 2009. Bacigalupi, who has written other speculative works set in Laos, uses the genre of speculative fiction as a way to avoid the pressure of representing his settings in a "genuine" way, and instead, he asks readers to rely on social realist novels as examples of "a pure literary window into Thai culture" (Bacigalupi). Like Le Guin and others before him, Bacigalupi's use of the speculative genre allows him to avoid the responsibility of depicting Southeast Asia as a real setting. He represents spaces like Bangkok to better understand "universal" issues of global warming and genetically modified crops. Issues more relevant to the region, such as democratic protest, American and Chinese military influence, tourism, nongovernmental organizations, etc., are of little concern.

Anglophone speculative fiction texts refocus the speculative element from the cultural magic found in Bacigalupi's work toward the implausible presence of global capital and violent imperial regimes. In a 2009 interview for the speculative fiction podcast *Rubber Dinosaur*, the writer Charles Tan outlined how Philippine speculative fiction can speak to real politics in ways that go beyond seeing Filipino/a culture as fantastical. The interviewer asks Tan what speculative fiction authors can "draw from Filipino culture . . . what should we find interesting, what should we investigate in your culture?" (Staggs). Instead of answering with examples of Filipino/a myths like the *aswang* (the Filipino/a ghoulish were-dog), Tan offers examples of "speculative" elements from Philippines' history, beginning with Spanish, American, and Japanese colonization, to the Marcos dictatorship and the People Power revolution. Rather than pull from "authentic" cultural myths, Tan views political events like People Power as "speculative," describing it as the fantastic election of a woman who was not even on the original ballot (Cory Aquino), which began an uprising where tanks and soldiers were defused with flowers and rosaries. When asked for more speculative elements, Tan mentions the ubiquity of owning cellphones without being able to afford landlines, and the micropayment and loan system supported by NGOs, both of which speak to "science fiction in a third world country" (Staggs). Tan's reinterpretation of the question "what can we draw from your culture?" challenges his audience to see the social relevancy of speculative fiction as an inheritor to the political projects of ethnic and anti-imperial fiction. Speculative fiction for Tan is not merely a recovery project of lost cultures, but a means to confront how "magic" impinges upon everyday logics.

YUSON'S "THE MUSIC CHILD"

Anglophone speculative fiction from Southeast Asia exposes and challenges the "speculating" gaze by writing from the point of view of the spectacle, of the one "being looked at," thus enabling readers to perceive the desires embedded within the gaze. In the Philippines, writers like Nick Joaquín, Alfred Yuson, and Charleston Ong have used nonrealist fictions to understand what possible forms of power are enabled by their expected performance of Filipino/a identity, questioning why some Filipino/a cultural practices are taken as "spectacle" and others as "backwards," some as "magical" and others as "primitive." Alfred Yuson's 1991 short story "The Music Child" depicts a Filipino American journalist, referred to only as "Pardner," who visits the Philippines to investigate the "dying issue" of muro-ami fishing, a business that once thrived in the Visayas (171). While investigating the ecological damage in the fishing villages, the journalist encounters stories of fishing companies exploiting young boys who are "packed in the hundreds in a small ship for months on end" and who occasionally disappear in the ocean, perhaps, "attacked by sharks" (172). Pardner becomes distracted, however, by the more exotic tale of a Visayas tribe that plays "violins with strings made of human hair." The journalist abandons his story of the fishing boys to follow these rumors toward the mountains, hoping to "come up with a story that should titillate the punks in Frisco" (176). Once he finds the village, the journalist encounters the fantastical tale of a mestizo "music child" who "never spoke but sang his every phrase, and mimicked to perfection all the bird sounds and jungle calls" (176).

In Yuson's story, the legend of the music child, juxtaposed with the fishing boys, questions the nature of the fantastic by examining how select cultural practices are marked as "spectacle," while stories of violence and exploitation, which can seem just as spectacular, do not warrant the same spectatorship. Like Robert Aguinaldo in Yuson's *Great Philippine Jungle Energy Café*, the Anglophone journalist becomes a stand-in for writers who focus on the fantastic elements of a culture (even their own) to cater to Western audiences. Yet Yuson's story also shows how historical events like the appropriation of land may appear just as fantastic, and may bring the reader closer to the reality of contemporary globalization. The "otherworldly," in the case of the fishing boys, exposes the anxieties at the heart of imperial encounters. As Yuson himself stated in a 2005 lecture, his use of nonrealist elements reflects how the contemporary "real world" has become an absurd parody that can only be seen as farcical, with "its lightness of tone and winking worldview, its comic turns" (*If a Filipino Writer* 47).[9] Such "comic turns" refer to the quasi-revolutionary events in the Philippines: the EDSA revolution in 1986, the subsequent People's Power movement in 2001 that toppled Joseph Estrada's administration, and the attempts to cast out his successor, Gloria Macapagal-Arroyo. For Yuson, to write fiction in this climate has made the writer "quixotic," "idealistic and impractical," who aspires for a "less exciting and less intrigue-ridden socio-political life" (ibid., 46).

Pardner's desire to write about the "spectacular" music child means marginalizing other realities. The child's mestizo father, Don Julio, attempts to recruit Pardner for a resistance movement against the state-protected multinational logging companies that have decimated the nearby forest, and threatened to "wipe out all resistance" (181). Don Julio tells the story of his resistance, presuming that the American journalist wants "to record all of this" for Western media. But Pardner only hopes to write about the fabled music child, even though the resistance too resembles a fantastic story: "I wondered whether I had just heard a tall tale. We were nearing the end of the twentieth century, after all. Bad guys didn't just show up and kill off recalcitrant natives. It couldn't happen.... Did these things still happen?" (182). As with the fishing boys, capitalist exploitation and imperial violence are seen as unreal, but at the same time, they do not entrance the Western reader like the hair-stringed violins and the mythical music child. Thus the fantastic elements that would remind the viewer of present-day imperial regimes are routinely suppressed. Given the liberal and multicultural discourses buttressing such regimes, these reminders of imperial violence seem *too* implausible, as events that "couldn't happen," not in "the twentieth century" (182).

Yuson's story makes visible the difference between the otherworldly elements that go unrecognized, and those fantastic elements that pluralist governmentality makes hypervisible. Though both the story of the resistance and the story of the music child seem similarly fantastic, one gets marked as "spectacle" (as that which deserves spectators), while the other is simply marked as "implausible." In juxtaposing both the "spectacle" and the "implausible," Yuson's story exposes the imperial desires that mark them as opposing elements, which will only distract Pardner from discovering a spectacle that will please his American audience. His impulse to deny the "implausible" afterlife of imperial violence in the Philippines is co-constituted by his desire for the "authentic," in this case, for a village child imbued with folkloreish magic.

At the end of "The Music Child," Pardner finds that all the rumors of the music child's abilities to mimic any sound are true. But the journalist is still unsatisfied. The boy has changed since the rumors. He goes by the name Luisito, he is mestizo, he has grown older and wiser, and no longer sings to mimic "the monsoon wind, and rustle of stalks," but sings "The Star-Spangled Banner" and "God Save the Queen" (176, 183). Like those who transition, Luisito is cast as "inauthentic," and is rather seen as "a great mimic, repeating exactly what he hears," though he also "makes up his own music, chanting epic tales of courage and gallantry" (184). Speaking in multiple languages, the boy mimics in order to create, to add "his own touches of whimsy cutting it here and there to suit his taste for the game, his own special game" (184). As spectacle, Luisito was presumed by the American to be frozen in time, but his growth and maturity make him aware of his own role as a spectacle, allowing him to satisfy the journalist's desire for magic while also speaking in his own tongue.

When the soldiers and logging companies return to decimate the valley, the boy's association with mimicry becomes a different kind of spectacle, one that does not praise the West, but reiterates the sounds of violence. Luisito mimics what he hears, and sings "his version of the rifle shots," documenting the oppression of the present so that others can continue to hear it (185). As Pardner flees, he hears the boy replicating the sounds of "running feet, shouts, gunshots, screams of pain" (185). The boy mimics the "fantastical" destruction that Pardner could only recognize as implausible. As the soldiers' victory nears, the music child creates a "hymn of fury that soon dissolved into vibrant waves of lament ... [praising] the bravery taking place around him" (187). The boy's voice, soon to be made silent, refuses to be recognized as simply an exotic spectacle or as a victim of historical suffering. His song creates an "ineradicable memory," loud and projected into the future.

Yuson's juxtaposition of capitalist reappropriation of land and the music child pushes readers to meditate on the very desires and discourses that make some aspects of the foreign into spectacle and others into obscure and implausible events. This theme contrasts with Anglo-American speculative fiction texts, which often focus on the magic of other cultures to "speculate upon" another culture as a stand-in for the "otherworldly," enabling them to construct new worlds while conveying other cultures as definitively antimodern. Similarly, Anglophone novels like Han Ong's *Fixer Chao*, Lydia Kwa's *This Place Called Absence*, and Peter Bacho's *Cebu* reinvent historical memory to expose the desires of their own readers, who seek an authentic representation. Yet because these texts are so often given the genre branding of nationalist literatures (Filipino, Asian American), their meanings are often obscured by the desire to see the Other as a spectacle of their identity. This book has made a case for seeing transitive culture through the antireal in order to see how these texts think through their own national and ethnic genres. In a region where American militarized and economic imperialisms converge in highly complex ways, such speculative fiction suggests that the manifestations of imperial violence—extreme inequalities, exploitation, and state and militarized violence—are so obscured that they can be mediated only through the fantastic. The "spectacle" in these fictions is located in the very contradictions of imperial logics themselves, logics of racial harmony and global multiculturalism, which continue to produce our preferred reality.

ANGLOPHONE SPECULATIVE FICTION

In 2005, Yuson's "The Music Child" was reprinted in the third volume of the *Philippine Speculative Fiction* anthology, shifting the story's genre from magical realism to speculative fiction, a genre that has taken hold in Southeast Asian Anglophone cultures as a transnational phenomenon that focuses on the spectacular processes, relationships, and hierarchies within Southeast Asia.[10] As a recent phenomenon, Anglophone speculative fiction does not refuse nationalist identity categories so much as reinterpret them as no longer belonging to the nation-state. In 2012, international attention came to Philippine anthologies when *Lauriat: A Filipino-Chinese Speculative Fiction Anthology* was published by Lethe Press in the United States, indicating that although the anthology carries the branding "Philippine" in its title, it takes the term "Filipino" outside of its authentic or nationalist assumptions. In the fourth volume of the *Philippine Speculative Fiction* series, the editor Dean Alfar considered the impact of speculative fiction in Philippine Anglophone writing as having created "a venue for Filipino writing of the fantastic sort, even as we struggle against the labels [and] deliberately break the barriers of genre."

Stories from these anthologies illustrate a focus on the body as racialized and gendered, rather than on the subjectivities of an identity. The short story "Keeping Time" by the Filipina Singaporean writer F. H. Batacan is narrated by a scientist hoping to cure a disease caused by a miracle "fat-reduction" enzyme that was put in the world's water supply, only to eventually hardwire infected bodies for starvation (12). When all the world's population becomes infected with the disease, only the richest and most obese people continue to survive, finally reaching their ideal bodily image before wilting into desiccated carcasses. Another story, Mia Tijam's "The Ascension of Our Lady Boy," features a young gay migrant living near Los Angeles who discovers that he can communicate with the chickens on his family's farm. Through repeated conversations with the chickens, the boy learns that on every forty-fourth day of their lives, they hold an orgiastic party similar to a Greek bacchanalia, though none of the chickens suspect that they will all be slaughtered on the forty-fifth day (49). The speculative element of the chicken's lives mirrors the narrator's own when he escapes to Manila to be courted by rich Filipinos, only to find rejection as his body ages, and he must live in abject poverty after the value of his body has withered away. In both stories "Keeping Time" and "The Ascension of Our Lady Boy," race is cast alongside its function as a bodily form, one of ever shifting value.

In the realm of high fantasy, Anglophone speculative fiction reflects upon the position of the colonial gaze within a world absent of realist racial identities, wherein the position of the colonial Other seems just as precarious as the position of the racialized colonial subject. M.R.R. Arcega's story "The Singer's Man" imagines a world unlike Anglo-Saxon-based universes, but one that also seems to have little relation to Filipino/a myths or beliefs. "The Singer's Man" instead attempts to reflect the complex globalized world by attempting to avoid a simple Tolkien-inspired universe where Anglo-Saxon myths are replaced with "magical" Filipino/a myths. The text's proper nouns of places and people, like "Derezn," "Gomergin," and "Harun" seem not to relate to any particular mythos. The story follows a singer from a faraway tribe who visits the Harun people, where the story's narrator, Derezn, agrees to assist her on her travels, fascinated by her music. As he says, "Her way was change. . . . She knew songs from many distant tongues, and though I did not know the words, I listened" (85). Her songs are passed down myths from other cultures, yet when such stories travel, they produce revolutionary moments causing immense change. When she encounters the slaves of the "Black Flower people," she sings "in their language in an otherworldly voice, of change," inspiring them to rebel against their masters, provoking a revolution that is later called "The Singer's War" (87).

"The Singer's Man" can be seen as a "mega-text" like those of Tolkien or Le Guin, with a full universe imagined by the author, yet Arcega's fantasy also fulfills Anna Sanchez's hope for Philippine speculative fiction in "resist[ing] the folly of mere mimicry" by imagining "a counter mega-text" (45). This "counter mega-text" comments upon other "mega-texts" by reflecting on the political and social function of speculative fiction, as the story becomes less focused on the world's different ethnic groups, and more on the singer's songs themselves, which match multiple tongues but are always in "an otherworldly voice." The songs create social upheavals despite the Singer's intentions, which are simply to find her long lost "sibling of the heart" (86). Because they are translated, the songs are always seen as foreign, threatening the conventional social orders long established throughout "the continent" (90). The story meditates on the position of the Anglophone speculative fiction writer as occupying a space between the colonial subject and the colonial Other, as the singer sings in an "otherworldly" tone, but her songs speak to political situations across worlds. Indeed, the story's ending can be seen as a call to arms for Anglophone speculative writers. After the singer is rejected by her "sibling," she disappears into the mist, and the narrator returns home, left with the singer's songs and a reputation of being "The Singer's Man" who is now known "as a bringer of change, of new ways of thinking" (91).

Reminiscent of the work of black science fiction writers in the United States like Octavia Butler, Samuel R. Delany, and Colson Whitehead, Anglophone speculative fiction stories like "The Singer's Man" expose the multilayered anxieties at the heart of racial prejudice: fears of people of color as sexually aberrant, as diseased, as unrestrained by attempts to control their bodies. The singer's desire for "change" makes her aberrant, while her culture is depicted as a foreign contagion made worse through the sexual lust for her "sibling" that motivates her to travel. Indeed, many of the stories printed in the *Philippine Speculative Fiction* series like "The Singer's Man," "Keeping Time," and "The Ascension of Our Lady Boy," refocus the speculative element from cultural "magic" toward the racialized body as vulnerable to bodily decay, sexual aberrance, and contagion. Rather than directly compare such bodies to white or colonial identities, these stories focus on the multicontextual violences that attempt to control it.

AUTHORIAL TRANSITION

Though works of Anglophone speculative fiction often distance their characters and authors from national identities, they remain under genre tags that retain nationalist terms like "Singaporean" and "Philippine." One of the *Philippine Speculative Fiction* anthology's main editors and proponents, Charles Tan, is known internationally for his speculative fiction blog, *The Bibliophile Stalker*, where Tan views speculative fiction as providing a space to transition among recognizable identities through metaphor and allegory, whereas, as he claims, most "national" or "ethnic" realist literature demands that "you can't write about cultures that aren't your own" ("No Foreigners Allowed"). For Tan, speculative fiction opens up the "possibility of genuine insight when an external party writes about another culture," because when there is "distance and a lack of presumptions, fresh perspectives arise." Tan's advocacy of cross-cultural writing has sparked controversy, with some naming Tan as an ally of "defensive white writers" who seek to mine inspiration from the mythos of others (Deepa). Tan, like many Philippine speculative fiction writers, is of mixed ancestry (Chinese Filipino), and speaks within an experience of hybrid backgrounds and imperial encounters that have so far not been incorporated into global nationalist identities. For a transcultural writer like Tan, to be able to write about another culture through a recognizable label like speculative fiction may enable one to write at all. Indeed, as many speculative fiction authors come from transcultural, mixed race, and Anglophone backgrounds, their ascribed identity is not their experience, and writing about their "spectacular" cultural traditions can seem just as strange as writing about "foreign" ethnic groups. Tan's *Philippine Speculative Fiction* anthologies have held to this perspective by encouraging open defiance of genre conventions as a means of reinterpreting and innovating upon the everyday reality of Filipino/a identity. As Tan's coeditor Dean Alfar writes in the series's first volume, in order to "create the fantastic,"

> We must write literature that unabashedly revels in wonder, infused with the culture of our imagination—which means being Filipino and, at the same time, surrendering that very same limiting notion—being more than Filipino, unleashing the Filipino of our imagination, divorcing and embracing the ideas of identity, nationhood and universality. We need to do magic. (viii)

The "magic" mentioned here is in imagining new forms of Filipino/a identity while still participating in an antiracist project. In this sense, Philippine speculative fiction can be read as an expression of transitive culture, as it pushes the limits of Filipino/a identity, expanding it to account for racial and cultural mixture, as well as the ongoing histories of imperial and neocolonial dominance—simply put, it reinvigorates and transforms a national identity against imperial projects.

The views of speculative fiction authors like Charles Tan and Dean Alfar in "going beyond" one's national, ethnic, and racial identity sound similar to views of white literary authors who claim the artistic privilege to write the life-stories of others. In 2015, the publication of Michael Derrick Hudson's poem in that year's *Best American Poetry* set off a storm of criticism against the poet, who published under a Chinese name, Yi-Fen Chou, simply because it would increase the likelihood of his poem's publication. The anthology's editor, Sherman Alexie, called the name a "subterfuge" that had fooled him into selecting an act of "colonial theft" (Flood). A year later, at the 2016 Brisbane Writers Festival, Lionel Shriver, the author of thirteen novels including *We Need to Talk about Kevin* and *The Mandibles*, gave an infamous speech defending the right of writers—implicitly white writers—to voice characters of ethnic, cultural, or sexual identities other than their own.[11] "Otherwise," Shriver says, "all I could write about would be smart-alecky 59-year-old 5-foot-2-inch white women from North Carolina" (Nordland). In response, the Sudanese-born writer Yassmin Abdel-Magied, who had walked out of Shriver's speech, penned an article claiming Shriver's monologue was "a celebration of the unfettered exploitation of the experiences of

others, under the guise of fiction" (Nordland). This debate became an annual ritual among the successful white literary establishment when it again emerged in
2017 after the Canadian writer Hal Niedzviecki argued that Canada should have a
"cultural appropriation prize" aimed at encouraging white and middle-class writers to "relentlessly explore the lives of people who aren't like you" (8). Claiming
that "the readers will know" if a work incorporates other cultures respectfully,
Niedzviecki also neglected to mention the fact that the literary establishment
so often caters to white and middle-class readers, who likely would *not* know.
Worse, the article prefaced an issue of *Write* magazine focused on the work of
indigenous authors who themselves were against cultural appropriation.[12]

The arguments for cultural appropriation by writers like Gudson, Shriver, and
Niedzviecki seem to overlap with those of Anglophone speculative fiction writers, as both seem to practice what Chen Kuan-Hsing has called "critical syncretism," where identification is not with the colonizer (like assimilation) or with
the self (as with multiculturalism), but through imagining oneself as Other. As
Chen writes, critical syncretism can offer a deimperializing political practice
through the intent "to become others, to actively interiorize elements of others
into the subjectivity of the self so as to move beyond the boundaries and divisive positions historically constructed by colonial power relations" (98). Critical
syncretism sees identities as divisive and in need of being breached, yet it keeps
those identities intact as objects to be overcome. Indeed, both sets of artists seem
aligned in "overcoming" identity politics, or at least replacing it through "a system of multiple reference points that can break away from the self-reproducing
neocolonial framework" (Chen 101). But if both sets of authors seem to practice critical syncretism, it is because Chen's term has been undertheorized. What
matters is not choosing to write about others, but *how* one writes about others
aesthetically, and *why* one does so within one's own position vis-à-vis contemporary pluralist structures.

Though the position of writers like Gudson, Shriver, and Niedzviecki may
seem similar to that of speculative fiction authors like Dean Alfar and Charles
Tan, their comments come within a literary culture that is envisioned as racially
diverse, but is heavily dominated by a tradition of white authors writing from the
perspectives of people of color. One could say in terms of real diversity, literary
culture is bottom of the barrel, but it is a barrel where the bit of colored oil has
floated to the top.[13] Indeed, to speak of the privilege of the author to write about
Others remains myopically focused on the right of white writers to write about
people of color. Though Gudson, Shriver, and Niedzviecki speak in universals
about what is allowed for all people, their examples and main agendas are about
the white privilege to colonize the stories of Others—a practice that has rarely
been out of fashion. Conversely, Anglophone speculative fiction authors seek
not to "write the Other's story" or to pass as another ethnicity, but to transition
among stories as a means of unsettling, broadening, or otherwise transforming

the associations of the identities assigned to them since birth (Chinese, Filipino, American). Here Chen's critical syncretism seems most questionable, for it centers on the need to actively shift "the objects of identification" to create a "liberating form of subjectivity" (100). But the objects of identity are already shifting, always in motion and responding to crisis. The writers who advocate and practice appropriation differ from Anglophone speculative authors not in their objects but in their *aesthetic modalities*: one reinscribes racial and gendered identities within the manageable borders of pluralist governmentality, the other punctures given notions of ethnic identity with the ineffable presence of transition; one attempts intimate portrayals of others to tell a story "that sells"; the other maintains a distance that questions the audience's very desire to read that story; one is made to impress us with its authenticity, the other plays in speculation.

ON BEING KAWIKA

To illuminate the differences between what I am calling "speculative transition" and the cultural appropriation represented by Gudson, Shriver, and Niedzviecki, I want to turn briefly to my own experiences as an artist writing speculative fiction under an "ethnicized" pen name that has allowed me to waver among many different identities: Filipino American, scholar, American expatriate, and itinerant artist. In 2011, I began publishing my short fiction under the name Kawika Guillermo. I had used Kawika as a name since my mother first revealed that it was the name she intended for me to have (Guillermo is her birth name). But before I was born, she decided against making Kawika my legal name, as it sounded too feminine and too ethnic. Since then I have used it as a character name when I role-play in online chat groups, as a gamer tag when I play online games, and as the name I give when I travel and prefer to remain anonymous. Now I continue to employ the name for my fiction to separate my art from my scholarship, to give recognition to my queerness and to my Hawaiian and Filipino (Ilocano, Visayan) heritage, and to distance myself from myself. On the one hand, "Kawika" has made me accountable to diasporic histories and marginal roots, while on the other hand, my work has constantly been read as the "authentic" or "inauthentic" representation of the Filipino American or Hawaiian male.

Transitioning into Kawika has forced me to confront the ambiguities of ethnic passing within the literary market. In 2011, after publishing my first story as Kawika, I was immediately offered the chance to coauthor a romantic novel based on the Amish experience. But the novel would not be published under either of my names. Instead, my prospective coauthor and I would write collectively under an Amish pseudonym, Ava Troyer. The novel would be an autobiography of Ava Troyer's experience leaving the Amish community for the romance and buzz of New York City. I knew nothing about the Amish community, and the invitation to write a fake autobiography under an Amish pseudonym was a startling introduction into the world of literary colonization. It became clear that taking on ethnic pseudonyms was the norm in the literary world, and I became increasingly anxious that, by using a pseudonym, I had marked myself as the kind of author who fakes names, steals stories, and ethnicizes myself in order to publish. I nearly excised the name, but then I also could not readopt my so-called "real" name, "Christopher B. Patterson," my scholarship name that heads published articles, a name originally meant to assimilate me into a white, Christian society. The feeling of distance remains, whether I see my father-given name, Christopher B. Patterson, which hides my racial and sexual difference, or whether I see my mother-given name, Kawika Guillermo, which amplifies my difference with its curious combination of "Kawika," the native Hawaiian word for the colonizer's name "David," and Guillermo, the first name of the Spanish friar for whom my family once worked in the Philippines.

Given my own mixed feelings about my pen name, in interviews, I've trained myself to give snarky responses to questions about it. In 2012, I was interviewed about my short story "Reunion," which follows an elderly German woman after the fall of East Prussia who waits for the Red Army to capture her. *Smokelong Quarterly*'s Brian Wicks asked about my name, and I responded:

> "Guillermo" is my mother's family name, who is third-generation Ilocano, and "Kawika" is the name she wanted to give me. The name is also a nod to Winnifred Eaton, the first Asian American fiction writer, who was part Chinese but called herself Onoto Watanna so she could write romances about Japanese geishas. If anyone at the time had thought to translate her name, they would have found "Onoto Watanna" meant something like "to change a name." She had a sense of humor, and I thought it would be funny to have a name that read "exotic" while writing about things like Nazis. (Wicks and Guillermo)

My decision to write under a pen name seemed natural in Asian diasporic literary cultures, where authors had a tradition of emphasizing their Asian-sounding middle names (Maxine Kingston can become Maxine "Hong" Kingston), and, as Shirley Geok-lin Lim writes, it can be common to transition from name to name depending on context ("'Geok Lin' in English school and 'Shirley' in my home") (*Among the White Moon Faces* 18). But by 2014, after I had graduated with my Ph.D., my attitude toward my pen name had changed dramatically. I felt that my colleagues suspected me to be a mixed race Asian attempting to fake "real" Asianness, who, like the mixed race Onoto Watanna, had adopted a pen name to self-orientalize. A regional journal interviewed me after they featured one of my stories about traveling in Malaysia, and the inevitable question about my name came up again. This time I responded tersely: "My mother's maiden name is Guillermo. Kawika is what she named me. Like most any name, I had no choice in the matter and don't really care for it" (Williamson).

My pen name took on new meanings as more of my work was published in speculative fiction journals. As a rejection of the presumptions of "Kawika," I have never written from the realist point of view of a Filipino citizen or Hawai'ian local. Instead, I've struggled to do the opposite, to write from a view of versatility that captures a person's story anchored within the speculative style of non-ownership. My story "The Last of Its Kind" in *Mothership: Tales from Afrofuturism and Beyond* (2013) is about the last magician seeking to kill the last dragon, two combating minorities entrenched in their magical difference. My story "No Name Islands," in *Amok: Asia-Pacific Speculative Fiction* (2014), is viewed through the eyes of a tourist beckoned to protect a young refugee in the futuristic islands of Mindanao. My story "Strange Gifts" (2012) in *decomP* follows a gang of young men living at the top floor of a vertical city upon the Puncak Jaya Mountain in Indonesia. The story depicts these boys' daily competitions to grab propaganda canisters that parachute into the city from a distant civil war. My short story "The Bear" (2015), in *LONTAR: The Journal of Southeast Asian Speculative Fiction*, follows a eunuch as he chases his young female charge around a dystopian underground in a futuristic Malaysia. The story revisits themes of bodily social control found in Southeast Asia and China, as only the eunuch can be trusted to handle children, while the child herself has been habituated by "the party" to rely upon a cocktail of addictive drugs.

I index my own fiction as a means of showing how thinking of myself as a speculative fiction author has enabled me to maneuver among the demands of my mixed-race identity, as well as my many other experiences as a traveler, expatriate, migrant, and American, experiences that neither of my names conjure. Besides those discussed above, I have published stories from the point of view of white female sex workers (in *Feminist Studies*), a young Korean American lesbian (in *Tayo Literary Magazine*), a dead person (in *Crack the Spine*), and a fashion-forward gerbil (in *The Monarch Review*). Even when I write in a socio-realist style, I prefer the speculative branding, as it immediately speaks from a position of distance. As an author I must remain aware that this detachment can sometimes take the form of pitiless market-driven commodity, a colonial subterfuge that reproduces white literary culture. Indeed, even in the transpacific Anglophone, the turn to speculative fiction as a brand can sometimes take cynical forms that deploy mythical histories while ignoring present-day imperial conflicts.[14] But my own speculative transitions have also offered a form of detachment from the trappings of the self, a means to criticize the self, to compare the self, to see outside, to refuse the gaze that demeans or steals from others. This distance does not reject authenticity, but transforms what we think of as authentication. Fakeness, speculation, transition, too, are forms of authenticating one's presence, and engaging with our material reality by revealing the implausible.

I do not identify as Kawika. Instead, I see the name as invoking a process of transition to live up to the name of my grandparents, to make something of the name my mother chose, to earn the name that was taken from me. Through the name's distancing I confront my own experiences as a descendant of mestizo Chinese Filipino/as, Polynesians, Irish, and Germans, who has lived and traveled extensively in Asia, who still maintains much of the Western gaze. When I write as Kawika I am not free—I feel the burden of history, the weight of unrequited pasts. Kawika becomes not a person but a ghost, taunting me in a cynical voice, "you're a fake, this name means nothing to you, you are a plastic glossy face, a cardboard cutout, an empty house." But this ghost comes from the future as much as it does the past. And it does not always mean me harm.

THE SPECULATIVE AND THE TRANSITIVE

This chapter formulated an aesthetics of transition not by seeing "above" or "beyond" genre, but by reading texts within the genre expectations of speculative fiction. Anglophone speculative fiction takes on a recognizable genre label, and uses it "as a shield against censorship and [as] a means of transgressing taboos" (Sanchez 42–43). Indeed, like ethnicized subjects who transition, these texts seem unreal, and "have no place in the turmoil of local socio-political realities," making their own self-branding appear as an oxymoron (ibid. 41). Yet these speculative texts also expose alternative logics to genres based on political identities (African American, Asian American) and genres based on themes or content (science fiction, fantasy). Speculation enables authors to transgress reader expectations of national or ethnic identity by instead expressing how identities fluctuate within the larger context of pluralist governmentality. In refusing to melt into this structure, such texts account for unseen connections and contradictions, where the author herself stands as both a critic of imperial governance and a product of imperial encounter.

Undefined and unrecognized by Western audiences, transpacific Anglophone literature writes back from spaces of transition, where multiple identities can be imposed at once, but as soon as one expects them to sing of their homeland's monsoon winds, like the music child, they sing instead of "bullets" through a "hymn of fury" (Yuson, "Music Child" 184). Coming from a region decimated by imperial projects and global capitalist extraction, these writers and their texts have received far too little attention by literary scholars who seek to mine the American, British, or "global" experience. To assume that transpacific Anglophone writing is irrelevant to understanding our own cultures erases the histories of imperial violence that produced "us" and "them" in the first place. This book has tried to account for such cultures, to recognize them as a viable aesthetic mode and as strategies that have the potential to dismantle the complex overlapping of imperialist, capitalist, and state regimes, which all rely on pluralist categories in order to function.

CONCLUSION
Identity, Authenticity, Collectivity

> To give an example of the way in which critical languages can sometimes weigh us down, consider the fact that we have become adept within postmodernism at talking about "normativity," but far less adept at describing in rich detail the practices and structures that both oppose and sustain conventional forms of association, belonging, and identification.
> —Judith Halberstam, *In a Queer Time and Place*

> Any real change implies the breakup of the world as one has always known it, the loss of all that gave one an identity, the end of safety.
> —James Baldwin, "Faulkner and Desegregation"

> They made us into a race. We made ourselves into a people.
> —Ta-Nehisi Coates, *Between the World and Me*

I remember well my first academic conference for two reasons. First, I remember couch-surfing at a frat house in Spokane, Washington, where I practiced my presentation outside in the freezing cold to avoid getting a secondary high from the marijuana smoke permeating the beer-stained couch I was to sleep on that night. Second, I recall attending the conference and seeing the critique of identity in action. I had cursory knowledge of identity critique, of course, but I had yet to witness its celebration within the academy through the distancing effect of "critical languages." I remember sitting in on panels whose every member derided identity as a faulty framework because it spoke to no true subjectivity—whether black, Latino/a, Asian, or white. Identity was said to bind us like a straitjacket, to limit our potential, and to keep us enmeshed within a labor hierarchy that would only cease to exist if we all, uniformly, woke up to its perils.

I was taken in. Up until that point, I was a mixed race white-Polynesian-Chinese-Filipino who spoke no Tagalog and did not discover my Filipino heritage until I was a teenager ("hapa haole" before that). I was raised in a working-class family of janitors, truck drivers, and fire-and-brimstone Protestants (both of my grandfathers were preachers). I was told to lie and tell anyone who asked of my race that I was "mostly white." As a teenager, I had worked menial jobs as a custodian, cashier, fast-food cook, and the like, where I formed ties with black, Latino/a, Filipina/o, and white working-class communities, and I was playfully called a "banana" or an "oreo." It was not until I attended that conference that I felt my dissociations had some greater purpose. I was outside of the ethnic straitjacket.

Years later, when working on a dissertation that was to become this book, I began to understand the disturbing irony of that conference. The scholars who had slept in the expensive conference hotel, who practiced their presentations in exclusive work groups, whose faces were featured in the conference program next to long bios detailing their publications, who wore name tags displaying their university affiliation, their tenure status, and their educational background—these were the same scholars lecturing on the false trappings of identity, and warning of the perils for those who dared reproduce it. And there I sat in the back row, an unknown student fast accumulating massive student debt, who had spent three long years fighting my way into graduate school.

I start with this example not to disparage any academics or their work, but to account for the not uncommon social imaginary that identity and its critiques have reiterated within our current moment. It is an imaginary of competing hierarchies, where some of us claim to be "Asian American," "Pacific Islander," and "queer" in order to gain recognition where none exists, or where its alternatives ("chink," "island hopper," "faggot") offer only ridicule; meanwhile, others, in so claiming this identity, feel only limited by it, as other identities have been made available ("global nomad," "academic," "professor," "artist"). The gray area between claiming an identity and being limited by it is implicitly an area separated by class, education, global sensibilities, and the like. The conference example, however crudely, illustrates the gray area as the only area that exists. It insists that the ability to publicly deny the importance of identity is conditioned by a culture that too operates through recognized modes of belonging (post-structural language, political arguments, a tenure-track position, affiliation to a well-known American university). To fault identity as form because it does not speak to one's "true subjectivity" ignores the processes through which identities are made and remade. What I experienced at that conference was not so much a revelation, but the beginnings of a long transition toward a new academic hierarchy wherein I was to start all over from the bottom. Like the hierarchies outside of it, the academic imaginary promised progress based on merit. It promised a belonging among a new group who, out of affordance or refuge, felt the need to cast some identities aside.

Transitive Cultures has approached questions of identity first by exposing their function within multiple modes of pluralist governmentality, which is not simply dismantled because one refuses identity, nor does it break apart at the sign of an unincorporated, critically minded subject whose identity appears ambiguous—especially when such figures already employ the privilege of the elite cosmopolitan or the flexibility of the business class traveler. Pluralist governmentality always seeks new identities to incorporate, new ambiguities to beam its policing flashlight upon. Each revealed identity fuels its mission to include the unincluded, to make itself appear progressive and future-oriented. "Confounding the system" with identity after identity is a loss cause. It underestimates how pluralist governmentality itself is already flexible—that lauded word!—how it shifts forms from the local to the global, so that what cannot figure in a city might have a deep recognizable history in a nearby small town. It operates across oceans, where a state characterized as inclusive and diverse (Singapore, the United States) will appear from the outside as one based on exclusion and divisive factioning. Within this framework, I have sought to explore how transitive cultures navigate these contexts by appropriating the lens of power to achieve tactical victories, to live well, and to flourish as one can.

This book has not attempted to dismantle notions of identity or identity politics so much as to show how transition makes the hierarchies that organize these concepts visible. What transitive cultures teach us is to see identity as neither an essential part of ourselves, nor as a "subjectless" tool that contains a particular political criticism. Rather, it demonstrates how the tactic of transitioning among identities has remained a cultural practice that, unlike "strategic essentialism,"[1] reveals an aesthetic form, an affective function, and new collectivities. In this sense, identity functions as a means of everyday communication not only between subjects and the world, but among subjects and the various audiences they could simultaneously be addressing in different coded grammar. This book has not attempted to expose authenticity as a "false trapping" so much as to understand the forms of resistance, management, and flourishing that appear in contexts where authenticity remains dominant. We can neither fully reject authenticity, nor can we dismiss it, but we can understand what emerges through its presumptions. We can understand how seeing cultural objects and practices as either "authentic" or "inauthentic" constitute and reproduce each other, making transition more and more difficult to recognize.

This book has attempted to examine transition as a cultural practice that maneuvers within the authentic/inauthentic binary. In its most applicable formulation, transition means three things about identity itself: 1) In being intersectional, identities are also multiple, contextual, and comparative. One does not merely have overlapping gender, racial, and class identities (as in a Venn diagram). One also transitions into multiple (and intersectional) identities, from big (Asian American) to small (Ilocano) to seemingly contradictory (white and Asian).

2) Identities are not merely political modes of recognition (an identity politics) reliant upon symbolic objects (objects of identification), but resemble modalities through which one experiences pleasure, love, and intimacy. Identities are not mere swaps of clothing, but open us up to deeper connections, and to new collectivities that better respond to injustice. Authenticity thus need not drive fetish or stereotype. Instead, transition urges us to see authenticity as authentication, as the ability to authenticate one's own presence within a space that may have otherwise excluded us. 3) Identities (like genres), do not tell us *who* or *what* we are so much as *when* and *where* we are. We are city-folk in the counties, district-folk in the cities, street-identified in the districts. When asked the question "what are you," we don't respond with a given, because it always depends on who's asking. We are Chinese to white people, mixed hapa to our own communities, and just plain American to our grandparents. It is too often the (white) audience, not us, who presumes to think of us in such simplistic terms, as people trapped in our identities. Identity tells us just as much about the audience who desires to know that identity as it does about the person being identified .

In a way, all of the above descriptions are obvious because they have always been a part of our everyday practice. Before we ever read an academic text, we were accounting for our time and place, we were identifying with multiple histories and desires (for what is more desirable than the Other in all its multitude?). And because we are categorized broadly as "ethnic" or "people of color," many of us can play with who we are—we find no monolithic, racial essence in the identities we match ourselves with, but rather, a means of reaching out to others with the modes of recognition that we share together. Critiques of our identity and authenticity should thus cause us to question the basis of that very critique—*how* does critiquing this particular identity help us in this moment, and *why* does the critic feel the need to expose something that, collectively, was already present in the way we have transitioned to and from this identity? These questions in mind, we can see transitive cultures not as another form of identity begging to be included (and thus tolerated), nor as a superior mode of living with difference, but as an everyday practice of dealing with the imperial gaze of those who might otherwise vilify us, as well as a way of reaching out to those who might ally with us. As Paulo Freire writes, transitivity is a mode of critical engagement when one does not have the methods or capabilities to outright organize and resist the dehumanizing hierarchies inherent in imperial dominance. Freire invokes transitive consciousness as an ability to grasp at larger themes of power in order to "intervene in reality instead of remaining mere onlookers" (5). Like transitive consciousness, transitive cultures do not name a political entity or position, but lay the critical groundwork for imaginative and creative collectives to emerge.

One can find these traits of transitive culture within the origins of "the Asian American," an identity that formed to reject racist notions of the Orient (and

"Orientals"). At a time when some groups were seen as "model minorities"—some as farmers, some as factory workers, some as suspected communists or sympathizers, and some as "the enemy"—"Asian American" constructed an identity that enabled new forms of transition wherein people could imagine themselves as part of a collectivity that took American belonging as its starting point. As with other coalitional identities—Malaysian, Singaporean, Filipina/o—what has become particularly troublesome about Asian American identity is not so much its exclusion of others who don't quite fit, but the anthropological basis of that exclusion where identity merely defines particular bodies. The use of Asian American in this way has resulted in its depoliticized staying power within institutions that appropriate the term to give themselves an aura of diversity. An identity that once galvanized people who had very little in common except for having migrated from the same continent can now appear to legitimate grant reports and to categorize new migrants who become Asian American as soon as they step into the United States. When identities that were once imaginative and politically active become exclusionary and cemented onto particular bodies—such as when the Association of Asian American Studies, in 2004, decided to indefinitely table a ballot regarding a proposed name change to "the Association for Asian/Pacific Islander American Studies"—identities become hard, toughened from decades of group association (Hsu, "Guåhan (Guam), Literary Emergence"). Appeals to tradition replace real histories of mixture and imagination, and dismiss contemporary contexts where U.S.-controlled capital circulation and militarization across the Asia-Pacific make new coalitions ever more crucial.

What this means then is not that concepts of identity and authenticity are useless, but that their political power comes through active and aggressive imaginative work aimed at reinvigoration, reframing, and remaking. It means looking critically at our context and imagining what collectivities (old and new) might be made and remade to combat the injustices of our time. Given that so many identities emerged to collectivize groups against imperial violence, the strategy of pluralist governmentality has not been to erase difference, but to take control of its innovations, to stymie the imaginative impulse by seeing new identities as already existing objects hidden within the dark—objects that the imperial state must brighten, celebrate, and make tolerable. Transition upsets this notion of identity. In the spotlight of pluralism transition appears monstrous, flashing into different forms every time light is cast upon it. Transition thus becomes devalued as the traits of an individualist chameleon, detached and merely appropriating others' cultures.

This book has attempted to invoke transitive culture as a way of recognizing how seemingly disparate groups share cultural practices of transition fostered through networks and histories that transgress national borders. Transitive cultures defy pluralist governmentality not by refusing visible racial or gendered markers, but by cohering strategies, tactics, and practices of transition that enable individuals to maneuver among the norms of identity. It takes back the power of imagination by reinvigorating and legitimizing new imaginings of the self and our relationships with others. It revokes the authority of imperial power by invoking our own modes of authentication, opening space for new clusterings, new social bonds, new routes for intimacy and pleasure, new politics for unionization, and new collectives for the future.

ACKNOWLEDGMENTS

Transitive Cultures was written from 2007 to 2017 in sites across the transpacific: Seattle, Kailua, Seoul, Nanjing, Hong Kong. It was made possible by relationships that were a mixture of the scholarly, the personal, and the itinerant. Friends, family, colleagues, mentors, and loved ones all contributed to its development.

Various intellectual communities have grounded this book and provided a discursive space for its arguments: The Asian American Studies Research Collective, including Simeon Man, Michael Hodges, Vanessa Au, and Alan Williams; For a Democratic University, including Ariel Wetzel and Caitlin Palo; the University of Washington English graduate student community, especially Christopher Martin, Bob Hodges, and Allen Barros; the Critical Filipino/Filipina Studies Collective, especially Michael Viola, Valerie Francisco, Amanda Solomon, and Freedom Siyam; and my dissertation writing group, including Jessie Kindig and Annie Dwyer. I have also gained from two years working with the Seattle Asian American Film Festival, and frequent collaborations with the Simpson Center for the Humanities. Su-Ching Wang provided enduring support during the formative years of this manuscript, and her devotion to social justice left an imprint in its pages.

The mentorship and kindness I have gained as part of the Asian American Studies community has helped sustain my belief in this project. I will always be grateful for the sacrifices these mentors made for me: Robyn Rodriguez, Steve Sumida, Rick Bonus, Vicente Rafael, Moon-Ho Jung, Eng-Beng Lim, Priti Ramamurthy, Guy Beauregard, Cathy Schlund-Vials, Martha Cutter, Catherine Fung, Eric Tang, and Martin Joe Ponce. Devoted mentors in Las Vegas sparked my thinking on ethnic and Asian literature, and I thank Marc Smerek, Felicia Campbell, and Vincent Perez. Many fiction writers have fueled my ongoing belief in literature, and I consider each of them crucial to my development as both artist and scholar: Shirley Geok-lin Lim, Madeleine Thien, M. Evelina Galang, Ken Liu, R. Zamora Linmark, Peter Bacho, Shawn Wong, Jose Dalisay, and Vu Tran.

The support from my dissertation committee throughout my time at the University of Washington was unwavering. Chandan Reddy, thank you for your probing questions and steadfast support. Gillian Harkins, thank you for your frank feedback and your openness as a mentor. Francisco Benitez, thank you for your invaluable advice and your persistence in pushing my arguments further. To my chair, Alys Weinbaum, your example as a scholar and professor convinced me to stay in graduate school numerous times. Your belief in holding my work to a high standard has pushed me to perform at my peak, and your constant support has rescued me in moments of self-doubt.

I was fortunate to find support from a number of grants, fellowships, and awards. I am grateful to Beverly Butcher at the New York Institute of Technology in Nanjing, China, who helped me earn awards for necessary visits to Singapore, Malaysia, Taiwan, Indonesia, and the Philippines. Thanks to this funding, I was able to foster relationships with scholars in Asia who influenced this work and provided an intellectual community during its stages of revision: Wen Jin and Celina Hung in Shanghai, Alvin Wong in Seoul, Oscar Campomanes and Ferdinand Lopez in Manila, and Andy Wang and Chien-ting Lin in Taiwan. I am also grateful to the online communities of scholars, particularly those who allowed me to interview them for the *New Books in Asian American Studies* podcast: Vernadette Gonzalez, LeiLani Nishime, Thuy Linh Tu, Rick Baldoz, Erin Khue Ninh, and Denise Cruz.

Revisions and final editing for this book were done in Hong Kong, where I began as a postdoctoral fellow in the Centre for Cultural Studies at Chinese University of Hong Kong. I thank Song Hwee Lim, Pang Laikwan, and Elmo Gonzaga who provided meaningful conversations that directed revision. My colleagues at Hong Kong Baptist University, especially John Erni, Tan Jia, Daisy Tam, and Lucetta Kam, have given constant flashes of insight that caused me to shift linguistic registers. Other academics and writers in Hong Kong have provided much needed counterpoints and references that made their way into the manuscript, including Elizabeth Ho, Grace Wang, Jeffrey Mather, Doretta Lau, Jason Coe, Kenneth Huynh, Charlotte Frost, and Collier Nogues. My research assistants, Jeff Chow Jung Sing, Patricia Choi, Pamela Wong, and Yicen Liu relieved much of the editorial burden. My bold acquisitions editor, Lisa Banning, deserves much credit for seeing this manuscript's budding though unpolished potential.

Portions of this book were previously published in different form, and have been substantially revised for the purposes of this book. Sections of chapter 3 appeared in *Melus: Multi-ethnic Literature of the United States* 39, no. 1 (2014, 149–172), and in *Queer Sex Work*, edited by Nicola Smith, Mary Laing and Katy Pilcher (Routledge, 2015, 53–63). A portion of chapter 4, including the concept "global imaginaries," appeared in *MANUSYA: Journal of Humanities*18 (2011, 49–69). Parts of chapter 5 appeared in *WorkingUSA* 15, no. 1 (2012, 87–102). Some of the concepts from chapter 6 on speculative fiction appeared in a collaborated article with Y-Dang Troeung in *Concentric: Literary and Cultural Studies* 42, no. 1 (March 2016, 73–98). A grant from Hong Kong Baptist University helped support the final stages of the revision process.

My partner and challenger, Y-Dang Troeung, has been indispensable for her emotional honesty, companionship, passion, and intellect. Through her, I have engaged with brilliant minds whose work influenced the manuscript's final revisions, including Donald Goellnicht, Phanuel Antwi, Christopher Lee, Anida Yoeu Ali, Helen Hok-Sze Leung, Christine Kim, Thy Phu, Nadine Attewell, and Vinh Nguyen. Y-Dang has been my trusted teacher, my most attentive listener, and my truest friend. I dedicate this book to her and our newborn son, Kai Basilio Troeung. You both invigorate me every day with the seeds for a more hopeful future.

I'd like to thank my family. First my father, Samuel James Patterson, and all my loved ones in Portland whose faith I long rejected, but whose lifelong search for moral justice and meaning in times of loss has always underpinned my own (re)search. Finally, this book, like many academic projects, came from the desire to understand those closest to me: my brother, Cameron Patterson in Seoul; my sister, Chanel Guillermo in San Antonio; my mother, Dion Guillermo Glenn in Las Vegas; and the rest of the Guillermo tribe in Oahu. Your mobility, flexibility, and ability to transition for all our sakes, showed me early on how identity, race, and gender work in the everyday, across cities, continents, and islands. You provided the kernels of this manuscript by being your many selves.

NOTES

INTRODUCTION

1. Lee Shin decorates his house with "calligraphy, banners, flute, and decorated dragon" ("Wicks, Diaspora and Identity" 12).

2. As Maniam writes in "The New Diaspora," "the problem for the Malaysian writer is in making the crossover to the other cultures, to get to know better the people of other races to be able to write about them" (40).

3. "Transpacific," as defined by Janet Hoskins and Viet T. Nguyen, signifies a study that charts how the rise of Asian countries "is tied to a complicated history of competition, conflict, and negotiation with the west, with each other, and with their own minorities" (12).

4. As Vijay Mishra has put it, the chameleon represents "placing an old skin with a new one through molting, dispensing with singular narrative forms" (*Literature of the Indian Diaspora* 51–52).

5. Instead of taking "a posture of adjustment" (5), Freire advocates for "the development of an especially flexible, critical spirit" (6). This spirit, which he calls transitive, is attuned to transitional epochs and accounts for the contradictions that emerge "between the ways of being, understanding, behaving, and valuing" (6).

6. I am in agreement here with Alexander G. Weheliye, who argues that methods employing "agency" and "resistance" too easily assume full, coherent subjects, rather than allowing for "a more layered and improvisatory" subjectivity (2).

7. Scott uses the term "metis," broadly understood as "a wide array of practical skills and acquired intelligence in responding to a constantly changing natural and human environment" (*Seeing Like a State* 313). I use "transitive" similarly, but in specifically responding to pluralist contexts.

8. As Jay Prosser writes, transsexuals speaking of themselves as such constitute a paradox: "If the goal of transsexuality is to pass as not transsexual, what does it mean to come out and speak as a transsexual?" (317)

9. As Judith Halberstam has argued, the transgender body has been a contradictory site where, on one hand, it has "emerged as futurity itself, a kind of heroic fulfillment of postmodern promises of gender flexibility" (*In a Queer Time and Place* 18), and on the other hand, marks the success of years of gender activism, where it is kept alive "as a meaningful designator of unpredictable gender identities and practices" (ibid. 21).

10. Amy L. Brandzel calls this a split between coalitional and intersectional politics with anti-coalitional, anti-intersectional politics. Brandzel sides with the former, arguing for "a political coalitional present to dismantle the heteronormative, whitenormative, and colonialnormative structures of U.S. culture and politics" (316).

11. Women of color feminism and queer of color feminism are two other sites of critique that have focused on the intersections "of race, gender, sexuality, and class in forming social practices" (Ferguson 4).

12. One only needs browse websites to see this term employed by companies and universities who base their diversity on multiple denominations of Christianity or different white ethnic backgrounds.

13. Kallen claimed the melting pot of "Americanism" was in fact synonymous with "Anglo-Saxonism," of people who were expected to be "individualist, English-speaking ... [and] devoted to laissez-faire" economics ("Democracy versus the Melting Pot" 6).

14. In Canada, "multiculturalism" emerged in a 1965 preliminary report, and became used formally in the 1988 Canadian Multicultural Act. Multicultural legislation also passed in Australia in 1972 to cope with the growing number of Asian immigrants. For more on Canadian multiculturalism, see chapter 3.

15. Critics like Michael Warner have similarly pointed out how "consumer capitalism makes available an endlessly differentiable subject," encouraging ethnicity and difference through the consumption of products, brands, and cultural icons (384–385).

16. The 1965 Immigration Act and the 1980 Refugee Act continued the shift away from an assimilationist-style social system toward a pluralist/multiculturalist one.

17. As Neda Atanasoski puts it, contemporary imperialism "is contingent on multiculturalism as a value system and mode of knowledge about the world ... through which the sanctity of human diversity is declared" (5).

18. Furnivall pointed to this as the main drive toward colonial pluralism, since in such a diverse society "the disorganization of social demand allows the economic process of natural selection by the survival of the cheapest to prevail" (310).

19. The colonial powers' system of pluralism was comprised of persons in "separate racial sections" to induce low labor costs, but who thought of themselves as "an aggregate of individuals" whose "social life is incomplete" (Furnivall 306).

20. The lasting violence of imperial powers like the Romans and Greeks, for Herder, was due to assimilative projects that imposed an artificial set of values that violated "the organic unity of the original culture" (White 172).

21. This absence of bureaucratic, normalizing forces has often been credited to various characteristics, such as archipelagos or "lowlands and highlands" (Reid), cultivated traditions of state resistance or anarchy (Scott, *Seeing Like a State*), or precolonial political forms of "galactic structures" of autonomous "satellite principalities" (Lieberman , "Local Integration" 485).

22. While cultural diversity is often the point of departure for studies of Southeast Asia (Wolters), some historians have seen this diverse construct of precolonial Southeast Asia as more of a Western imagining than a historical fact (since "precolonial" already suggests the absence of a hegemonic state/culture). Yet the conceptions of post-independence Southeast Asia as pluralist have been more firmly established, since the very structure for multicultural governance was reinforced by Western colonial regimes that practiced "divide and conquer" rule (Emmerson).

23. According to Anthony Reid, these nationalist forms were unlike those seen in Europe, where ethnic and state nationalisms "mutually reinforce each other to create cultural homogeneities," rather these semi-autonomous ethnic nationalities were often anti-imperial in more of a local (against state nationalism) than a foreign sense (against overseas colonization) (12).

24. Chinese became identified as traders or "Jews of the East," while other ethnicities were divided into groups of soldiers, subjects, or rivals (Reid 89).

25. Furnivall's *Colonial Policy and Practice*, often seen as a great forerunner to multiculturalist discourse, in fact illuminates how pluralist societies replace spirituality and cultural traditions with the desire for commerce, wealth, and the worship of "Mammon," the god of money.

26. Overseas Chinese governments in Taiwan (the Kuomintang) and Singapore (the People's Action Party) were seen by the People's Republic as "running dogs," who chose Americanism (signified through capitalism and Western culture) over economic equality.

27. Here I am thinking of Raymond Williams's definition of formations as "conscious movements and tendencies (literary, artistic, philosophical or scientific)" that are not identified through formal institutions (119).

28. This legacy of producing "state nationalism" through multiculturalist policies continues today with the "1Malaysia" campaign.

29. The contemporary mestizo class makes up less than 4 percent of the population (Capelli et al.), yet mestizos still garner over half of the country's personal income (Demko, Agel, and Boe).

30. The export of Filipina/o bodies has brought significant economic gains in the form of remittances, an estimated $18.76 billion in 2010 (Remo).

31. As Weheliye writes, diaspora discourse relies upon a nationalist comparative method that makes national borders and linguistic differences appear as ontological "truths," rather than as "structures or institutions" (31).

32. As Martin J. Ponce has argued, Anglophone literature in places like the Philippines complicates approaches to reading minority literature, which privilege race and nation, because they are shaped by "overlapping forces of colonialism, imperialism, and migration" (18).

33. In 1989, the Singaporean scholar Tai A. Koh criticized scholars who see Anglophone novels as "unworthy of consideration," and noted that most literary critics were unable to fully consider "the historical and cultural context in which such works are written and the reading is conducted" (277).

34. In Singapore, for example, ethnic Chinese are expected to learn Mandarin as their ethnic language, even though most Singaporean Chinese have spoken Chinese Hokkien or Hakka.

35. As the collaborator T. H. Padro de Tavera wrote in a letter to Douglas MacArthur, "[T]hrough [English] agency we may adopt its principles, its political customs, and its peculiar civilization, that our redemption may be complete and radical" (Constantino and Constantino, *Neocolonial Identity* 67).

36. In my sixth chapter, I shift the generic conceptions of these novels toward speculative fiction to better account for their critiques of authenticity.

37. Baldwin writes, "[T]he white man's motive was the protection of his identity; the black man was motivated by the need to establish an identity" (394).

CHAPTER 1   MULTIRACIAL CLANS IN COLORFUL MALAYA

1. As scholars like Robert Hefner and Philip Holden have pointed out, colonial pluralism in Malaya only had the effect of making racial differences more rigid, more segregated, and more incorporable into a colonial division of labor (Hefner 42).

2. As Neela's uncle warns her brother: "She's a slut, she will spoil our blood" (5).

3. Others include novelist Lee Kok Liang and the poets Ee Tiang Hong and Wong Phui Nam.

4. For the literary scholar Philip Holden, Fernando's text mourns an "idealized space of multicultural knowledge ... [that] can only be located now in the past, in the English-medium colonial school" ("Colonialism's Goblins" 166).

5. See Hefner (12); Raihanah ("Multiculturalism" 68); and Reid (41).

6. Supported by unionized workers and radicalized students, the alliance sought an anticolonialist agenda in the spirit of cross-cultural protest (Chua and Kian-Woon 89).

7. Singapore's entry into the Federation of Malaysia in 1963 thus came with the assumption that "Malaysian" identity would be an integrative "neutral" name distinct from any race (Reid 105).

8. Shirley Geok-lin Lim writes that she was taught by British teachers to see Chinese as "unpatriotic, brutal, and murderous" (*Among the White Moon Faces* 70).

9. As Shirley Geok-lin Lim writes in her memoir, "After May 13, most events in Malaysia, whether public or domestic, were, and possibly still are, inevitably charged with a racialized dimension, whether in civil service or private business, whether professional or personal, economic or literary" (*Among the White Moon Faces* 211).

10. The riots, which led to a state of emergency, the suspension of Parliament, and at least 196 reported killings, stemmed from the heated rhetoric of political campaigning.

11. Fernando was a migrant from Sri Lanka who studied in Britain and lived much of his life in Singapore and thus seems oddly positioned as a Malaysian author.

12. The first English poetry collection, Wang Gungwu's *Pulse*, mentioned saris and sarongs, but lamented, "Life there is here, but machine-life." Arthur Yap's collections *Only Lines* (1971), *Commonplace* (1972), and *Down the Line* (1980) met with awards and acclaim, but reflected the author's disapproval for "poems with a political basis or a social basis, commenting upon society as such" (qtd. in S. G. Lim, *Nationalism and Literature* 18).

13. In Singapore, English-language theater and poetry has been more prominent than the short story and the novel, due to the great amount of censorship once placed on the literary arts, which restrict "issues of race, especially inter-racial relations" (Chua and Kian-Woon 95).

14. Fernando moved to Kuala Lumpur to become the head of the English department at the University of Malaya in 1967.

15. As Peter Nazareth has observed, the protagonists contrast the "multicultural world that seeks to 'sell' the multiculturalism instead of exploring it honestly and profoundly" (96).

16. Her strokes "manipulat[e] the brush as an extension of her hand; her hand as an extension of her will; her will, the expression of her being" (15).

17. Fernando went so far as to state, "I do not want to write about my own ethnic group—I have none" ("Truth in Fiction" 225)

18. Though English use has continued in private institutions and colleges, *bahasa melayu* or Malay still functions as the Malaysian national language.

19. Shirley Geok-lin Lim has written of Tok Said's racial ambivalence as "the core message of Fernando's fiction" (*Writing S.E. Asia in English* 143).

20. Roderick Ferguson defines historiography as when "the writing of history . . . is not simply a scholarly practice," but also "connotes practices of socialization, conventions that work to establish a community of interpreters" (153).

21. Other sources include *Memoirs of a Malayan Family*, *Hikayat Hang Tuah*, and *Syonan* (My Story) by M. Shinozaki.

CHAPTER 2   SO THAT THE SPARKS THAT FLY WILL FLY IN ALL DIRECTIONS

1. As the historian Vicente Rafael has written, the aftermath of the EDSA revolution of 1986 "brought about the reaffirmation of social hierarchy" rather than a reversal of it (*White Love* 198).

2. Myra Mendible sees Rosca's festival "as a symbolic and literal site of transgression," though I focus here on its symbolism (4).

3. Bhabha states that "colonial hybridity is not a problem of genealogy or identity between two different cultures . . . [it] is that the difference of cultures can no longer be identified or evaluated as objects of epistemological or moral contemplation" (114).

4. Dirlik writes that "the hybridity to which postcolonial criticism refers is uniformly between the postcolonial and the First World, never, to my knowledge, between one postcolonial intellectual and another" (342).

5. As the historian Rey Ileto has pointed out, even Marcos responded to communists who identified with Bonifacio "by portraying himself as another Emilio Aguinaldo." Similarly, President Joseph Estrada "portray[ed] himself as a latter-day Bonifacio, [and] succeeded in drawing a massive following from the poorer classes despite his lack of sincerity in this identification" ("Philippine" 229).

6. Alongside these descriptions, photographs displayed individuals and groups in their "natural state," and reduced cultural differences into "an ordered range of variations and a set of representative figures" (Rafael, *White Love* 38).

7. I have found no serious literary narrative in English dedicated to the subject of the Moros conflict.

8. Pheng Cheah has had similar critiques of hybridity in the context of global capitalism, naming it a "theory of resistance that reduces the complex givenness of material reality to its symbolic dimensions and underplays the material institution of capitalist oppression at a global systematic level" (94).

9. "Buhawi of the Bisayas: The Revitalization Process and Legend-making in the Philippines" by Donn V. Hart (1967).

10. The prominence of English in secondary schools has also vernacularized English just as the late nineteenth-century *ilustrados* attempted to nationalize Spanish, making English also "a medium of nationalist identification" (Rafael, *White Love* 199).

11. A transvestite tells her he wishes he could kill Colonel Amour, but "I don't have the guts. I could help you, though, if you really want to do it. There are about a hundred of us here … we all are marvelous gossips [and] I should be able to tell you where he is at any given time" (139).

12. In a meeting with his father and the governor of the island K, Adrian remains silent while his father plans his future in managing the island as a tourist destination (40).

13. Eliza and Anna talk in "snatches of Spanish, English, and Tagalog, mixed with some mathematical language" (35).

14. The handkerchief gives him powers that cause bullets to bounce off his braided vest.

15. Myrdal authored the influential book *An American Dilemma*.

16. Yu Cheng Co is also the name of a prominent banking family in the Philippines.

17. In 1988, Benedict Anderson called the Philippines political system "so spectacularly different" from other countries in Southeast Asia because of this clan politics, which he called a politics of "political dynasties" ("Cacique Democracy").

18. In this case, the blind Cebuano mistress Teresa makes love to Leon by attempting to "measure its contours" (133).

19. Yu Cheng Co takes "the cool celestial pose of efficacious martial attack … his kicks supreme and prosperous as would befit the mighty image of the Middle Kingdom" (134).

CHAPTER 3   LIBERAL TOLERANCE AND ASIAN MIGRANCY

1. Steven D. Levitt charts the growth of homicide rates in urban cities as beginning in 1980 and peaking between 1990 and 1993.

2. Ahmed uses "performativity" as defined by J. L. Austin and Judith Butler, and similarly shows how race is performative in that it is "brought into existence by being repeated over time."

3. According to the *Seattle Times* in 2011, "In Seattle, 66 percent of all residents" consider themselves "non-Hispanic white" (Turnball and Mayo). In Portland, it was 72 percent, the highest in the country.

4. The African American candidate, Norm Rice, was elected mayor of Seattle for two terms from 1989 to 1997, and Washington's Chinese American governor, Gary Locke, had wide popularity throughout the 1990s.

5. Patricia O'Connell Killen and Mark Silk have named the Pacific Northwest the "none zone," in reference to the amount of people who check the "none" box for religious affiliation. In addition to the "none" box, Killen and Silk also point out that the region is home to "the lowest level of illiteracy in the nation (13.5 percent of adults without a high school degree), and a relatively high level of advanced education (26.6 percent with a bachelor's degree)" (26).

6. Section 19 of Canada's 1976 Immigration Act restricts those "whose admission would cause or might reasonably be expected to cause excessive demands, within the meaning assigned to that expression by the regulations, on health or prescribed social services" as well as persons who are "unable or unwilling to support themselves and those persons who are dependent on them for care and support."

7. Most of Seattle's minority populations are socially segregated in the lower-income southeast districts ("Seattle's Population"). According to the 2001 "Gender and Minority Inclusion Tables," only 2.3 percent of University of Washington students were African American, and only 3.3 percent were Latino/a.

8. As Larissa Lai has pointed out, in Vancouver, multiculturalism has efficiently depoliticized cultural politics so that "the radical and productive aspects of [identity politics] have been largely contained, and . . . what remains effective is its conservatizing function" (138).

9. Will Kymlicka compares the liberal tolerance of the United States and Canada to the "hypercommunitarian" model of group rights common in Singapore and Malaysia (Kymlicka, "Two Models" 96).

10. While scholars read *Cebu* as an intimate portrayal of the Filipino American, reviewers seem to account more for its ambiguity. *Kirkus Reviews* states, "Bacho writes with a light touch, lending an ambiguity to his narration that can be frustrating but is more usually intriguing" ("*Cebu* by Peter Bacho"). Indeed, one can also observe contradictory Amazon .com reviews, where one reviewer claims that Bacho's novel "provides an intimate look into the distant, brash, and passionate demeanor of the Filipino psyche," while another reviewer claims "Peter Bacho's book made me laugh out loud. . . . His dry sense of humor is just the right touch" ("*Cebu* [Paperback]").

11. E. San Juan writes that Bulosan's *manongs* are mediated by the "residual memory of the national liberation struggle of millions of Filipinos against Spanish colonialism and US imperialism" (558).

12. "Affect" for Clare Hemmings refers not to emotions, but to a "state of being," and places the individual in "a circuit of feeling and response, rather than opposition to others" (552).

13. While affect studies has been criticized for its "over-aestheticization" and its tendency to be "diagnostic rather than prescriptive in nature" (Pruchnic 165), affects, for Massumi, hold "a key to rethinking postmodern power after ideology" by revealing an ideology's "real conditions of emergence" (104).

14. Relationships based on *utang na loob*, according to historian Vicente L. Rafael, are "based on the sensed incommensurability between the gift that is received and its return, particularly if the gift is unsolicited" ("Confession" 334).

15. As Ileto wrote, according to Filipino "official interpretation of history," McArthur's liberation justified decades of colonial rule, as it "meant the recovery of a lost age of happiness under America's tutelage" ("Philippine" 226).

16. My definition contrasts its use by Manfred Steger (*Rise of the Global Imaginary*), who saw it as a way of moving past ideological and national landscapes. The global imaginary is rather an instance of the particular positing itself as universal—an imperial technique for creating and dictating "the global."

17. As Gayatri Gopinath has argued, the public visibility of diasporic subjects is vital in erasing the "hidden economies" of domestic labor (60).

18. For Tina Chen, Asian American identity is neither "essentialized [n]or constructed," but considers "the mutually constitutive dimensions of identity and performance" in producing "personhood" (8).

19. Francis reveals later that her income comes from a legal settlement with her uncle who molested her as an adolescent (164).

CHAPTER 4   JUST AN AMERICAN DARKER THAN THE REST

1. Halberstam writes that "the transgender body has emerged as futurity itself, a kind of heroic fulfillment of postmodern promises of gender flexibility" that reflects the global elite's association with flexibility at the level of identity and personal choices (*In a Queer Time* 18).

2. As Martin Manalansan and Lisa Duggan describe it, the homonormative is middle-class and white, and bases equality on domestic privacy, and bases freedom on the freedom to consume.

3. Ellen Wu writes that bringing statehood to Hawaii would sketch the territory "as proof of American multiracial 'democracy at work'" and would create a "vital link to Asia" (211).

4. Similarly, Oscar Campomanes has sought to redefine Filipino American as a politically resistant identity that can remain unabsorbed by nationalist rubrics while reflecting a (neo) imperial history.

5. In Stephen Sohn's essay on *Gold by the Inch*, he identifies the narrator's desire for Thong as a disguised attempt at denying his own complicity as a sex tourist ("'Valuing' Transnational Queerness").

6. Pratt writes, "I use these terms ["autoethnography" and "autoethnographic expression"] to refer to instances in which colonized subjects undertake to represent themselves in ways that engage with the colonizer's own terms . . . autoethnographic texts are those the others construct in response to or in dialogue with those metropolitan representations" (7).

7. Urry writes of "sensescapes" as discursively mediated senses of spaces that "signify social taste and distinction, ideology and meaning" ("Transports of Delight" 243).

8. As Ponce writes, the second person in *Rolling the R's* "shifts the politics of representation away from the burden of portraying 'social diversity' and toward an implication of readers themselves" (171).

9. Being identified as "Joe," as Vernadette Gonzalez has put it, is to be seen as participating in tourist and militaristic acts that are "refracted through desires to identify with masculinities that have been mobilized in the service of extraterritorial domination" (7).

10. This attitude toward English may be a subtle reference to Shirley Geok-lin Lim's memoir, where she describes her father as being "possessed by Western images," and speaking only English to his children (*Among the White Moon Faces* 42).

11. The extent to which the *bakla* and feminine Filipino gay is a colonial imagined stereotype remains a contentious issue and has yet to resolve with academic consensus. Clearly, however, figures of feminine gays and *baklas* are rampant in Philippine cinema as well as in daily visual culture, and cannot be a mere American fetish.

12. This quote, and these thoughts on arrival, were brought to my attention during a reading by Madeleine Thien and Rawi Hage.

13. Joshua Guzmán writes that for Muñoz, brownness persists "in the here-and-now as the materiality of everyday life," while queer utopia is always on the horizon and not-yet-here (60).

CHAPTER 5   MUTANT HYBRIDS SEEK THE GLOBAL UNCONSCIOUS

1. Since "mere repetition would not attract an audience" (Neale 50), "any instance of a genre will be necessarily different" (Tzvetan Todorov qtd. in Chandler 3).

2. As Robert Allen has observed, "for most of its 2,000 years, genre study has been primarily a function of 'typecasting' done by scholars who would cast a book into a genre as a species is cast into a genus" (qtd. in Chandler 1).

3. John Fiske described this as "inescapable intertextuality," and used the example of a car chase invoking an action film (115).

4. As C. J. Wee writes, the novel exemplifies an era wherein "artistic and technocratic culture need not be a monoculture; multicultural or interstitial cultures are welcome now" (201).

5. As Viet Thanh Nguyen points out, rather than lead to what Immanuel Kant called a "perpetual peace," cosmopolitanism "may also be just as useful for war as for peace" (*Nothing Ever Dies* 271). Similarly, Paul Gilroy warns of cosmopolitanism's implications for war against "intolerable" peoples, a form of "armored cosmopolitanism" (59–60).

6. Robbins hopes that multicultural education, valued through the cosmopolitan ideal, can help to keep violent incidents like the first Iraq War from taking place.

7. Affective labor includes the immaterial labor of the service industry, of housemaids, nannies, and sex workers, and transfers value from the labor in producing a commodity to the laborer's very dispositions and attitudes, her moods and affective capacities, and her ability to "get along" with clients (Clough 24).

8. Cheryl Narumi Naruse has argued that *Mammon Inc.* invokes the bildungsroman genre "with a transnational and neoliberal twist," which she describes as "coming-of-career" novel that can be read alongside recently published novels like *Crazy Rich Asians*, as well as "Aravind Adiga's *The White Tiger* (2008), Tash Aw's *Five Star Billionaire* (2013), Mohsin Hamid's *How to Get Filthy Rich in Rising Asia* (2013), and Dave Eggers's *The Circle* (2013)" (97).

9. As Pamela Butler and Jigna Desai have written, "collapsing of all chick lit into one category may indicate an inability to recognize difference not only within the genre, but between different feminisms as well" (4).

10. Daniel P. S. Goh compares Christianity in South Korea and the Philippines to Singapore where it has helped "make sense of the spiritual telos of the post-colonial nation and engage the developmental ethos of the Singapore state" (57).

11. In articulating multiple global imaginaries, I follow Stuart Hall in considering how nations and ethnicities also claim universality by revising their localism as a "dominant particular" ("Old and New Identities" 67).

12. In his reading of Ong's work, Francisco Benitez considers how the novels' (and author's) biculturalism suggests ways to avoid seeing identity/subjectivity as "autonomous act of autobiography" (338).

13. Jeffrey Partridge, in his book *Beyond Literary Chinatown*, analyzes marketing techniques for Asian American novels, and highlights themes of transportation and hidden demons with their source in the family's past (8).

14. As the writer E. San Juan points out, "the Philippines today is the largest exporter/supplier of affordable domestics—about ten million Filipino/a Overseas Contract Workers (OCWs), out of eighty-seven million Filipinos at home shuttle back and forth" (*In the Wake of Terror* xxi).

15. The structural adjustment of the 1970s Philippines left a foreign debt of over $42.8 billion by 1982, the same year that Marcos signed Executive Order 797, which created the Philippine Overseas Employment Administration, a government agency used to monitor, supervise, and collect remittances from Filipino/a migrants overseas (R. Rodriguez 13).

16. As Eleanor Ty points out, this immigrant dream is ironic, since these products "are now manufactured through transnational labor, so that what William's family covets is very likely produced in his own or other Asian countries by using cheap laborers" ("Abjection" 130–131).

CHAPTER 6   SPECULATIVE FICTION AND AUTHORIAL TRANSITION

1. Williams proceeds from genre to concepts of form, the "trans-individual author," and "commitment" and "alignment."

2. Genres for Williams are generalities made out of three basic components: "(i) *stance*; (ii) *mode of formal composition*; (iii) *appropriate subject-matter*" (183, italics in original).

3. Eric Tang refers to the hyperghetto as "a hybrid of the impoverished and racially segregated neighborhood" that resembles extensions of refugee camps and prisons, and has functioned "as a site of captivity" (10).

4. Darko Suvin distinguished science fiction and "fantastic genres" like speculative fiction through a rubric of believability and empirical evidence, claiming that "fantastic genres" are "ensembles of fictional tales without empirical validation" (viii).

5. Gomez writes, "[S]peculative fiction is a way of expanding our ideas of what human nature really is, allowing us to consider all aspects of ourselves" (954).

6. The list includes clichés like "#14: White protagonist is given wise and mystical advice by Holy Simple Native Folk" and "#3: Visitor to alien planet ignores information about local rules, inadvertently violates them, is punished" ("Stories We've Seen Too Often").

7. More examples include *The Digest of Philippine Genre Stories*, *Story Philippines*, the anthologies *Nine Supernatural Stories* and the *Philippine Speculative Fiction* series, which has been nominated for the Manila Critics' Circle National Book Award and is now in its eleventh volume.

8. "Technologizing Orientalism" defines techno-orientalism as "the phenomenon of imagining Asia and Asians in hypo- or hypertechnological terms in cultural productions and political discourse" (Roh, Huang, Niu 2).

9. From Yuson's lecture on *Don Quixote*'s influence on Philippine literature.

10. As this chapter was written, Yuson expanded the story into a novel, *The Music Child and the Mahjong Queen* (2016), where Luisito survives and moves to Japan.

11. Shriver's example of political correctness was of a sombrero party at Bowdoin College that was spoiled by instigators who took pictures of the white students and shamed them over social media (Nordland).

12. Despite many leading authors coming to Niedzviecki's defense, the preface set setting off outrage among writers of color and resulted in Niedzviecki's resignation as editor of the Writers' Union of Canada magazine..

13. According to a 2015 Diversity Baseline Survey of eight review journals and thirty-four major publishers, 79 percent of the literary industry identifies as white, with 82 percent as editors, and 89 percent as book reviewers ("Where Is the Diversity in Publishing?").

14. See my review of Verena Tay's short story collection, *Spectre*, which Tay herself describes as a way to engage with "the bizarre and the fantastical," in order to "increas[e] the potential of these tales to be sold under the supernatural and/or horror categories that do very well in the Singaporean context" (Patterson, "Verena Tay").

CONCLUSION

1. In the 1980s, Gayatri Spivak saw strategic essentialism as an approach to temporarily adopt an essentialist position in order to act as a collective, and to appropriate the idea of anti-essentialism upheld by poststructuralist critics. Spivak herself has disavowed this term, and indeed, the term for me too easily presumes an "inside" and "outside" to essentialist thinking about the Other and the self.

WORKS CITED

Acton, Lord. "Nationality." *Mapping the Nation*. Ed. Gopal Balakrishnan. London: Verso, 1996. 17–38.

Adorno, Theodor W., and Max Horkheimer. *Dialectic of Enlightenment: Philosophical Fragments*. Ed. Gunzelin Schmid Noerr. Stanford, CA: Stanford UP, 2002.

Ahmed, Sara. "Declarations of Whiteness: The Non-Performativity of Anti-Racism." *Borderlands e-journal* 3.2 (2004).

Alfar, Dean F. "Introduction." *Best of Philippine Speculative Fiction IV, 2009*. Ed. Charles Tan. Manila: Kestrel IMC, 2009.

———, ed. *Philippine Speculative Fiction*. Pasig City, Philippines: Kestrel IMC, 2006.

Anderson, Benedict R. O'G. "Cacique Democracy and the Philippines: Origins and Dreams." *New Left Review* 169 (1988): 3–31.

———. *Imagined Communities: Reflections on the Origin and Spread of Nationalism*. London: Verso, 1991.

Appiah, Anthony. *Cosmopolitanism: Ethics in a World of Strangers*. New York: W. W. Norton, 2006.

Arcega, M.R.R. "The Singer's Man." *Philippine Speculative Fiction: Literature of the Fantastic, Vol. 3*. Ed. Dean F. Alfar, and Nikki Alfar. Pasig City: Kestrel IMC, 2007. 84–91.

Bacho, Peter. *Cebu*. Seattle: U of Washington P, 1991.

Bacigalupi, Paolo. "I Am Paolo Bacigalupi, Author of Hugo Award-Winning THE WINDUP GIRL, and National Book Award Finalist SHIP BREAKER. AMA." *Reddit.com*, 18 Dec. 2012. https://www.reddit.com/r/writing/comments/152jap/i_am_paolo_bacigalupi_author _of_hugo_awardwinning/.

Baldoz, Rick. *The Third Asiatic Invasion: Empire and Migration in Filipino America, 1898–1946*. New York: New York UP, 2011.

Baldwin, James. "The Art of Fiction: Interview with James Elgrably." *Paris Review* (Spring 1984): 91.

———. "Faulkner and Desegregation." *Partisan Review* (Fall 1956): 568–573.

———. "Stranger in the Village" from *Notes of a Native Son. The Norton Reader: An Anthology of Nonfiction*. Ed. Linda H. Peterson, John Brereton, Joseph Bizup, Anne Fernald, and Melissa Goldthwaite. 13th ed. New York: W. W. Norton, 2012. 387–396.

Balibar, Étienne, and Immanuel M. Wallerstein. *Race, Nation, Class: Ambiguous Identities*. London: Verso, 1991.

Barthes, Roland. *S/Z*. New York: Hill and Wang, 1974.

Batacan, F. H. "Keeping Time." *Philippine Speculative Fiction Sampler (online)*, 2008. http://philippinespeculativefiction.com/batacan.html.

Beatty, Paul. *The Sellout*. New York: Farrar, Straus and Giroux, 2015.

Benedicto, Bobby. "The Haunting of Gay Manila: Global Space-Time and the Specter of Kabaklaan." *GLQ: A Journal of Lesbian and Gay Studies* 14.2/3 (2008): 317–338.

Benfer, Amy. "'Fixer Chao' by Han Ong." *Salon*, 20 Apr. 2001.

Benitez, Francisco. "Diasporic and Liminal Subjectivities in the Age of Empire: 'Beyond Biculturalism' in the Case of the Two Ongs." *Filipino Studies: Palimpsests of Nation and Diaspora*. Ed. Martin F. Manalansan and Augusto Espiritu. New York: NYU P, 2016. 333–354.

Benjamin, Walter. *Illuminations*. New York: Harcourt, Brace & World, 1968.

Berlin, Isaiah. *Vico and Herder: Two Studies in the History of Ideas*. New York: Viking Press, 1976.

Bernards, Brian. "Beyond Diaspora and Multiculturalism: Recuperating Creolization in Postcolonial Sinophone Malaysian Literature." *Postcolonial Studies* 15.3 (2013): 311–329.

Bhabha, Homi K. *The Location of Culture*. London: Routledge, 2004.

Bourne, Randolph S., and Olaf Hansen. *The Radical Will: Selected Writings, 1911–1918*. Ed. Olaf Hansen. New York: Urizen Books, 1977.

Brandzel, Amy L. *Against Citizenship: The Violence of the Normative*. Urbana: U of Illinois P, 2016.

Brown, Wendy. *Regulating Aversion: Tolerance in the Age of Identity and Empire*. Princeton, NJ: Princeton UP, 2006.

Buckingham, David. *Children Talking Television: The Making of Television Literacy*. London: Falmer Press, 1993.

Butler, Judith. *Bodies That Matter: On the Discursive Limits of "Sex."* New York: Routledge, 1993.

Butler, Pamela, and Jigna Desai. "Manolos, Marriage, and Mantras: Chick-Lit Criticism and Transnational Feminism." *Meridians: Feminism, Race, Transnationalism* 8.2 (2008): 1–31.

Cacho, Lisa Marie. "You Just Don t Know How Much He Meant: Deviancy, Death, and Devaluation." *Latino Studies* 5.2 (2007): 182–208.

Campomanes, Oscar. "On Filipinos, Filipino Americans, and U.S. Imperialism: Interview with Oscar V. Campomanes." *Positively No Filipinos Allowed: Building Communities and Discourse*. Ed. Antonio T. Tiongson, Edgardo V. Gutierrez, and Ricardo V. Gutierrez. Philadelphia: Temple UP, 2006. 26–42.

Capelli, Cristian, James F. Wilson, Martin Richards, Michael P. H. Stumpf, Fiona Gratrix, Stephen Oppenheimer, Peter Underhill, Vincenzo L. Pascali, Tsang-Ming Ko, and David B. Goldstein. "A Predominantly Indigenous Paternal Heritage for the Austronesian-Speaking Peoples of Insular Southeast Asia and Oceania." *American Journal of Human Genetics* 68.2 (2001): 432–443.

"*Cebu* by Peter Bacho." *Kirkus Reviews*. 20 May 2010.

"*Cebu* [Paperback]" *Amazon.com*, 2012.

Chakrabarty, Dipesh. *Provincializing Europe: Postcolonial Thought and Historical Difference*. Princeton, NJ: Princeton UP, 2008.

Chan, Pian Sharon, and Ashley Bach. "Venting Nickels Suggests Secession." *Seattle Times*, 18 Apr. 2008.

Chandler, Daniel. "An Introduction to Genre Theory." http://visual-memory.co.uk/daniel/Documents/intgenre/chandler_genre_theory.pdf.

Cheah, Pheng. *Inhuman Conditions: On Cosmopolitanism and Human Rights*. Cambridge, MA: Harvard UP, 2006.

Chen Kuan-Hsing. *Asia as Method: Toward Deimperialization*. Durham, NC: Duke UP, 2010.

Chen, Tina. *Double Agency: Acts of Impersonation in Asian American Literature and Culture*. Stanford, CA: Stanford UP, 2005.

Chiu, M. Y. "Imagining a Nation: Lloyd Fernando's *Scorpion Orchid* and National Identity." *New Zealand Journal of Asian Studies* 5.2 (2003): 47–55.

Chng, Joyce. "A Matter of Possession." *Crossed Genres*, 20 Jul. 2009. http://crossedgenres.com/archives/009/a-matter-of-possession-by-joyce-chng/.

Chomsky, Noam. "Modern-Day American Imperialism: Middle East and Beyond." *Chomsky. Info*, 24 Apr. 2008. https://chomsky.info/20080424/.

Christian, Barbara. "The Race for Theory." *Cultural Critique* 6 (1987): 51–63.

Chua, Beng Huat. "Being Chinese Under Official Multiculturalism in Singapore." *Asian Ethnicity* 10.3 (2009): 239–250.

———. "The Cost of Membership in Ascribed Community." *Multiculturalism in Asia*. Ed. Will Kymlicka and Baogang He. Oxford: Oxford University Press, 2005. 170–185.

———. "The Cultural Logic of a Capitalist Single-Party State, Singapore." *Postcolonial Studies* 13.4 (2010): 335–350.

———, and Kwok Kian-Woon. "Social Pluralism in Singapore." *The Politics of Multiculturalism: Pluralism and Citizenship in Malaysia, Singapore, and Indonesia*. Ed. Robert W. Hefner. Honolulu: U of Hawai'i P, 2001.

Chua, Lawrence. *Gold by the Inch*. New York: Grove P, 1998.

Clough, Patricia Ticineto. "Introduction." *The Affective Turn: Theorizing the Social*. Ed. Patricia Clough and Jean O'Malley. Durham, NC: Duke UP, 2007. 1–33.

Coates, Ta-Nehisi. *Between the World and Me*. New York: Spiegel & Grau, 2015.

Cœdès, George. *The Indianized States of Southeast Asia*. Honolulu: East-West Center Press, 1968.

Constantino, Renato. "The Miseducation of the Filipino." *The Philippines Reader: A History of Colonialism, Neocolonialism, Dictatorship, and Resistance*. Ed. Daniel B. Schirmer and Stephen Rosskamm Shalom. Boston: South End Press, 1987. 45–49.

———. *The Philippines: A Past Revisited*. Quezon City: Tala Pub. Services, 1975.

Constantino, Renato, and Letizia R. Constantino. *Neocolonial Identity and Counter-consciousness*. London: Merlin Press, 1978.

Cruz, Denise. *Transpacific Femininities: The Making of the Modern Filipina*. Durham, NC: Duke UP, 2012.

Cruz, Jon. "From Farce to Tragedy: Reflections on the Reification of Race at Century's End." *Mapping Multiculturalism*. Ed. Avery Gordon and Christopher Newfield. Minneapolis: U of Minnesota P, 1996. 19–39.

Deepa, D. "An Open Letter to Charles Tan." *Dreamwidth*, 21 Apr. 2010. https://deepad.dreamwidth.org/50595.html.

Demko, George J., Jerome Agel, and Eugene Boe. *Why in the World: Adventures in Geography*. New York: Anchor Books, 1992.

Diamond, Catherine. "Maturation and Political Upheaval in Lloyd Fernando's *Scorpion Orchid* and Robert Yeo's *The Singapore Trilogy*." *Comparative Drama* 36.1 (2011): 125–144.

Dirlik, Arif. "The Postcolonial Aura: Third World Criticism in the Age of Global Capitalism." *Critical Inquiry* 20.2 (1994): 328–356.

Dubey, Madhu. "Speculative Fictions of Slavery." *American Literature* 82.4 (2010): 779–805.

Duggan, Lisa. "The New Homonormativity: The Sexual Politics of Neoliberalism." *Materializing Democracy: Toward a Revitalized Cultural Politics*. Ed. Dana D. Nelson and Russ Castronovo. Durham, NC: Duke UP, 2002. 175–194.

Edwards, Brent H. *The Practice of Diaspora: Literature, Translation, and the Rise of Black Nationalism*. Cambridge, MA: Harvard UP, 2003.

Ee, Tiang H. *I of the Many Faces*. Malacca: Wah Seong Press, 1960.

Elliott, Jane, and Gillian Harkins. "Introduction Genres of Neoliberalism." *Social Text* 31.2 115 (2013): 1–17.

Emmerson, Donald K. "'Southeast Asia': What's in a Name?" *Journal of Southeast Asian Studies* 15.1 (1984): 1–21.

Eng, Chuah Guat. "The Translator as Agent of Nation Building: Lloyd Fernando's *Scorpion Orchid* Revisited." Paper presented at Found in Translation: A Common Voice in a Multicultural World Conference, Kuala Lumpur, 23–25 July 2010. http://fass.um.edu.my/departments/english/anuvaada/PAPERS/CHUAH.pdf.

Eng, David L. *Racial Castration: Managing Masculinity in Asian America.* Durham, NC: Duke UP, 2001.

Examined Life. Dir. Astra Taylor. Zeitgeist Films, 2010.

Ferguson, Roderick A. *Aberrations in Black: Toward a Queer of Color Critique.* Minneapolis: U of Minnesota P, 2004.

Fernando, Lloyd. *Cultures in Conflict: Essays on Literature and the English Language in South East Asia.* Singapore: Graham Brash, 1986.

———. *Scorpion Orchid.* Kuala Lumpur: Heinemann Educational Books (Asia), 1976.

———. "Truth in Fiction." *Perceiving Other Worlds.* Ed. Edwin Thumboo. Singapore: Times Academic Press for Unipress, 1991. 220–225.

Feuer, Lewis S. "From Pluralism to Multiculturalism." *Society* 29.1 (1991): 19–22.

Fiske, John. *Television Culture.* London: Routledge, 1987.

Flood, Alison. "White Poet Used Chinese Pen Name to Gain Entry into *Best American Poetry.*" *Guardian,* "Poetry." 8 Sept. 2015.

Foucault, Michel. *Society Must Be Defended: Lectures at the Collège de France, 1975–76.* Ed. Mauro Bertani and Alessandro Fontana. Gen. eds. François Ewald and Alessandro Fontana. Trans. David Macey. New York: Picador, 2003.

———. *The Birth of Biopolitics: Lectures at the Collège de France, 1978–79.* Ed. Michel Senellart. Gen. eds. François Ewald and Alessandro Fontana. Trans. Graham Burchell. Basingstoke: Palgrave Macmillan, 2008.

Freire, Paulo. *Education as the Practice of Freedom in Education for Critical Consciousness.* New York: Continuum. 1973.

Fujita-Rony, Dorothy B. *American Workers, Colonial Power: Philippine Seattle and the Transpacific West, 1919–1941.* Berkeley: U of California P, 2003.

Furnivall, J. S. *Colonial Policy and Practice: A Comparative Study of Burma and Netherlands India.* 1910. Reprint. Cambridge: Cambridge UP, 1970.

Gairola, Rahul. "Occupy Education: An Interview with Gayatri Chakravorty Spivak." *Politics and Culture* (Sept. 2012). https://politicsandculture.org/2012/09/25/occupy-education-an-interview-with-gayatri-chakravorty-spivak/.

Ganesan, N. "Liberal and Structural Ethnic Political Accommodation in Malaysia." *Multiculturalism in Asia.* Ed. Will Kymlicka and Baogang He. Oxford: Oxford University Press, 2005. 136–151.

Garcia, J. Neil C. *Slip/pages: Essays in Philippine Gay Criticism, 1991–1996.* Manila: de La Salle University, 1998.

Gertsch, Sabra. "Census Bureau: 98118, the Most Diverse Zip Code in US." *KOMO 4 News,* 5 Apr. 2010.

Gilroy, Paul. *Postcolonial Melancholia.* New York: Columbia UP, 2006.

Goh, Daniel P. S. "State and Social Christianity in Post-Colonial Singapore." *Sojourn: Journal of Social Issues in Southeast Asia* 25.1 (2010): 54–89.

Goh, Robbie B. H. "Writing 'the Global' in Singapore Anglophone Fiction: Language, Vision, and Resonance in Hwee Hwee Tan's Fiction." *China Fictions, English Language Literary Essays in Diaspora, Memory, Story.* Ed. Robert Lee. Amsterdam: Rodopi, 2008. 239–258.

Gomez, Jewelle. "Speculative Fiction and Black Lesbians." *Signs: Journal of Women in Culture and Society* 18.4 (1993): 948–955.

Gonzaga, Elmo. *Globalization and Becoming-Nation: Subjectivity, Nationhood, and Narrative in the Period of Global Capitalism.* Diliman, Quezon City: U of the Philippines P, 2009.

Gonzalez, Vernadette V. *Securing Paradise: Tourism and Militarism in Hawai'i and the Philippines.* Durham, NC: Duke UP, 2013.

Gopinath, Gayatri. *Impossible Desires: Queer Diasporas and South Asian Public Cultures*. Durham, NC: Duke UP, 2005.

Grewal, Inderpal. *Transnational America: Feminisms, Diasporas, Neoliberalisms*. Durham, NC: Duke UP, 2005.

Gudeman, Roxane Garvey. "Multiculturalism in Malaysia: Individual Harmony, Group Tension." *Malaysia: Crossroads of Diversity in Southeast Asia*. Ed. Ahmed I. Samatar and Margaret Beegle. St. Paul, MN: Macalester College, International Studies and Programming, 2002. 138–160.

Guevarra, Anna R. *Marketing Dreams, Manufacturing Heroes: The Transnational Labor Brokering of Filipino Workers*. New Brunswick, NJ: Rutgers UP, 2010.

Guillermo, Kawika. "The Bear." *LONTAR: The Journal of Southeast Asian Speculative Fiction* 5 (2016): 22–30.

———. "The Last of Its Kind." *Mothership: Tales from Afrofuturism and Beyond*. Ed. Bill Campbell and Edward Austin Hall. Greenbelt, MD: Rosarium Publishing, 2013. 39–40.

———. "No Name Islands." *Amok: Asia-Pacific Speculative Fiction*. Ed. Dominica Malcolm. Oakland, CA: Solarwym Press, 2014. 113–116.

———. "Strange Gifts." *decomP Magazine* (November 2012). http://www.decompmagazine.com/strangegifts.htm.

Guzmán, Joshua J. "Notes on the Comedown." *Social Text* 121 (2014): 59–68.

Halberstam, Jack/Judith. *In a Queer Time and Place: Transgender Bodies, Subcultural Lives*. New York: NYU P, 2005.

———. *The Queer Art of Failure*. Durham, NC: Duke UP, 2011.

Hall, Stuart. "Old and New Identities, Old and New Ethnicities." *Culture, Globalization, and the World System: Contemporary Conditions for the Representation of Identity*. Ed. Anthony D. King. U of Minnesota P, 1991. 41–68.

———. "What Is This 'Black' in Black Popular Culture?" *Black Popular Culture*. Ed. Michele Wallace and Gina Dent. New York: New Press, 1992. 21–33.

Hart, Donn V. "Buhawi of the Bisayas: The Revitalization Process and Legend-Making in the Philippines." *Studies in Philippines Anthropology: Essay in Honor of H. Otley Beyer*. Ed. Mario Zamora. Quezon City: Alemar Phoenix Press, 1967.

Haskell, Edward F. *Lance: A Novel About Multicultural Men*. New York: John Day Company, 1941.

Hau, Caroline. "The Filipino Novel in English." *Philippine English: Linguistic and Literacy*. Ed. Lourdes S. Bautista and Kingsley Boulton. Hong Kong: Hong Kong UP, 2008. 317–336.

———. *Necessary Fictions: Philippine Literature and the Nation, 1946–1980*. Quezon City: Ateneo de Manila UP, 2000.

———. *On the Subject of the Nation: Filipino Writings from the Margins, 1981–2004*. Quezon City: Ateneo de Manila UP, 2004.

Hefner, Robert W. *The Politics of Multiculturalism: Pluralism and Citizenship in Malaysia, Singapore, and Indonesia*. Honolulu: U of Hawai'i P, 2001.

Heinlein, Robert A. "Science Fiction: Its Nature, Faults, and Virtues." *The Science Fiction Novel: Imagination and Social Criticism*. Ed. Basil Davenport. Chicago: Advent Publishers, 1959. 14–48.

Hemmings, Clare. "Invoking Affect: Cultural Theory and the Ontological Turn." *Cultural Studies* 19.5 (2005): 548–567.

Herder, Johann G. *J. G. Herder on Social and Political Culture*. Ed. and trans. F. M. Barnard. London: Cambridge UP, 1969.

Hildebrand, Laura. "Speculated Communities: The Contemporary Canadian Speculative Fictions of Margaret Atwood, Nalo Hopkinson, and Larissa Lai." Master's thesis, University of Ottawa, 2012.

Ho, Jennifer A. *Racial Ambiguity in Asian American Culture*. New Brunswick, NJ: Rutgers UP, 2015.

Holden, Philip. "Colonialism's Goblins: Language, Gender, and the Southeast Asian Novel in English at a Time of Nationalism." *Journal of Postcolonial Writing* 44.2 (2008): 159–170.

———. "Interrogating Multiculturalism and Cosmopolitanism in the City-State: Some Recent Singapore Fiction in English." *Mobilities* 5.2 (2010): 277–290.

———. "Rajaratnam's Tiger: Race, Gender, and the Beginnings of Singapore Nationalism." *Journal of Commonwealth Literature* 41.1 (2006): 127–140.

———, and Daniel P. S. Goh. "Introduction." *Race and Multiculturalism in Malaysia and Singapore*. Ed. Daniel P. S. Goh, Matilda Gabrielpillai, Philip Holden, and Gaik Cheng Koo. London: Routledge, 2009.

Hoskins, Janet, and Viet T. Nguyen. *Transpacific Studies: Framing an Emerging Field*. Honolulu: U of Hawai'i P, 2014.

Hsu, Hsuan L. "Guåhan (Guam), Literary Emergence, and the American Pacific in Homebase and from Unincorporated Territory." *American Literary History* 24.2 (2012): 281–307.

———. "Mimicry, Spatial Captation, and Feng Shui in Han Ong's *The Fixer Chao*." *MFS: Modern Fiction Studies* 52.3 (2006): 675–704.

Huang, Betsy. *Contesting Genres in Contemporary Asian American Fiction*. New York: Palgrave Macmillan, 2010.

———. "Premodern Orientalist Science Fictions." *MELUS: Multi-Ethnic Literature of the United States* 33.4 (2008): 23–43.

Ileto, Reynaldo C. "Philippine and the Politics of Memory." *Positions: East Asia Cultures Critique* 13.1 (2005): 215–235.

———. "The 'Unfinished Revolution' in Philippine Political Discourse." *Southeast Asian Studies* 31.1 (1993): 162–182.

Isaac, Allan P. *American Tropics: Articulating Filipino America*. Minneapolis: U of Minnesota P, 2006.

Ivison, Duncan. "Introduction: Multiculturalism as a Public Idea." *The Ashgate Research Companion to Multiculturalism*. Ed. Duncan Ivison. Farnham, UK: Ashgate Publishing Group, 2010. 1–16.

Jacobson, Matthew Frye. *Special Sorrows: The Diasporic Imagination of Irish, Polish, and Jewish Immigrants in the United States*. Berkeley: U of California P, 1995.

Jeyaretnam, Philip. "Hub, Spoke, or Rim: Singapore Literature in the Asia-Pacific." *Sharing Borders: Studies in Contemporary Singaporean and Malaysian Literature. Writing Asia*, Vol. 2. Ed. Mohammad A. Quayum and Wong Phui Lam. Singapore: National Library Board and Singapore Arts Council, 2009. 164–169.

Jin, Wen. *Pluralist Universalism: An Asian Americanist Critique of U.S. and Chinese Multiculturalisms*. Columbus: Ohio State UP, 2012.

Joaquín, Nick. *Culture and History: Occasional Notes on the Process of Philippine Becoming*. Metro Manila, Philippines: Solar Pub. Corp., 1988.

———. *The Woman Who Had Two Navels: A Filipino Novel*. Manila: Solidaridad Pub. House, 1972.

Jose, F. Sionil. "Filipino English—The Literature As We Think It." *Writing Asia, the Literatures in Englishes*, Vol. 1. Ed. Edwin Thumboo and Rex I. Sayson. Singapore: Ethos Books, 2007. 14–22.

Kallen, Horace M. *Culture and Democracy in the United States*. New York: Boni and Liveright, 1924.

———. "Democracy versus the Melting-Pot: A Study of American Nationality." http://www.expo98.msu.edu/people/kallen.htm. Originally published in *The Nation*, 25 Feb. 1915.

———. *What I Believe and Why-Maybe: Essays for the Modern World*. New York: Horizon, 1971.

Keong, Neil Khor Jin. "A History of the Anglophone Straits Chinese and Their Literature." *Sharing Borders: Studies in Contemporary Singaporean-Malaysian Literature*. Vol. 2. Ed. Mohammad A. Quayum and Wong Phui Nam. Singapore: National Library Board and Singapore Arts Council, 2009.

Killen, Patricia O'Connell, and Mark Silk. *Religion and Public Life in the Pacific Northwest: The None Zone*. Walnut Creek, CA: AltaMira, 2004.

Kim, Jodi. *Ends of Empire: Asian American Critique and the Cold War*. Minneapolis: U of Minnesota P, 2010.

Koh, Tai A. "Self, Family, and the State: Social Mythology in the Singapore Novel in English." *Journal of Southeast Asian Studies* 20 (1989): 273–287.

Kramer, Paul A. *The Blood of Government: Race, Empire, the United States, and the Philippines*. Chapel Hill: U of North Carolina P, 2006.

———. "Power and Connection: Imperial Histories of the United States in the World." *American Historical Review* 116.5 (2011): 1348–1391.

Kwa, Lydia. *This Place Called Absence*. New York: Kensington, 2002.

Kymlichka, Will. "Neoliberal Multiculturalism." *Videolectures.net*, Mar. 2011. http://videolectures.net/ffeminent_kymlicka_neoliberal/.

———. "Two Models of Pluralism and Tolerance." *Toleration: An Elusive Virtue*. Ed. David Heyd. Princeton, NJ: Princeton University Press, 1996. 81–105.

———, and Baogang He. *Multiculturalism in Asia*. Oxford: Oxford University Press, 2005.

Lai, Larissa. "The Identity of the Body Has Not Yet Been Confirmed." "Active Geographies: Women and Struggles of the Left Coast," Ed. Jo-Anne Lee and Rita Wong. Special issue of *West Coast Line* 58 (2008): 137–139.

Lai, Paul. "Autoethnography Otherwise." *Asian Canadian Writing beyond Autoethnography*. Ed. Eleanor Ty and Christl Verduyn. Waterloo, ONT: Wilfrid Laurier UP, 2008. 55–70.

Laurie, Clayton D. "'The Chinese Must Go': The United States Army and the Anti-Chinese Riots in Washington Territory, 1885–1886." *Pacific Northwest Quarterly* 81.1 (1990): 22–29.

Laya, Juan C. *His Native Soil*. Quezon City: Kayumanggi Publishers, 1972.

Lee, Christopher B. *The Semblance of Identity: Aesthetic Mediation in Asian American Literature*. Stanford, CA: Stanford UP, 2012.

Lee, Regina. "Theorizing Diasporas: Three Types of Consciousness" *Asian Diasporas: Cultures, Identities, Representations*. Ed. Robbie B. H. Goh and Shawn Wong. Hong Kong: Hong Kong UP, 2004. 53–76.

Le Guin, Ursula K. "Why Are Americans Afraid of Dragons?" *The Language of the Night: Essays on Fantasy and Science Fiction*. Ed. Ursula K. Le Guin and Susan Wood. New York: Putnam, 1979. 39–45.

Levitt, Steven D. "Understanding Why Crime Fell in the 1990s: Four Factors That Explain the Decline and Six That Do Not." *Journal of Economic Perspectives* 18.1 (2004): 163–190.

Lieberman, Victor. "Local Integration and Eurasian Analogies: Structuring Southeast Asian History, c. 1350–c. 1830." *Modern Asian Studies* 27 (1993): 475–572.

———. *Strange Parallels: Southeast Asia in Global Context, c. 800–1830*. New York: Cambridge UP, 2003.

Lim, Eng-Beng. *Brown Boys and Rice Queens: Spellbinding Performance in the Asias*. New York: NYU P, 2014.

Lim, Shirley Geok-lin. *Among the White Moon Faces: An Asian-American Memoir of Homelands*. New York: Feminist P, 1997.

———. "The English-Language Writer in Singapore." *Singaporean Literature in English: A Critical Reader.* Ed. Mohammad A. Quayum and Peter C. Wicks. Serdang: Universiti Putra Malaysia Press, 2002. 33–58.

———. *Joss and Gold.* New York: Feminist P, 2001.

———. *Modern Secrets.* Sydney, Australia: Dangaroo P, 1989.

———. *Monsoon History.* London: Skoob Books, 1994.

———. *Nationalism and Literature: English-Language Writing from the Philippines and Singapore.* Quezon City: New Day Publishers, 1993.

———. *Writing S.E./Asia in English: Against the Grain, Focus on Asian English-Language Literature.* London: Skoob Books, 1994.

Lim, Su-chen C. *Fistful of Colours.* Singapore: EPB Publishers, 1993.

Linmark, R. Zamora. *Leche: A Novel.* Minneapolis: Coffee House P, 2011.

———. *Rolling the R's.* New York: Kaya/Muae, 1995.

Locke, Alain. *The Philosophy of Alain Locke: Harlem Renaissance and Beyond.* Ed. Leonard Harris. Philadelphia: Temple University Press, 1989.

Lonely Planet. "China House: Top Choice International in George Town." *Lonely Planet Malaysia,* August 2016. https://www.lonelyplanet.com/malaysia/george-town/restaurants/china-house/a/poi-eat/1386936/357010.

Lowe, Lisa. *Immigrant Acts: On Asian American Cultural Politics.* Durham, NC: Duke UP, 1996.

Lundberg, Jason E. *Fish Eats Lion: New Singaporean Speculative Fiction.* Singapore: Math Paper P, 2012.

Mabalon, Dawn Bohulano. *Little Manila Is in the Heart: The Making of the Filipina/o American Community in Stockton, California.* Durham, NC: Duke UP, 2013.

Manalansan, Martin F. "Beyond Authenticity: Rerouting the Filipino Culinary Diaspora." *Eating Asian America: A Food Studies Reader.* Ed. Martin Manalansan, Robert J.-S. Ku, and Anita Mannur. New York: NYU P, 2013. 288–302.

Mandal, Sumit K. "Boundaries and Beyond: Whither the Cultural Bases of Political Community in Malaysia?" *The Politics of Multiculturalism: Pluralism and Citizenship in Malaysia, Singapore, and Indonesia.* Ed. Robert W. Hefner. Honolulu: U of Hawai'i P, 2001. 141–181.

———. "Reconsidering Cultural Globalization: The English Language in Malaysia." *Third World Quarterly—Journal of Emerging Areas* 21.6 (2000): 1001–1012.

Maniam, K. S. *In a Far Country.* London: Skoob Books, 1993.

———. "The New Diaspora." *Globalisation and Regional Communities: Geoeconomic, Sociocultural, and Security Implications for Australia.* Ed. Donald H. McMillen and Donald Hugh. Toowoomba, Australia: USQ Press, 1997. 18–23.

Marcuse, Herbert. "Repressive Tolerance." *The Essential Marcuse: Selected Writings of Philosopher and Social Critic Herbert Marcuse.* Ed. Andrew Feenberg and William Leiss. Boston: Beacon, 2007. 32–62.

Martell-Gámez, Alpha. "Arizona's SB 1070 Law: An Affront to US Migrant Rights." *Multicultural Politic,* 8 June 2010. http://www.tmponline.org/2010/06/08/arizonas-sb-1070-law-an-affront-to-us-migrant-rights/.

Martinez-Sicat, Maria T. *Imagining the Nation in Four Philippine Novels.* Diliman, Quezon City: U of the Philippines P, 1994.

Massumi, Brian. "The Autonomy of Affect." *Cultural Critique* 31.0 (1995): 83–109.

Mazza, Cris, and Jeffrey DeShell. *Chick-Lit: New Women's Fiction Anthology.* Normal, IL: FC2, 1995.

McKay, Steven C. "Filipino Sea Men: Constructing Masculinities in an Ethnic Labour Niche." *Journal of Ethnic and Migration Studies* 33.4 (2007): 617–633.

McLagan, Elizabeth. "The Black Laws of Oregon, 1844–1857." *Blackpast.org*, 9 Aug. 2012. http://www.blackpast.org/perspectives/black-laws-oregon-1844-1857.

McMahon, Suzanne. *Echoes of Freedom: South Asian Pioneers in California, 1899–1965: An Exhibition in the Bernice Layne Brown Gallery in the Doe Library, University of California, Berkeley, July 1–September 30, 2001.* Berkeley: Center for South Asian Studies, University of California, Berkeley, 2001.

Melamed, Jodi. "Reading Tehran in Lolita: Making Racialized and Gendered Difference Work for Neoliberal Multiculturalism." *Strange Affinities: The Gender and Sexual Politics of Comparative Racialization.* Ed. Grace Kyungwon Hong and Roderick A. Ferguson. Durham, NC: Duke University UP, 2011. 76–112.

———. *Represent and Destroy: Rationalizing Violence in the New Racial Capitalism.* Minneapolis: U of Minnesota P, 2011.

———. "The Spirit of Neoliberalism: from Racial Liberalism to Neoliberal Multiculturalism." *Social Text* 24.4 (2006): 1–24.

Mendible, Myra. "The Politics and Poetics of Philippine Festival in Ninotchka Rosca's State of War." *International Fiction Review* 29.2 (2002): 30–38.

Mishra, Vijay. *The Literature of the Indian Diaspora: Theorizing the Diasporic Imaginary.* New York: Routledge, 2007.

———. "Multiculturalism (2003)." *The Year's Work in Critical and Cultural Theory.* Ed. Martin McQuillan. New York: Oxford University Press, 2005. 182–204.

Mohanty, Chandra T., Ann Russo, and Lourdes Torres. *Third World Women and the Politics of Feminism.* Bloomington: Indiana UP, 1991.

Morse, Ruth. "Novels of National Identity and Inter-National Interpretation." *Singaporean Literature in English: A Critical Reader.* Ed. Mohammad A. Quayum and Peter C. Wicks. Serdang: Universiti Putra Malaysia Press, 2002. 60–77.

Muñoz, José Esteban. "The Brown Commons: The Sense of Wildness." JNT Dialogue 2013: José Muñoz and Samuel Delany (Part 1/4). Youtube.com, 1 Apr. 2013. https://www.youtube.com/watch?v=F-YInUlXgO4.

———. *Cruising Utopia: The Then and There of Queer Futurity.* New York: NYU P, 2009.

———. *Disidentifications: Queers of Color and the Performance of Politics.* Minneapolis: U of Minnesota P, 1999.

———. "Feeling Brown: Ethnicity and Affect in Ricardo Bracho's *The Sweetest Hangover (and Other STDs)*." *Theatre Journal* 52.1 (2000): 67–79.

———. "Feeling Brown, Feeling Down: Latina Affect, the Performativity of Race, and the Depressive Position." *Signs: Journal of Women in Culture and Society* 31.3 (2006): 675–688.

Naruse, Cheryl Narumi. "Hwee Hwee Tan's *Mammon Inc.* as Bildungsroman; or, The Coming-of-Career Narrative." *Genre* 49.1 (2016): 95–115.

Nazareth, Peter. "Fistful of Colours (Brief Article)." *World Literature Today* 67.4 (1993): 905–906.

Neale, Steve. *Genre.* London: British Film Institute, 1980.

Negri, Antonio, and Michael Hardt. "Value and Affect." *boundary 2: An International Journal of Literature and Culture* 26.2 (1999): 77–88.

Newton, Pauline T. "Lloyd Fernando's Circle: An Interview with Marie Fernando, Wife of Lloyd Fernando." *Asiatic* 2.2 (2008): 101–110.

Ng, Andrew. "Nation and Religion in the Fiction of Lloyd Fernando." *Sharing Borders: Studies in Contemporary Singaporean-Malaysian Literature. Writing Asia*, Vol. 2. Ed. Mohammad A. Quayum and Wong Phui Nam. Singapore: National Library Board and Singapore Arts Council, 2009. 114–127.

———. "The Vision of Hospitality in Lloyd Fernando's *Scorpion Orchid*." *Journal of Postcolonial Writing* 44.2 (2008): 171–181.

Nguyen, Tan Hoang. *A View from the Bottom: Asian American Masculinity and Sexual Representation*. Durham, NC: Duke UP, 2014.

Nguyen, Viet Thanh. *Nothing Ever Dies*. Cambridge, MA: Harvard UP, 2016.

———. *Race and Resistance: Literature and Politics in Asian America*. Oxford: Oxford UP, 2002.

Niedzviecki, Hal. "Winning the Appropriation Prize." *Write* (Spring 2017): 8.

Nietzsche, Friedrich Wilhelm, and Walter Arnold Kaufmann. *Beyond Good and Evil; Prelude to a Philosophy of the Future*. Trans. Walter Kaufmann. New York: Vintage Books, 1966.

Nordland, Rod. "Lionel Shriver's Address on Cultural Appropriation Roils a Writers Festival." "Book Review," *New York Times*, 12 Sept .2016.

Ommundsen, W. "Sex and the Global City: Chick Lit with a Difference." *Contemporary Women's Writing* 5.2 (2011): 107–124.

Ong, Aihwa. *Flexible Citizenship: The Cultural Logics of Transnationality*. Durham, NC: Duke UP, 1999.

———. *Neoliberalism as Exception: Mutations in Citizenship and Sovereignty*. Durham, NC: Duke UP, 2006.

———. *Spirits of Resistance and Capitalist Discipline: Factory Women in Malaysia*. Albany: SUNY P, 1987.

Ong, Han. *Fixer Chao*. New York: Farrar, Straus and Giroux, 2001.

"O'Reilly: 'War' on Christmas Part of 'Secular Progressive Agenda' That Includes 'Legalization of Narcotics, Euthanasia, Abortion at Will, Gay Marriage." *Media Matters for America*, 21 Nov. 2005. https://www.mediamatters.org/video/2005/11/21/oreilly-war-on-christmas-part-of-secular-progre/134262.

Pantoja-Hidalgo, Cristina. *Coming Home*. Pasig City, Philippines: Anvil Pub, 1997.

Parreñas, Rhacel Salazar. *Servants of Globalization: Women, Migration, and Domestic Work*. Stanford, CA: Stanford University Press, 2001.

Partridge, Jeffrey F. L. *Beyond Literary Chinatown*. Seattle: University of Washington Press, 2007.

Patterson, Christopher B. "Beyond the Stigma: The Asian Sex Worker as First-World Savior." *Queer Sex Work*. Ed. Nicola Smith, Mary Laing, and Katy Pilcher. London: Routledge, 2015. 53–63.

———. "Cosmopolitanism, Ethnic Belonging, and Affective Labor: Han Ong's *Fixer Chao* and the Disinherited." *WorkingUSA* 15.1 (2012): 87–102.

———. "The Filipino American in Spaces of Liberal Tolerance: Satire and Reciprocity in Peter Bacho's *Cebu*." *MELUS: Multi-Ethnic Literature of the United States* 39.1 (2014): 149–172.

———. "Global Imaginaries and Global Capital: Lawrence Chua's *Gold by the Inch* and Spaces of Global Belonging." *MANUSYA: Journal of Humanities* 18 (2009): 49–69.

———. "Verena Tay, *Spectre: Stories from Dark to Light*." *Asiatic: An International Journal of Asian Literatures, Cultures, and Englishes* 9.1 (2015): 221–224.

———, and Troeung, Y-Dang. "The Psyche of Neoliberal Multiculturalism: Queering Memory and Reproduction in Larissa Lai's *Salt Fish Girl* and Chang-rae Lee's *On Such a Full Sea*." *Concentric: Literary and Cultural Studies* 42.1 (Mar. 2016): 73–98.

Pérez, Hiram. *A Taste for Brown Bodies: Gay Modernity and Cosmopolitan Desire*. New York: NYU P, 2015.

Philip, Susan. "Interculturalism in the Early Malaysian English-language Theatre." *Sharing Borders: Studies in Contemporary Singaporean-Malaysian Literature. Writing Asia*, Vol. 2.

Ed. Mohammad A. Quayum and Wong Phui Nam. Singapore: National Library Board and Singapore Arts Council, 2009. 95–113.

Pisares, Elizabeth H. "Payback Time: Neocolonial Discourses in Peter Bacho's *Cebu.*" *MELUS: Multi-Ethnic Literature of the United States* 29.1 (2004): 79–97.

Pison, Ruth J. L. *Alternative Histories: Martial Law Novels As Counter-Memory.* Diliman, Quezon City: U of the Philippines P, 2005.

Ponce, Martin J. *Beyond the Nation: Diasporic Filipino Literature and Queer Reading.* New York: NYU P, 2012.

Pratt, Mary Louise. *Imperial Eyes: Travel Writing and Transculturation.* London: Routledge, 1992.

Preston, Peter. "A World Away from Texas." *Guardian,* 28 Feb. 2010.

Prosser, Jay. "Transgender." *Lesbian and Gay Studies: A Critical Introduction.* Ed. Andy Medhurst and Sally R. Munt. London: Cassell, 1997. 309–326.

Pruchnic, Jeff. "The Invisible Gland: Affect and Political Economy." *Criticism* 50.1 (2008): 160–175.

Quayum, Mohammad A. "Editor's Introduction." *Sharing Borders: Studies in Contemporary Singaporean-Malaysian* Literature. *Writing Asia,* Vol. 2. Ed. Mohammad A. Quayum and Wong Phui Nam. Singapore: National Library Board and Singapore Arts Council, 2009. 11–35.

———. "Self-refashioning a Plural Society: Dialogism and Syncretism in Malaysian Postcolonial Literature." *New Zealand Journal of Asian Studies* 9.2 (2007): 27–46.

Rafael, Vicente L. "Confession, Conversion, and Reciprocity in Early Tagalog Colonial Society." *Comparative Studies in Society and History* 29.2 (1987): 320–339.

———. *White Love: And Other Events in Filipino History.* Durham, NC: Duke UP, 2000.

Raihanah, M. M. "Malaysia and the Author: Face-to-Face with the Challenges of Multiculturalism." *International Journal of Asia Pacific Studies* 5.2 (2009): 43–63.

———. "Multiculturalism and the Politics of Expression: An Appraisal." *European Journal of Social Sciences* 7.3 (2009): 63–70.

Rajan, Kaushik Sunder. *Biocapital: The Constitution of Postgenomic Life.* Durham, NC: Duke UP, 2006.

Ralston, Meredith L, and Kiefer Sutherland. *Selling Sex in Heaven.* Halifax, NS: Ralston Productions, 2005.

Realuyo, Bino A. *The Umbrella Country.* New York: Ballantine Books, 1999.

Reddy, Chandan. *Freedom with Violence: Race, Sexuality, and the US State.* Durham, NC: Duke UP, 2011.

Reid, Anthony. *Imperial Alchemy: Nationalism and Political Identity in Southeast Asia.* Cambridge: Cambridge UP, 2010.

Remo, Michelle. "Overseas Filipinos' Remittances Hit $18.76b in 2010." *Philippine Daily Inquirer,* Asia News Network, 16 Feb. 2011.

Reynolds, Craig. "A New Look at Old Southeast Asia." *Journal of Asian Studies* 54.2 (1995): 416–446.

Ricœur, Paul. *The Course of Recognition.* Cambridge, MA: Harvard UP, 2005.

Robbins, Bruce. "Comparative Cosmopolitanism." *Social Text* 31/32 (1992): 169–186.

Rodríguez, Dylan. "Asian-American Studies in the Age of the Prison Industrial Complex: Departures and Re-Narrations." *Review of Education, Pedagogy, and Cultural Studies* 27.3 (2005): 241–263.

———. *Suspended Apocalypse: White Supremacy, Genocide, and the Filipino Condition.* Minneapolis: U of Minnesota P, 2010.

Rodriguez, Robyn M. *Migrants for Export: How the Philippine State Brokers Labor to the World.* Minneapolis: U of Minnesota P, 2010.

Roh, David, Betsy Huang, and Greta A. Niu. "Technologizing Orientalism: An Introduction." *Techno Orientalism: Imagining Asia in Speculative Fiction, History, and Media.* Ed. David Roh, Betsy Huang, and Greta A. Niu New Brunswick, NJ: Rutgers UP, 2015. 1–19.

Rosca, Ninotchka. *State of War: A Novel.* New York: W. W. Norton, 1988.

Rose, Jacqueline. *States of Fantasy.* Oxford: Clarendon Press, 1996.

RuPaul, Andres Charles, and E. Alex Jung. "Real Talk with RuPaul." *Vulture.com,* 23 Mar. 2016. http://www.vulture.com/2016/03/rupaul-drag-race-interview.html.

Safran, William. "Diasporas in Modern Societies: Myths of Homeland and Return." *Diaspora* 1.1 (1991): 83–99.

Said, Edward W. *Culture and Imperialism.* London: Vintage, 1993.

———. *Orientalism.* New York: Vintage, 1979.

———. *Representations of the Intellectual: The 1993 Reith Lectures.* New York: Pantheon, 1994.

Saldívar, Ramón. "Historical Fantasy, Speculative Realism, and Postrace Aesthetics in Contemporary American Fiction." *American Literary History* 23.3 (2011): 574–599.

San Juan, E. *After Postcolonialism: Remapping Philippines–United States Confrontations.* Lanham, MD: Rowman & Littlefield, 2000.

———. "Beyond Identity Politics: the Predicament of the Asian American Writer in Late Capitalism." *American Literary History* 3.3 (1991): 542–565.

———. *In the Wake of Terror: Class, Race, Nation, Ethnicity in the Postmodern World.* Lanham, MD: Lexington Books, 2007.

———. "The Paradox of Multiculturalism: Ethnicity and Identity in the Philippines." Universitat Wien, 1999. https://www.univie.ac.at/ksa/apsis/aufi/ethno/paradox.htm.

———. *The Philippine Temptation: Dialectics of Philippines–U.S. Literary Relations.* Philadelphia: Temple UP, 1996.

Sanchez, Anna Felicia C. "Waiting for Victory: Towards a Philippine Speculative Fiction." *Journal of English Studies and Comparative Literature* 10.1 (2010): 37–48.

Saranillo, Dean. "Colonial America: Rethinking Filipino 'American' Settler Empowerment in the U.S. Colony of Hawai'i." *Positively No Filipinos Allowed: Building Communities and Discourse.* Ed. Antonio T. Tiongson, Edgardo V. Gutierrez, and Ricardo V. Gutierrez. Philadelphia: Temple UP, 2006. 124–144.

Schlund-Vials, Cathy J. *War, Genocide, and Justice: Cambodian American Memory Work.* Minneapolis: U of Minnesota P, 2012.

Scott, James C. *Seeing Like a State: How Certain Schemes to Improve the Human Condition Have Failed.* New Haven: Yale UP, 1998.

———. *Weapons of the Weak: Everyday Forms of Peasant Resistance.* New Haven: Yale UP, 1985.

"Seattle's Population and Demographics." Department of Planning and Development, City of Seattle, 2013. https://www.seattle.gov/opcd/population-and-demographics.

See, Sarita E. *The Decolonized Eye: Filipino American Art and Performance.* Minneapolis: U of Minnesota P, 2009.

Sharrad, Paul. "Alienation, Self-Realisation, and Community in K. S. Maniam." *Sharing Borders: Studies in Contemporary Singaporean-Malaysian* Literature. *Writing Asia,* Vol. 2. Ed. Mohammad A. Quayum and Wong Phui Nam. Singapore: National Library Board and Singapore Arts Council, 2009. 65–79.

Shaw, Linda. "The Resegregation of Seattle's Schools." *Seattle Times,* 1 June 2008.

Shih, Shu-mei. "Global Literature and the Technologies of Recognition." *PMLA* 119.1 (2004): 16–30.

———. "Toward an Ethics of Transnational Encounters, or, 'When' Does a 'Chinese' Woman Become a 'Feminist'?" *Minor Transnationalism.* Ed. Françoise Lionnet and Shu-mei Shih. Durham, NC: Duke UP, 2005. 73–108.

————. *Visuality and Identity: Sinophone Articulations Across the Pacific*. Berkeley: U of California P, 2007.

————, and Françoise Lionnet, eds. *Minor Transnationalism*. Durham, NC: Duke UP, 2005.

Silva, Catherine. "Racial Restrictive Covenants: Enforcing Neighborhood Segregation in Seattle." *Seattle Civil Rights & Labor History Project*, n.d. http://depts.washington.edu /civilr/covenants_report.htm.

Sohn, Stephen Hong. *Racial Asymmetries: Asian American Fictional Worlds*. New York: NYU Press, 2014.

————. "'Valuing' Transnational Queerness: Politicized Bodies Are Commodified Desires in Asian American Literature." *Transnational Asian American Literature: Sites and Transits*. Ed. Shirley Geok-lin Lim. Philadelphia: Temple UP, 2006. 100–122.

Spivak, Gayatri. *In Other Worlds: Essays in Cultural Politics*. London: Methuen, 1987.

Stackhouse, John, and Patrick Martin. "Canada: 'A Model for the World.'" *The Heritage Society*, 2 Feb. 2002. http://ismaili.net/timeline/2002/20020202a.html.

Staggs, Matt. "Matt Talks with Charles Tan, the 'Bibliophile Stalker.'" *Rubber Dinosaur Podcast*, iTunes, 27 June 2009.

Star Wars Episode IV: A New Hope. Dir. George Lucas. Twentieth Century Fox, 1977.

Steger, Manfred B. *The Rise of the Global Imaginary: Political Ideologies from the French Revolution to the Global War on Terror*. New York: Oxford UP, 2008.

Stein, Marc. *Encyclopedia of Lesbian, Gay, Bisexual, and Transgender History in America*. New York: Charles Scribner's Sons/Thomson Gale, 2004.

"Stories We've Seen Too Often." *Strange Horizons*, 10 Mar. 2012. http://strangehorizons.com /submit/fiction-submission-guidelines/stories-weve-seen-too-often/.

Suvin, Darko. *Metamorphoses of Science Fiction: On the Poetics and History of a Literary Genre*. New Haven: Yale UP, 1979.

Syjuco, Miguel. *Ilustrado*. New York: Farrar, Straus and Giroux, 2010.

Tadiar, Neferti X. M. "Domestic Bodies of the Philippines." *Journal of Social Issues in Southeast Asia* 12.2 (1997): 153–191.

————. "(Miracle): The Heretical Potential of Nora Aunor's Star Power." *Signs: Journal of Women in Culture and Society* 27.3 (2002): 703–741.

Tan, Charles. *Lauriat: A Filipino-Chinese Speculative Fiction Anthology*. Maple Shade, NJ: Lethe Press, 2012.

————. "No Foreigners Allowed." *Bibliophile Stalker*. Blogspot, 21 Apr. 2010. http://charles -tan.blogspot.hk/2010/04/essay-no-foreigners-allowed.html.

Tan, Hwee Hwee. "Comparing Yourself with Others." Wordpress, 1 Aug. 2012. http:// hweehweetan.com/comparing-yourself-with-others/

————. "Ginger Tale." *Time* magazine (Asia) 159.21 (2002): 66.

————. "Launch of New Christian Blog by Hwee Hwee Tan." Wordpress, 12 Mar. 2012. http://hweehweetan.com/launch-of-new-christian-blog-by-hwee-hwee-tan/.

————. *Mammon Inc.* London: Penguin, 2001.

————. "Peace That Transcends All Understanding." Wordpress, 13 Sept. 2012. http:// hweehweetan.com/peace-that-transcends-all-understanding/.

Tang, Eric. *Unsettled: Cambodian Refugees in the New York City Hyperghetto*. Philadelphia: Temple UP, 2015.

Tay, Eddie. *Colony, Nation, and Globalisation: Not at Home in Singaporean and Malaysian Literature*. Hong Kong: Hong Kong UP, 2010.

————. "The Dispersal of Eurasian Identity and the Ethics of Remembrance: Rex Shelley's Eurasian Quartet." *Sharing Borders: Studies in Contemporary Singaporean-Malaysian*

Literature. *Writing Asia*, Vol. 2. Ed. Mohammad A. Quayum and Wong Phui Nam. Singapore: National Library Board and Singapore Arts Council, 2009. 146–157.

Taylor, Quintard. "Blacks and Asians in a White City: Japanese Americans and African Americans in Seattle, 1890–1940." *Western Historical Quarterly* 22.4 (1991): 401–429.

Teodoro, Luis V. *Out of This Struggle: The Filipinos in Hawaii*. Honolulu: U of Hawai'i P, 1981.

Thumboo, Edwin. *Perceiving Other Worlds*. Singapore: Times Academic P, 1991.

Tijam, Mia. "The Ascension of Our Lady Boy." *Philippine Speculative Fiction: Literature of the Fantastic*, Vol. 3. Ed. Dean F. Alfar and Nikki Alfar. Pasig City: Kestrel IMC, 2007. 46–56.

Tope, Lily Rose. "State of Engagement: Filipino and Singaporean Women Writers in English Engage the State." *Asiatic: An International Journal of Asian Literatures, Cultures, and Englishes* 1.1 (2007): 1–15.

Tupas, T. Ruanni. "World Englishes or Worlds of English?" *Philippine English: Linguistic and Literary Perspectives*. Ed. Maria L. S. Bautista and Kingsley Bolton. Hong Kong: Hong Kong UP, 2008. 67–81.

Turnball, Lornet, and Justin Mayo. "Census Ranks Seattle among Whitest Big Cities." *Seattle Times*, 23 Apr. 2011.

"Two-Day Conference Examines City's 1907 Race Riot." *Vancouver Courier*, 31 Aug. 2007.

Ty, Eleanor. "Abjection, Masculinity, and Violence in Brian Roley's *American Son* and Han Ong's *Fixer Chao*." *MELUS: Multi-Ethnic Literature of the United States* 29.1 (2004): 119–136.

———. *Unfastened: Globality and Asian North American Narratives*. Minneapolis: U of Minnesota P, 2010.

Ty-Casper, Linda. *Awaiting Trespass: A Pasion*. New York: Readers International, 1985.

Urry, John. *Mobilities*. Cambridge: Polity, 2007.

———. *The Tourist Gaze: Leisure and Travel in Contemporary Societies*. London: Sage, 1990.

———. "Transports of Delight." *Leisure Studies* 20.4 (2001): 237–245.

Warner, Michael. "The Mass Public and the Mass Subject." *Habermas and the Public Sphere*. Ed. Craig J. Calhoun. Cambridge, MA: MIT P, 1992. 377–401.

Warren, James F. *Ah Ku and Karayuki-san: Prostitution in Singapore, 1870–1940*. Singapore: Oxford UP, 1993.

Washima Che Dan, and Norita Omar. "Writing Malaysia in English: A Critical Perspective." *Sharing Borders: Studies in Contemporary Singaporean-Malaysian* Literature. *Writing Asia*, Vol. 2. Ed. Mohammad A. Quayum and Wong Phui Nam. Singapore: National Library Board and Singapore Arts Council, 2009. 151–170.

Wee, C. J. "Creating High Culture in the Globalized 'Cultural Desert' of Singapore." *TDR/The Drama Review* 47.4 (2003): 84–97.

———. "The Indigenized West in Asian Multicultures: Literary-Cultural Production in Malaysia and Singapore." *Interventions: The International Journal of Postcolonial Studies* 10.2 (2008): 188–206.

Weheliye, Alexander G. *Habeas Viscus: Racializing Assemblages, Biopolitics, and Black Feminist Theories of the Human*. Durham, NC: Duke UP, 2014.

Weinbaum, Alys E. *Wayward Reproductions: Genealogies of Race and Nation in Transatlantic Modern Thought*. Durham, NC: Duke UP, 2004.

Wesling, Meg. *Empire's Proxy: American Literature and U.S. Imperialism in the Philippines*. New York: NYU P, 2011.

"Where Is the Diversity in Publishing? The 2015 Diversity Baseline Survey Results." *Lee and Low Books*, "The Open Book," 26 Jan. 2016. http://blog.leeandlow.com/2016/01/26 /where-is-the-diversity-in-publishing-the-2015-diversity-baseline-survey-results/.

White, Richard. "Herder: on the Ethics of Nationalism." *Humanitas* 18 (2005): 166–181.

Wicks, Brian, and Kawika Guillermo. "Smoking with Kawika Guillermo." *Smokelong Quarterly*, 26 Mar. 2012.

Wicks, Peter. "Diaspora and Identity in the Fiction of K. S. Maniam." *Atlantic Literary Review* 3.4 (2002): 115–127.

———. "A Dream Shattered: Lloyd Fernando's Literary Vision of Malaysia." *Asian Culture Quarterly* 28.2 (2000): 49–53.

Williams, Raymond. *Marxism and Literature*. Oxford: Oxford UP, 1977.

Williamson, Kris. "January 2014 Featured Author Interview with Kawika Guillermo." *Anak Sastra*, no. 14, 29 Jan. 2014.

Wolters, O. W. *History, Culture, and Region in Southeast Asian Perspectives*. Singapore: Institute of Southeast Asian Studies, 1982.

Wong Phui Nam. "Out of the Stony . . . A Personal Perspective on the Writing of Verse in English in Malaysia." *Perceiving Other Worlds*. Ed. Edwin Thumboo. Singapore: Published by Times Academic Press for Unipress, 1991. 170–178.

Wu, Ellen D. *The Color of Success: Asian Americans and the Origins of the Model Minority*. Princeton, NJ: Princeton UP, 2014.

Wynter, Sylvia, and Greg Thomas. "ProudFlesh Inter/Views Sylvia Wynter." *PROUD FLESH: A New Afrikan Journal of Culture, Politics & Consciousness* 4 (2006): 1–36.

Yap, April T., and Lara Saguisag. *Nine Supernatural Stories*. Diliman, Quezon City: U of the Philippines P, 2005.

Young, Crawford. *The Politics of Cultural Pluralism*. Madison: U of Wisconsin P, 1976.

Yuson, Alfred A. *Great Philippine Jungle Energy Cafe: A Novel*. 1988. Reprint. Diliman, Quezon City: U of the Philippines P, 1996.

———. *Lush Life: Essays, 2001–2010*. España, Manila: U of Santo Tomas P, 2011.

———. "The Music Child." *Philippine Speculative Fiction: Literature of the Fantastic*, Vol. 3. Ed. Dean F. Alfar and Nikki Alfar. Pasig City: Kestrel IMC, 2007. 171–187.

———. *The Word on Paradise: Essays 1991–2000 on Writers and Writing*. Pasig City, Philippines: Anvil, 2001.

———, Vicente G. Groyon, and F. S. José. *If a Filipino Writer Reads Don Quijote: Three Lectures*. Manila: Los libros del Instituto Cervantes, 2007.

Žižek, Slavoj. "Catastrophic But Not Serious." *FORA.tv, The Conference Channel*. Graduate Center, CUNY, 2011

———. "Multiculturalism; or, the Cultural Logic of Multinational Capitalism." *New Left Review* 97.225 (1997): 28–51.

———. *The Sublime Object of Ideology*. London: Verso, 1989.

———. "Tolerance as an Ideological Category." *Critical Inquiry* 34 (2008): 660–682.

INDEX

Page numbers in italics indicate figures and page numbers followed by n indicate notes.

ABOUT THE AUTHOR

CHRISTOPHER B. PATTERSON (Ph.D., University of Washington) is an assistant professor of Humanities and Creative Writing at Hong Kong Baptist University. He writes fiction under the name Kawika Guillermo.

Lightning Source UK Ltd.
Milton Keynes UK
UKHW03f1032140318
319426UK00001B/107/P